INTERNET MARKETING

Barbara G. Cox, Ph.D.
William Koelzer, C.B.C., A.P.R.

Partial charge full

Wilsonweb

http://imdb.com/

PEARSON

Prentice
Hall

Upper Saddle River, New Jersey 07458

Library of Congress Cataloging-in-Publication Data

Cox, Barbara G., 1946-
    Internet marketing/Barbara G. Cox, William Koelzer.
        p. cm.
    Includes index.
    ISBN 0-13-033628-9
     1. Internet marketing. I. Koelzer, William. II. Title.
HF5415.1265.C693 2003
658.8'4—dc21
                                    2002022992

Executive Acquisitions Editor: Elizabeth Sugg
Editorial Assistant: Cyrenne Boit de Freitas
Managing Editor: Mary Carnis
Production Management: Linda Zuk, WordCrafters Editorial Services, Inc.
Production Liaison: Brian Hyland
Director of Manufacturing and Production: Bruce Johnson
Manufacturing Manager: Ilene Sanford
Creative Director: Cheryl Asherman
Design Coordinator: Christopher Weigand
Formatting: Pine Tree Composition, Inc.
Marketing Manager: Leigh Ann Sims
Composition: Pine Tree Composition, Inc.
Printer/Binder: R.R. Donnelley & Sons
Net Effect Design: Rob Richman, La Fortezza Design Group
Cover Design: Christopher Weigand
Cover Printer: Phoenix Color Corp.

Pearson Education LTD, *London*
Pearson Education Australia PTY, Limited, *Sydney*
Pearson Education Singapore, Pte. Ltd.
Pearson Education North Asia Ltd., *Hong Kong*
Pearson Education Canada, Ltd., *Toronto*
Pearson Educacion de Mexico, S.A. de C.V.
Pearson Education—Japan
Pearson Education Malaysia, Pte. Ltd.

10 9 8 7 6 5 4 3 2 1
ISBN 0-13-033628-9

Contents

3 More Than a Pretty Face: Web Site Content   49

4 The Key to Stickiness: Interactive Functions   79

5 Look 'n' Feel: Site Appearance and Organization   111

Part 3   Getting Found   **141**

6   Portals, Vortals, Search Engines, and Directories   **145**

7   Internet Advertising of Your Web Site: Links, Banners, Tiles, and More   **173**

Preface

Participate in the Conversation

Listen.

Get a grip.

Lighten up.

Little doubt remains that the Internet continues to change the ways we do business. Certainly it has changed how we obtain information. Trillions of dollars in annual online purchases underscore the changes in buying behavior. But where do those revenues go? Who is doing the selling? And how do you assure that you are part of it?

Be part of the conversation.

Faster and less expensive modes of travel developed during the last century enabled people to meet face to face with more people. Telephones—until the advent of call distributors and multiple layers of "Press one for . . ."—enabled people to communicate by voice more frequently and more easily. The Internet has added new dimensions to human conversation, extending the reach and personal networks of the millions of people online. Internet users are asking questions and answering them *for each other*. If your company doesn't learn to participate in the conversation, you probably won't be part of that selling.

Participating in the conversation may require breaking out of some of the old ways—even the old ways that were successful. Mission statements and glossy brochures touting your glories do not, for the most part, convey what online users are looking for. They seek and require more than ivory-tower, self-important declarations. Your brochures are no longer sacred.

Why? Because the online world knows more—much more—than the pre-Internet world that relied on you for the "truth" about products and services and business. The online world has unprecedented access to people who have used those products and services: people with opinions, complaints, praise, advice, information. Your secrets are secret no more. They're on to you. They know about *spin*.

So, just how do you go about participating in this world? Recognize that your target market is full of *people*. Yes, you can still think about their group characteristics, needs, and priorities. But talk to them in "real" language. Drop the language of the hawker of wares or the authority from on high. Find ways to listen. (If you don't, someone else will.) And then respond in their language, without corporate puffery.

LISTEN

Recognize that your target market is full of people and the rest will follow. Ask these people what they know and what they need. If you listen, they'll communicate their ideas—for tightening your thresher's turn ratio, or making your claim form easier to use, or increasing the safety of your GK04692, or making better tasting biscuits. They'll tell you what they need and what they'll pay for. They'll tell you that the connection on your whats-it is weak, your bathrooms are too small, your Philly sandwich needs more cheese, your customer service department needs to add more weekend hours. And if you don't listen, they'll go and tell others.

That's the point. They go. No time to answer your e-mail? They'll ask somebody else. No time to listen? They'll tell somebody else. No time to consider their ideas? Someone else will. Good-bye.

Your clients and customers and employees and investors are loyal, you say? Loyalty? What loyalty? All gone loyalty. Online purchasers can change suppliers, channels of distribution, manufacturers, or bookkeeping services as easily as they can move a mouse or press a button. Listen. Talk. No time? Hear the click?

GET A GRIP

Take a hard look at who you are and what you do, your products and your services, and try to put them in perspective. If you do this honestly, some of what you see may be humbling. That's good. It will help you talk more honestly, more directly. It will help you listen.

How's your company management philosophy working for you? Are you still functioning as a holy hierarchy? You risk moving from hierarchy to anarchy if you continue. Conversation is a great leveler. Your company's internal communications, whether you've noticed or not, are being corrupted and subverted. People are talking. Let them. Better yet, help them. And, while you're at it, help them talk with the people in your marketplace. Otherwise the marketplace will go elsewhere. Or your people will.

LIGHTEN UP

This book is intended for people who want to become part of the conversation or who want to help others do so. It includes practical how-to Internet marketing information in straightforward language. You don't need a college degree in the theoretical foundations of commerce to benefit from these chapters. The concepts are straightforward. The procedures aren't difficult.

People who work as part of a marketing or customer service team will learn how to extend their effectiveness through Internet marketing. Those who are part of a nonmarketing team will learn why Internet marketing affects them, why they should care, and how they can help.

Entrepreneurs who run a small business or an independent professional building, or who hope to retain a client base will find out how to derive maximum benefit from their Internet marketing time and efforts.

Marketing consultants will discover a wealth of tools, tips, and insights to share with clients.

Students preparing to enter the marketing workplace will acquire the analytical tools and the practical skills valued by today's businesses.

> If you read only this page, but take away the message that Internet marketing is about people, about the conversation, and about taking yourself less seriously, we think you'll at least be headed in the right direction.

INTERNET MARKETING

It is the aim of *Internet Marketing* to avoid theoretical and highly technical discussions. We aim to provide useful, practical information in plain language. We also present the information in ways that make learning easy.

The four parts of the book address:

■ what e-commerce is all about

■ what Web sites should do and look like

■ how to increase the likelihood that people will find your Web site

■ how to use e-mail effectively

Each of the four parts opens with a list of terms and their definitions, enabling you to preview some of the Internet language presented in that section.

Each chapter begins with a section called "The Basics" and follows with more detail and explanation and how-to in a section called "Beyond the Basics." Various stops along the way—called "Try It," "Analyze It," or "You Decide" —provide activities to help learners evaluate their understanding or try out a technique or tool. Don't skip them. They're not difficult or time-consuming, and they really will help clarify understanding and improve skills.

Each chapter closes with a short summary to remind you of where you've been, followed by a list of review questions. Possible answers to the review questions are included at the back of the book.

There are two appendixes. The first is a checklist to help you plan and manago Internet marketing for your product, service, or business. The second is a list of Web sites that you might find helpful for various purposes. The book closes with a glossary of the terms presented throughout the book. Use it for quick reference, to test yourself, or to review the terminology.

ACKNOWLEDGMENTS

The authors are indebted to many friends and colleagues for various moments of help with this book

Elizabeth Sugg, as usual, was inspirational. She showed genuine interest in and appreciation for the work throughout its various stages.

Val Munei worked diligently and persistently to obtain and coordinate the many permissions required for the images used in this text. She had no idea at the outset how much patience would be required to complete the project.

We sincerely thank the individuals, companies, and one book-writing dog that generously allowed us to use their Web pages as examples for various concepts. They are cited in captions accompanying the figures showing their Web pages. Please visit their sites when you can.

Trying to keep up with changes on the Internet was quite a challenge, and our spouses and friends continually sent us their treasured Web finds. Some they treasured more than we did, but we are grateful nonetheless.

Finally, we thank all who offered suggestions, criticisms, or corrections. Text that is good, is good because of them. If errors have insinuated themselves into this book, the responsibility remains ours alone.

About the Authors

Barbara Cox, Ph.D., and William Koelzer, CBC, APR, write from a practical foundation in *Internet Marketing*. Both have built and managed successful Internet marketing programs, and they continue to direct many more.

Barbara Cox earned her doctorate in education and psychology from Stanford University. Her professional life includes work as educator at college/university level, corporate trainer, and textbook author. She has directed the work of marketing departments, including strategic planning, market research, direct response marketing, and public communications. She is the principal of Cox Marketing Services and associate faculty at Saddlebrook College in Mission Viejo, California. She and William Koelzer are the authors of *Internet Marketing in Real Estate* (Prentice Hall, 2001) and *Internet Marketing in Hospitality* (Prentice Hall, 2004).

William Koelzer applies more than thirty years of marketing experience to the creation of his work. He has owned his own marketing consulting and promotional firm, Koelzer & Associates, since 1979. He was Vice President of Cochrane Chase & Co., the largest full-service advertising agency in Orange County, California. Koelzer served major clients including Technicolor®, Carl's Jr.™ restaurants, Dos Equis™ beer, Armor All™, and AMF Voit®. He is the recipient of two PROTOS awards for Outstanding Achievement, from the Orange County Public Relations Society of America.

To contact the authors, send e-mail to Barbara at bgcox@cox.net or to Bill at mktg4u@cox.net.

Part One
Businesses on the Web

No longer considered a fad or a fancy, the Internet has infiltrated our lives—invited or not. From a quirky toy of university and government researchers, the online world has become required for American businesses. Consumers *expect* to find Web and e-mail addresses on everything from packaged goods to sports equipment, for every professional and store of every kind, for every company and organization large enough to have a business card and a telephone. Sites created for marketing and selling on the Web number in the millions (with billions of Web pages), some more effective than others.

Part One will familiarize you with the types of business Web sites being used today, their approaches to marketing in cyberspace, and how they serve very different purposes.

LEARNING THE LANGUAGE

The following terms are used in Part One. Familiarize yourself with them by reading the plain language definitions provided.

auction A site where visitors bid on items for sale. At a predetermined time, the auction closes and the high bidder "wins" the auction and pays the seller. Many variations are now available, but the significant player is eBay, at http://www.ebay.com.

B2B business-to-business. B2B sites are constructed to sell business products and/or services to other businesses

B2C   business-to-consumer. B2C sites are constructed by businesses to sell their products and/or services to consumers.

C2C   consumer-to-consumer. C2C sites are constructed by individuals to sell products and/or services to consumers. C2C selling also happens commonly on auction sites, such as eBay.com.

corporate identity site   A Web site whose purpose is to communicate with a company's employees and/or investors. Corporate identity sites promote their market positioning and philosophy, and present information on their history, size, leadership, dedications, etc.

customer relationship management (CRM)   A type of marketing based on the goal of building long-term relationships with customers or clients. Web sites built to support CRM goals provide features to communicate with visitors; engage them in "conversation"; demonstrate that they understand visitors' priorities, preferences, and needs; provide visitor-friendly ways to purchase items; provide fast or real-time communications between customer service or marketing representatives and visitors, and so forth.

portal   A Web site that serves as a gateway to the world of the Internet by providing a directory or directories of links, featured links, and a search engine or engines to help visitors find what they seek (or what the owner of the portal wishes them to find). Portals offer a very broad range of choices to help visitors locate almost anything imaginable on the Web.

product or service information site   A Web site that provides information on the features and benefits of products or services, but that falls short of helping visitors purchase those products or services.

transaction-oriented site   A Web site that provides some level of online purchasing capability so visitors can buy products or services, make reservations, or transact other business. Transaction-oriented sites emphasize the selling of their products or services, but fall short of providing visitor-friendly information and communications tools.

vortal   A "vertical portal": a Web site that serves as an Internet gateway to pages and sites related to a particular topic or interest.

Web page   A page in a site on the World Wide Web. Every Web page is identified by a unique address, or URL (Universal Resource Locator). A page is often considered to be 11 inches long, but actually pages can be very long, indeed, and can take up many paper pages when printed.

Web site   An organized, related, interconnected group of Web pages. Sites typically include a *home page*, which is the first page seen by someone entering the site, and subsequent pages reachable from the home page and internal links.

Types of Businesses, Types of Sites

Introduction to E-Commerce

Because the entry of a business into marketing on the Web can be so inexpensive and easily accomplished, thousands of companies and businesspeople add themselves to the Internet galaxy every day. Every type of business or organization imaginable has some type of Web presence. Every conceivable industry and every type of product or service is represented. From mega-billion-dollar corporations to kids selling lemons, they're there.

Businesses use the Internet to brand themselves and their products and services, working to occupy a clear position in the minds of the people in their marketplace. They create Web sites to sell themselves to investors and contributors, to sell ideas, to sell their wares, to sell their services. This chapter will introduce you to the approaches to marketing that businesses use on the Internet.

THE BASICS

The tremendous variety of approaches to marketing on the Internet makes their clearcut categorization difficult. Most Web sites have multiple goals and a number of strategies for reaching them. They have unique looks and operate differently. Nonetheless, most business-oriented Web sites fit roughly (not neatly) into one of four broad groups, although the "fits" are more a matter of emphasis than strict conformity to a particular category.

1. *Company or corporate identity sites.* These sites, often expansions of the familiar "capability brochures," are usually built for the stakeholders—the employees and investors—in the business. They promote their market positioning and their own philosophy, size, history, and other characteristics to attract and retain quality management, consistent workers, dedicated investors, and capable, knowledgeable, tough, or inspirational leadership. Sometimes corporate identity sites link to other sites developed by the business for product marketing, customer service, and other purposes.

2. *Product or service information sites.* Web pages and Web sites that present information about products and services also work to enhance positioning or increase public awareness. The primary purpose of these sites is not direct sales; such sites are more similar to general advertising than to direct response marketing.

3. *Transaction-oriented sites.* Millions of Web sites and Web pages sell the wares and services of the world to other businesses and to consumers. They may allow Web visitors to use an existing business account, charge to a credit card, use an online payment service, or place an order for later billing—but sell they do. Many are immediately recognizable as purveyors of something-or-other, with the site's pages devoted to the product's features, benefits, and pricing. Other sites combine an educational or informational mission with direct selling, such as an art museum site with pages of art history as well as means for visitors to make donations, reserve places in a museum tour, or make purchases from the gift shop.

4. *Relationship-building sites.* Creating, maintaining, and enhancing long-term relationships with customers and clients, including employees and investors, requires some action or interaction beyond a single sale. Working to ensure that clients are satisfied, committed to a particular product line, service, or company, requires repeated—or continuous—communication. Some sites emphasize this communication, working to keep clients informed and providing ways for those clients to communicate their thoughts, opinions, and questions to the marketing,

sales, customer service, and/or management representatives of the site's owner. Many technical help sites fall into this category.

Direct selling on the Internet is also popularly categorized as business-to-business (B2B), business-to-consumer (B2C), or consumer-to-consumer (C2C) selling. (See "Business Web Sites" section later in this chapter.)

BEYOND THE BASICS

What Business Web Sites Do

Let's look at four general categories of business Web sites and examine some of the issues involved in creating a Web site that will build a close and ongoing relationship with your target audience—whether employees, investors, or prospective or existing clients and customers. This information will provide a framework for your own decision-making about the goals, audience, and purpose for Internet marketing.

CORPORATE IDENTITY SITES

Many sites exist primarily to inform and influence target audiences favorably about the owner of the site. Such sites typically emphasize a firm or organization's mission, size, scope, services, revenue, profitability, stock market success, industry leadership, and so forth—in much the same way as an annual financial report would. In fact, much of what you find on corporate identity sites is there to influence Wall Street, stockholders, and investors, and to instill a sense of pride among company employees.

A corporate identity site is a *marketing positioning tool.* Its goal is not to sell a tangible object or a service, but rather to provide information that creates or reinforces a favorable opinion about the firm in the minds of site visitors—in other words, public relations. Corporate Web sites usually provide quick access to in-depth information about a company. When we viewed Cendant's site at http://www.cendant.com in mid-2002, the site was using several strategies to build its positioning. At that time, the strategies included the following:

1. Positioning text that read:

   > We are the homes you buy, the hotels and resorts you visit, the cars you rent and the services that you rely on . . . both on-line and off-line. At Cendant, we concentrate on growing our core businesses by providing highly focused services to franchisees, licensees, affinity partners and corporate clients. Our ability to continue our growth is based on our core competencies: building franchise systems, providing outsourcing solutions and delivering superior marketing.

This text displayed first, and visitors could read the statements while the graphics and other page elements loaded.

2. An image that reinforced the position and read "one of the foremost providers of travel-related & direct-marketing business and consumer services in the world."

3. A box showing Cendant's updates for investors. The text in this box scrolled, displaying various headlines that users can click on to access additional information.

4. Product logos along the bottom. These logos are those of various Cendant companies, and displaying their logos here helps visitors make the association between these more familiar businesses and Cendant. The screen capture shows only a few logos, but they alternate among the many Cendant companies.

5. Menu choices across the top and in the bars center-left that gave visitors access to much more detailed information about Cendant.

Analyze It   Visit http://www.cendant.com. What elements do you see today that Cendant uses to communicate its position?

MARKET GLOBALLY, MARKET LOCALLY

In their corporate identity Web site, corporate parents usually provide a list of subsidiaries or offices, along with street address, phone number, and often the e-mail address of each location (office, dealer, facility, franchisee, etc.), nationwide or worldwide. Some of these multilocation businesses also create a Web page or even a separate Web site for each location. The company logos shown on Cendant's opening page are active links to Web sites for those companies.

Other companies may provide a common database for their offices to share. This is extremely common in the shipping industry, where origin and destination offices must access shared information about rates, routes, and schedules. The use of a common database varies considerably, however, depending on the company's industry, structure, and inclinations. (For another example, see the discussion of Budget Blinds in Chapter 4.)

PRODUCT/SERVICE INFORMATION SITES

Similar to corporate identity sites, product or service information sites emphasize positioning products or services more than selling them. Some of these sites are posted by businesses that really do intend to sell their products directly, but haven't mastered the Internet marketing elements they need to use to accomplish that goal. These sites are akin to product brochures: They may give the business telephone number and perhaps the e-mail address, but they do not provide the interactive tools that are central to the Web's capacity for direct selling. These information-oriented Web sites reflect a product focus, but usually do not communicate urgency or establish a two-way information exchange with site visitors.

TRANSACTION-ORIENTED SITES

Many business sites focus almost exclusively on selling. They are transaction oriented and provide means for visitors to purchase items or make reservations online. The list includes good selling sites that present product or service features, benefits, prices, and incentives, and that emphasize the order-taking process without "going the extra mile" to add the tools and functions intended to build long-term relationships.

Small Web sites created for the purposes of selling an individual's crafts or a small manufacturer's one-of-a-kind products or local auto-repair services, for example, usually focus on convincing a visitor to make a one-time purchase or order, or to make a reservation.

CUSTOMER RELATIONSHIP MANAGEMENT (CRM) SITES

The CRM category of e-commerce site is the best model for many firms that want to conduct e-business. While a site in this category is a selling site, it transcends mere selling to "befriend" a prospect or customer in a powerfully appealing way. Such sites combine the best of product information and product selling Web sites with an appreciation of customers and a desire to establish a long-term relationship with them.

CRM sites work to educate visitors, providing ample information and sometimes even links to information on other sites. CRM sites typically offer many ways for visitors to communicate with the company and vice versa. Why? Because there is a happy immediacy in doing so, reminiscent of the service people used to give and get in the old fashioned small-town hardware store. These sites stand apart from the anonymity of most Web applications and seek to engage the visitor in an onsite activity. Many of them store a visitor's name and then greet each visitor by name and with new information related to that visitor's interests when he or she returns.

Interactive elements usually include a feature that enables a visitor to chat with a company representative, sign up for a newsletter, vote in a poll, and provide feedback to improve the site or enter a chat room with other site visitors. Free e-mail, a guest book for comments, free Web site offers, and free reports and updates (sent by e-mail) are popular elements.

Large businesses have studied purchasers and know precisely what they want and their buying habits. They know how likely people are to purchase product Y if they have purchased product X, and within what time frame. Smaller firms can develop such information, to a degree, from on-Web-site and e-mail polling, as well as from their own sales statistics.

In the next few paragraphs, we describe a few examples of CRM sites. Specific interactive functions are discussed in greater detail in Chapter 4.

ONLINE BANKING

Online banking was among the earliest and most successful Web-based services. Not only can users get information about bank offices and hours and locations, types of accounts, rates, terms, and other bank products, but they can also access their account information; transfer funds; pay bills; plan a reinvestment, retirement, or home loan refinance; and communicate with the bank. Investors can learn about bank assets and liabilities, stability, size, and investments.

NEWS AND ENTERTAINMENT

News and entertainment sites are usually tied to another media, such as television, films, magazines, or newspapers. Cnn.com, tvguide.com, Hollywood.com, usatoday.com, and austindailyherald.com are all examples. These sites keep visitors returning day after day for updates and current information, as well as for customer service regarding subscription, delivery, or other services. What do they gain by providing all this information? Increased ratings, circulation, and physical sales—which, in turn, help increase advertising sales.

LARGE STORES AND MANUFACTURERS

Some large stores and manufacturers are finding ways to personalize their Web sites. These sites usually encourage visitors to sign in or register for something or otherwise provide a name or nickname that the site can use when the visitor returns in the future. Amazon.com, for example, displays "Welcome back, [visitor name]." The entry page has "New books for [visitor name]" based on searches or purchases the visitor made on previous visits.

Another way sites personalize their interactions with visitors is to allow them to change the appearance of the Web page or some element of the page to suit their own taste. The site remembers the settings (by placing the information in a cookie file in the visitor's browser), and the settings are then used on subsequent visits. A variation of this tactic is the "try-on" feature used by clothing, automobile, hairstyle, make-up, and other sites. On these sites, visitors can change the look of the items for sale.

SHOPPING SERVICES

Sites that deal exclusively with helping Web users shop on the Web direct them to specific products or services or stores. StoreRunner.com (Fig. 1.1) (http://www.storerunner.com), for example, "searches millions of products from hundreds of your favorite stores, across more than 8,500 categories, in more than 85,000 local store locations." The revenue-producing strategies for such sites vary. Some send shoppers only to cooperating sellers and receive a commission or click-through fee in return. Others charge sellers a flat fee per month or make some other arrangement to be "found" by users

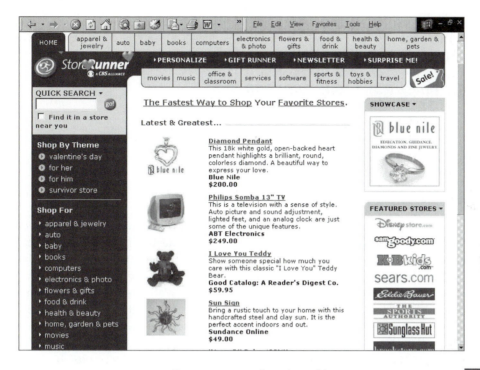

Screen capture from http://www.storerunner.com.   **Figure 1.1**

of the shopping site. Still others generate their revenues (or hope to) from advertising sales.

URL SELLING

Domain name sites are a combination of a vortal and an exchange site. You register the URLs you have for sale with the site, and then it acts as an interface between you and buyers, taking a commission for its service. Such sites also usually offer domain name registration, an escrow service, professional appraisal of a URL's value, checking of trademark conflicts, and more. The leaders in this field are GreatDomains (http://www.great domains.com) and Yahoo Domains (http://domains.yahoo.com). There are dozens of similar sites.

Do you have a domain name that you're not using, may never use, and would like to sell? Just register it with a domain name marketplace (or *exchange*) and—who knows?—you might get lucky and find a willing buyer. In late 1999, Web incubator eCompanies (http://www.ecompanies. com) set a domain name price record when it paid $7.5 million for Business.com.

| **Analyze It** | Visit http://www.pepsico.com, a Web site for Pepsico™. Name the elements that this site uses to position itself and to engage its Web visitors. Compare it to the Cendant Web site discussed earlier. |

Business Web Sites: B2C, B2B, C2C

Sites that market or sell products and services, whether order-takers or more person-oriented, generally fall into one of three business Web categories: business-to-consumer, business-to-business, or consumer-to-consumer. Some sell to both consumers and businesses.

BUSINESS-TO-CONSUMER SITES (B2C)

Business-to-consumer sites are probably the ones most familiar to the Web-using public. These sites, in almost every possible industry, market goods and services to you. Many stores—department, variety, books, cars, fabric, music, electronics, clothing, food, hardware, and many other types—that you know from in-person experience also have Web sites to sell merchandise. Other business-to-consumer sites have no "brick-and-mortar" facilities; they sell exclusively over the Internet. And not all business-to-consumer sites sell online. Some of them market goods and services that consumers purchase by telephone or from a local store or office. Examples include amazon.com and barnes&noble.com (books and related items), blooming dales.com and nordstrom.com (department stores), pontiac.com and lincoln.com (vehicles), staples.com and officemax.com (office supplies), and a host of others.

How much selling do business-to-consumer sites carry out? U.S. consumers spent $10.8 billion online in 2000, a 54 percent increase over the $7 billion spent in 1999, according to a survey by online research firm Jupiter Media Metrix.[1] During the 2000 holiday season, about 36 million consumers purchased online and spent an average of $304. About 35 percent of online buyers surveyed said they shopped at so-called "pure play" (sell solely online) retailers, while 37 percent said they shopped online with companies that also have physical stores or catalog services.

Tower Group projects that, by 2005, consumer-to-business (C2B) payments online will exceed 31 billion transactions—nearly eight times the projected person-to-person sales volume for that year.[2] Tower expects the C2B market to account for 88 percent of consumer-initiated online payments and 68 percent of corresponding value.

---

[1]http://www.emarketer.com/estatnews/enews/reuters/01_17_2001.rwntz-story-bcnetonlinespendingdc.html

[2]"You Down for C2B?" in *eMarketer Quick eStats Newsletter*, Issue 27, February 7, 2001. Visit http://about.reuters.com/investormedia/news_releases/art_31-1-2001_id515.asp for archive of news release.

According to NFO Interactive's (NFO) report, *The 2000 Online Retail Monitor*, in the United States, 42 percent of online shoppers are men and 52 percent are women.[3] (The remaining 6 percent are not identified.) Eighty percent of all U.S. Internet users have participated in at least one transaction online. NFO also reports that one-fourth of the online shopping population in the United States accounts for three-fourths of all online purchases. The remaining 75 percent of online shoppers purchase less frequently and tend to buy less expensive items. eMarketer concluded that in 2000, 37 percent of online shoppers were "regular buyers" who purchase items online at least every three months; 62.7 percent were buyers who bought at least one item online within the previous year.[4]

Online shopping is increasing in part simply because the number of household computers is growing. A recent Employment Policy Foundation (EPF) report indicated that 51 percent (54.5 million) of U.S. households have at least one computer.[5] Of those households 43.5 million have Internet access. The EPF predicts that by November 2002, 68 million U.S. households will have computers, and 66 million will also have Internet access.

Many high-ticket items are now purchased with online help. According to automotive industry research company Polk (http://www.polk.com), 60 percent of U.S. car buyers used the Internet to help with their purchase in 2000—up from 46 percent in 1999.[6]

BUSINESS-TO-BUSINESS SITES (B2B)

The B2B market is growing at an astonishing rate. Despite the economic downturn at the beginning of 2001 and a generally gloomy outlook for the dot-world at that time, companies around the globe will increase their spending on business-to-business (B2B) e-marketplaces (exchanges, auctions, etc.) from U.S. $2.6 billion in 2000 to $137.2 billion by 2005, according to Jupiter Research.[7] Goldman Sachs' estimates are more aggressive: it predicts that worldwide B2B spending will reach $4,500 billion by 2005—out of total online commerce spending of $60 trillion by that year. Furthermore, Goldman Sachs expects that 80 percent of B2B commerce worldwide will be conducted online over the next 20 years.[8]

---

[3] http://www.nfoi.com/nfointeractive/nfoipr01042001.asp
[4] http://www.emarketer.com/estatnews/estats/ecommerce_b2c/20010108_retail.html
[5] http://www.emarketer.com/estatnews/estats/edemographics/20010115_us_house.html
[6] *The eMarketer Quick eStats Newsletter.* Issue No. 12, 2001, 17 January 2001
[7] http://www.ecommercetimes.com/perl/story/6515.html
[8] Goldman Sachs Global Equity Research, "B2B: Just How Big is the Opportunity?" May 9, 2000. See http://www.gs.com/hightech/research/b2b-opp.pdf.

According to ActivMedia Research, "Most B-to-B websites are established for a dual purpose: to both sell products and services, either directly or indirectly (98%), and to provide information (73%). The primary means for creating a sale for 77% of sites is by stimulating customers to make an offline contact. Most B-to-B sites also provide pre-sale support and purchasing information (62%) and generate leads for staff to follow-up (60%) as ways to make a sale through their website."[9]

The same article claims the following B2B site function proportions:

- 33 percent of B2B sites market, but do not sell, products online

- 25 percent of B2B sites offer professional services

- 15 percent of B2B sites sell products at the site to business end-users

B2B SELLING ON AUCTION SITES

B2B auctions require precision of product description and specifications. Auction sites cannot succeed unless suppliers are clear about the products or services a buyer needs and the terms under which they are to be delivered. Many industrial products are technically complex. Many large exchange sites work closely with members of each client's purchasing organization to help specify their needs in detail and communicate them clearly to bidders before each auction.

AUCTION TIP! **BE SPECIFIC**

To a great extent, a firm's success with auction sites depends on how clearly it describes product functions, features, and benefits—not only from a technical standpoint, but from a marketing perspective as well.

TIP! **TORTURED TERMINOLOGY**

The terms *e-marketplace, B2B exchange site* and, frequently, *B2B auction site* were virtually interchangeable in the Spring of 2001, because many e-marketplace sites (designed specifically for businesses to sell to businesses) each incorporated many different selling methods. These methods ranged from simple buy/sell transactions to open auction, bid or sealed auction, barter, and other forms of commerce. The prevalent term, however, was *B2B exchange*, with *e-marketplace* becoming the generic term for any site dealing as a platform for B2B selling.

---

[9]"B-to-B Companies Go Online as a Matter of Survival: Value Found in Relationship Building, Not Profitability, August 15, 2000." Available online at http://www.activmediaresearch.com/magic/pr081500.html.

B2B auction sites vary widely. Some are narrowly focused, such as TekSell.com (http://www.teksell.com), which provides an online marketplace for serious IT (information technology) professionals to buy and sell new, remanufactured, and previously owned data, video, and voice equipment. Another niche auction/exchange site is operated by Tradeloop Corporation (http://www.tradeloop.com), an online marketplace for computer resellers, value-added resellers (VARs), brokers, and distributors.

Although most B2B auction sites operate in narrowly defined business segments, some span several broad segments. A pioneer in this realm is FreeMarkets (http://www.freemarkets.com). The firm conducts online auctions for industrial parts, raw materials, commodities, and services. In these auctions, suppliers compete in real time for the purchase orders of large buying organizations by lowering their prices until the auction is closed.

E-MARKETPLACES—B2B EXCHANGE SITES

While the year 2000 saw thousands of exchange sites appear almost overnight, the numbers diminished quickly. According to eMarketer (http://www.emarketer.com) analyst Steve Burtler, "Deloitte Consulting pegs the total at 1,500 exchanges worldwide, predicting that less than 500 will remain in three years' time. Forrester Research believes that only 181 B2B exchanges will exist by 2003."

According to an October 2000 report by The Boston Consulting Group (BCG), total U.S. e-marketplace revenues will approach $9 billion in the next four to five years, pointing to solid long-term revenue prospects for individual e-marketplaces.[10] "In five years' time, e-marketplaces serving America's largest industries should be expected to generate $350 million to $450 million in annual revenues, while e-marketplaces in most other industries will generate revenues of much less than $100 million. Only a small number of top performers will be able to exceed these revenue projections," says BCG in its report, "The B2B Opportunity: Creating Advantage Through E-Marketplaces." BCG also forecasts that, by 2004, business-to-business e-commerce will generate productivity gains equivalent to 1 to 2 percent of sales; by 2010, this figure could grow to 6 percent, or roughly $1 trillion. Nonetheless, the market will only support one to three major e-marketplaces within any given industry segment.

"Today, there are more than 700 e-marketplaces currently in operation. Most of them face an uphill battle to survive," says BCG Vice President Jim Andrew. "Ultimately, the U.S. B2B market will be characterized by a handful of e-marketplace giants that serve the overall needs of an industry; and scores of niche players serving a special segment within an industry or providing a specialized function across many industries."

---

[10]http://www.bcg.com/new_ideas/new_ideas_subpage28.asp

BCG notes that, in order to survive among so many competitors, e-marketplaces (B2B exchanges) will need to prove to potential participants that they have staying power and offer the best opportunity to maximize competitive advantage. BCG's report outlines five success factors that e-marketplaces need to create the critical mass or liquidity required of a viable business:

- Leave room for companies to differentiate themselves

- Stay cost-effective and focused on execution

- Clearly communicate to buyers and sellers the value that the e-marketplace creates

- Extend the offering to medium and small companies

- Be flexible about changing the business model

BCG's report, titled "The U.S. B2B Landscape Through 2004," is available in PDF format online at http://www.bcg.com/publications/files/B2BResearch.pdf.

What do you need to do if you intend to sell through online exchanges? Carefully review those serving your industry to be sure that the one or more that you choose will survive an exchange shakeout, should that happen. How? Talk to other firms that appear in those sites, interview owners of such sites, read industry news on e-marketplace sites, and talk to the executive directors of trade associations that serve your target audiences' industries. A B2B yellow pages (http://www.B2Byellowpages.com) helps users locate B2B Web sites. Its directory allows businesses to aggregate, locate, and publicize Web sites to other businesses.

CONSUMER TO CONSUMER (C2C)

CONSUMER AUCTION SITES

Most consumer-to-consumer sales take place through auction sites. In a Harris Interactive survey sponsored by The National Consumers League (NCL; see http://www.natlconsumersleague.org), 83 percent of online auction bidders have bought something in an online auction.[11] The report says that 75 percent of those buyers have spent an average $100 or less, and 21 percent have spent between $101 and $500.

In general, auction sites are just what you think they are. Sellers post items to sell and buyers post bids on them. The highest bidder wins the item that is for sale, assuming the bid meets an established minimum amount. The auction site takes a small commission from the seller's credit card account for each item sold. Buyers generally pay nothing to the auction site itself.

---

[11]Daily e-stat, 5 February 2001

EBAY

The largest C2C auction site today is eBay at http://www.eBay.com. It has been the model for auction sites that followed, including many now emerging to help *businesses* conduct e-commerce. Even though eBay is primarily a C2C service, its simplicity is well worth study by any business planning to buy or sell products in a B2B auction site.

At eBay and most other auction sites, users register and, if they intend to sell on the site, set up a means of payment, typically a credit card or a financial account enabling transfers of funds. Buyers explore a directory of categories or enter identifying words into the site's search engine and the site displays a list of such products for sale. Sellers pay for listing and selling items. eBay charges an insertion fee, usually between 25 cents and $2.00, depending on the opening bid, and a fee at the end of the auction, ranging from 1.25 percent to 5 percent of the final selling price. Additional fees also apply for enhancements such as bold font or featured placement. See http://pages.ebay.com/help/sellerguide/selling-fees.html for a complete explanation.

In November 2001, we searched for "scissors" and eBay displayed a list of 851 (up from 729 the previous June) auctions with the word "scissors" in the title and 3,876 (up from 2,965 the previous June) auctions with "scissors" in either the title or the description or both (Fig. 1.2). Most B2B exchange sites function much like eBay, although many B2B auctions are not conducted within a fixed time frame.

eBay's tutorial is excellent. Businesses planning to buy or sell in a B2B auction or exchange site will benefit by having the planning staff review the tutorial and even buy and sell some items on eBay. They will become familiar with the basic auction process, but will do so at far less monetary risk than they would incur in large "for-real" transactions involving B2B items costing thousands of dollars.

Visit eBay's sellers' guide at http://pages.ebay.com/help/sellerguide/index.html. Use the information linked from that page to answer the following questions.

Analyze It

1. What four types of auctions can sellers create on eBay?
2. List four tips that eBay offers its members for better selling.
3. How does the feedback program work?

Portals and Vortals

PORTALS

According to Internet-word-related online dictionary *Webopedia* (http://www.webopedia.com), a *portal* is "a Web site or service that offers a broad array of resources and services, such as Web-based e-mail, forums, search

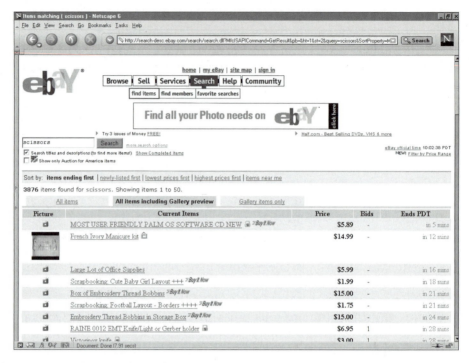

Figure 1.2   Results of searching for "scissors" on eBay. Screen capture from http://
search.ebay.com/search/search.dll?MfcISAPICommand=GetResult&
ht=1&SortProperty=MetaEndSort&query=scissors.
Reproduced with the permission of eBay Inc. Copyright © EBAY INC. All rights
reserved.

engines, and on-line shopping malls. The first Web portals were online services, such as America Online, that provided access to the Web, but by now most of the traditional search engines have transformed themselves into Web portals to attract and keep a larger audience."

Other large portals include Netscape's Netcenter (http://www. net scape.com), MSN (http://www.msn.com), Lycos (http://www.lycos.com), Yahoo! (http://www.yahoo.com), Excite (http://www.excite.com), NBCi.com (http://www.nbci.com), Webcrawler (http://www.webcrawler.com), and dozens more.

Portals—except for their search engines, which are mostly objective—dictate the content that you are able to find. They're helpful for new users to become acquainted with what is on the Web. However, they serve up only the portion of the Internet that they, not the users, deem most important. They do this in many cases because they gain income from advertisers by including links either to advertisers' sites or to their own properties or partnerships.

A portal's goal is to be set as users' default home page—used as an entry point to other Web destinations and returned to day after day. That is the proven way to gain site visits in large numbers. In addition, having numerous page views is essential in commanding higher rates for advertising links and banners that portals sell. Bottom line? The links on portals do not always direct users to the most relevant or informative site(s) on a particular topic. However, if your firm owns a portal, it can be a very powerful marketing tool called a *company vortal.*

VORTALS

Vortals are "vertical portals," that is, portals that focus on particular topics and help visitors find information relating to those topics. A good example is Findlaw.com at http://www.findlaw.com (Fig. 1.3).

The vortal FindLaw.com deals exclusively with legal matters. About itself, FindLaw says:

> FindLaw, the leading Web portal focused on law and government, provides access to a comprehensive and fast-growing online library of legal resources for use by legal professionals, consumers and small businesses. FindLaw's mission is to make legal information on the Internet easy to find. Visitors to the FindLaw site will find a broad array of features that

Figure 1.3

FindLaw.com. Screen capture from http://www.findlaw.com.

include Web search utilities, cases and codes, legal news, and community-oriented tools, such as a secure document management utility, mailing lists, message boards and free e-mail.

Vortals can prove valuable for small businesses. The collection of information and pages related to a given topic direct visitors to information that supports a firm's marketing position, products, or services. An example from the nonprofit world is diabetesportal.com (Fig. 1.4). This vortal is owned by DiabetesPortal.com, Inc., which supports the Insulin-Free World Foundation, a nonprofit organization, both of St. Louis, MO. "Diabetes Portal—the gateway to a cure" provides links to research information, news, discussions, interviews, helpful guides for living with diabetes, and, importantly, a shopping mall (http://www.diabeteswarehouse.com). The shopping mall site, also owned by DiabetesPortal.com, Inc., states that it pays a commission on sales made by purchasers who start their shopping at its Web page to help to find the cure for diabetes.

Figure 1.4   Diabetes portal. Screen capture from http://www.diabetesportal.com.

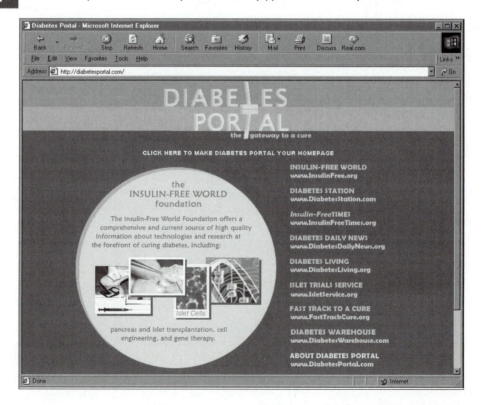

VORTAL OR PORTAL?

Some vortals target such a huge audience (e.g., all females) that it becomes a flip of the coin whether they should be called a *vortal* or a *portal*. A good example is iVillage at http://www.ivillage.com (Fig. 1.5), a site devoted almost exclusively to women's interests.

Figure 1.5

Vortal? Screen capture from http://www.ivillage.com.

Many online shopping malls focus on a particular type of item and might also be considered vortals. Strictly speaking, the distinction between the two tends to be that vortals provide links to news, information, guidance, and other helpful resources, whereas shopping malls link only or primarily to their dealers' selling pages or Web sites. Portals and vortals provide search engine tools and directories. See additional discussion of these functions in Chapter 6.

Analyze It

Your company manufactures and sells hygiene and health products for dogs. Your boss asks you to create a Web site to sell the products. You decide to create a vortal. Make a list of the types of information you would include or link to.

1. _____

2. _____

3. _____

Summary

Business Web sites vary widely in type and target audience. Four general categories are:

- Corporate identity sites
- Product/service information sites
- Transaction-oriented sites
- Customer relationship management (CRM) sites

Another way that business Web sites are categorized is according to who is doing the selling and the buying. The three common groups are:

- Business-to-consumer sites (B2C)
- Business-to-business sites (B2B)
- Consumer-to-consumer sites (C2C)

Portals and vortals are gateways to the world of Internet information. Portals are usually huge information sites with hundreds of links into Cyberspace. They usually include directories and/or search engines that are very broad in scope. Vortals are "vertical portals." They are more narrowly focused than portals, seeking to provide a gateway to Internet pages related to a particular topic, industry, or issue of interest.

Review Questions

1. What are the four general categories of business Web sites?
2. Who are the most common audiences for a corporate identity Web site?
3. Are product or service information Web sites built for high-pressure sales?
4. What feature is typical of a transaction-oriented Web site?
5. What distinguishes a relationship-building site from other sites?
6. In what way is an old-fashioned hardware store similar to a good transaction-oriented site?
7. List four interactive elements that a Web site can offer visitors.
8. Describe how typical C2C auction sites (such as eBay) work.
9. What percentage of online auction bidders have actually purchased something in an online auction?
10. List four features that portals offer visitors.
11. Why may the data that portals provide not always be objective?
12. Define a *vortal* and describe how it differs from a portal.
13. What purpose might a business have for constructing a vortal?

Part Two

Creating and Building an Internet Presence

Among the first questions we usually hear from businesses and professionals who are getting serious about Internet marketing are:

1. What should I put on my site?

2. What should my site look like?

3. How should my site be organized? Sometimes this question is phrased, How should my site work?

The answers to these questions take two forms. The first is direct. We'll give you a list of items to put on your site, a "Do and Don't" list about site appearance, and some models showing how sites are organized.

The second answer is, "It depends." It depends on how you wish to market your business, product, or services; how you wish to be perceived; whom you want to attract; and what you want visitors to do when they find you. In short, it depends on your *positioning* and your *goals*.

Part Two begins with a discussion of positioning. We'll help you decide how to differentiate your business and/or products or services from others, especially on the Internet. Then you'll learn the implications of positioning and the key principles for site content, functioning, appearance, and organization.

The chapters in Part Two are:

2. Standing Out from the Crowd: Positioning, Audience, and Goals

3. More Than a Pretty Face: Web Site Content

4. The Key to Stickiness: Interactive Functions

5. Look 'n' Feel: Site Appearance and Organization

LEARNING THE LANGUAGE

The following terms are used in Part Two. Familiarize yourself with them by reading the plain language definitions provided.

animated .gif A type of graphic that appears to move. An animated .gif combines several images, each slightly different from the previous one, that appear one after another automatically, giving the appearance of motion—similar to motion pictures.

audio books Books that are downloadable from the Internet or available on disk, that can be listened to by users through their computer's audio program. Similar to books on tape, audio books differ from e-books in that audio books are heard by users, whereas e-books are read by users.

autoresponder A function on a computer that sends an automated response to a command from a Web site or to an e-mail with a particular addressee or subject line.

bulletin board A Web page that displays messages submitted by users. Most bulletin boards are specific to a particular topic.

cgi form A form on a Web page filled in by Internet users and then sent to the owner of the Web site or some other designated recipient. Examples of cgi forms are guest books or surveys on the Internet. CGI is an acronym for Common Gateway Interface.

chat room A Web site function that allows a group of people to type statements in such a way that all members of the group can see everything written by every other member.

community site (1) A Web site featuring content that is primarily for or about a given city. In a broader sense, this term includes county, regional, and state sites. (2) A Web site created and maintained by a community of users, or a group of formally linked Web sites on a common topic. This book uses the phrase *community site* in the sense of the first of these two descriptions.

downloadable Capable of being copied from a computer connected to the Internet to a user's computer.

e-books Electronic books, downloadable from the Internet or available on disk, that can be read by various reading devices such as Adobe® Acrobat® eBook Reader™. E-books differ from audio books in that audio books are heard by users, whereas e-books are read by users.

.gif A file extension indicating a type of compressed file used for photos and other graphics on the Internet. .gif (pronounced "gif," as in *gift*) files are more frequently used for graphics than for photos. GIF is an acronym for Graphics Interchange Format.

home page The front or main page of a Web site. A home page often acts as a starting point leading to other documents stored at the site. A page that precedes the main, navigation-oriented, traditional home page is often called a *splash page*.

host (1) To store a customer's Web site on a server, thus making the site available to everyone with Web access. (2) A computer system that stores data, such as a Web site, and that is accessed by a user or users from a remote location.

.htm A file extension indicating a page prepared in hypertext markup language (html); one of the most common types of Web pages.

html Acronym for Hyper Text Markup Language, an authoring language used to create documents for viewing with an Internet browser.

interactive catalog A database of items with a "front end" that allows visitors to search for an item and provides some means of online ordering.

interactive functions Functions on a Web site that allow visitors to interact with the site. That is, visitors take some action (clicking on something, for example), and the Web site performs some action in response, usually clicking to go to another page (although technically causing the Web site to do something is not included in this definition since it is so common). Examples include visitors' adding items to shopping carts, using an online order form, participating in a chat room, or starting a video stream.

.jpg A file extension indicating a type of file used for photos and other graphics on the Internet. .jpg (pronounced "jay-peg") files are usually used for photos, but sometimes they are also used for graphics. .jpg files are compressed so that photos appear on the user's monitor more quickly. Photos compressed as .jpg files can be reduced to about 5 percent of their normal size, but some detail is lost in the compression. .jpg stands for Joint Photographic Experts Group, for which the compression technique is named.

link A connection between a location on a page and another location on the same or a different page on the Internet. When a user clicks on a link with the mouse, the location connected to the link is displayed. Text links are often underlined and shown in blue. Graphics can also be linked. When the mouse is pointed at a link, the mouse pointer usually changes to a pointing hand.

live chat or **live customer service** A Web site function that allows a user to communicate with a customer service representative or other person by typing messages back and forth. Compare with *chat room*.

mall A Web site consisting of many individually owned sections or *store fronts* selling products and services.

position, positioning A specific place held in the minds of the public or a given audience (or market segment) concerning a product or service. Chez LaFayette, for example, may have positioning as the best upscale French restaurant in a given town, whereas MacGregor's may be positioned as a family style, low-cost, easy-access fast food vendor. Positioning is similar, in many ways, to reputation.

server A computer or device on a network that manages that network's resources. Your Internet service provider and all the people who belong to it share the use of its servers. Basically, a server "serves" the e-mail and Web browsing needs of those who use it.

screen saver A program that displays animated graphics on a computer's monitor when the computer is turned on but has not been used for a period of time. Screen savers are small programs that can be easily downloaded.

shopping cart A selecting and ordering mechanism used on some sites that sell products and services. A shopping cart usually allows visitors to select items to put in the shopping cart or basket and later check out using a credit card or other payment mechanism.

streaming media Technology that transmits (streams) audio and/or video from a server to a user's computer. Streaming video is played on the user's computer as it is received from the server.

teleconferencing Voice conferencing using an Internet connection and a microphone and speakers connected to users' computers rather than to telephones.

UMPS Acronym for unique marketing positioning statement; a concise statement intended to express the characteristics that combine to make up your position. Examples are "Hershey— The Number One Chocolate Bar in the World" and "The Top-Selling Ocean-View-Home Real Estate Agent in Maine."

URL Acronym for Universal Resource Locator, the World Wide address of Web pages, Web images, documents, and other Web resources. For example, the URL for the main entry page of Burpee Seeds' site is http://www.burpee.com. Each page and image or graphic on the Internet has its own URL. The URL for Burpee's logo image on its home page is http://www.burpee.com/image/global/wwwlogo.gif. Learn more about URLs at: http://www.w3.org/Addressing/Addressing.html.

user-controlled catalog A catalog that allows users to custom design or select particular models, colors, or pieces. See http://www.makeoverstudios.com for an example.

video conferencing Similar to teleconferencing via the Internet, but allows transmission of video as well. Video conferencing can be used between two people or can connect several people in different locations at one time.

Webcasting Internet broadcasting; transmission of live or prerecorded audio and/or video to users connected to the Internet.

Web fax, Internet fax A Web site function that allows visitors to send a document from their computer to another person's fax machine.

Standing Out
from the Crowd
Positioning, Audience, and Goals

Just because Web marketing takes place on the Internet does not mean that the traditional principles of marketing can be set aside. The basic principles of market positioning, audience identification, and establishment of goals are every bit as important in Web marketing as in traditional marketing. In fact, developing an effective Web site or Internet marketing strategy requires certain key decisions about market position, audience or audiences, and goals for Internet marketing. Without good planning, a Web site can waste time and money. This chapter will help you make the necessary decisions.

THE BASICS

Defining Your Market Position

To stand out from competitors, your business or its product or service must have a marketing position—a *unique* marketing position. You must be perceived as different from others—as special. Otherwise your potential customers and clients will have no reason to select your products or services over those of your competitors. What characteristics or features or benefits make your company or product(s) or service(s) special? What distinguishes your customer service or the support your company provides for its products? Is there something different about the way you distribute or deliver your product? Does your product have unique packaging? Think of ways in which your products are different from those of your competitors—other companies in your industry—or at least different from what they claim. Is your service or product different from those of your competitor(s) in design, function, quality, or cost? Of course, those differences should be both positive and valuable to customers. Do any of the following phrases describe your business or product or service?

> The quality manufacturer in [your field]
> Friendly to first-time buyers
> The efficient company for busy executives
> The company with the easiest to use Web site
> The company with the largest sales force
> The company that attends the most trade shows
> The wholesaler with the most complete inventory
> The antique dealer who knows the most about Louis XV furniture
> The brokerage firm that accurately predicts NYSE shifts
> The realty firm that sells the most homes
> The bowling alley with the most lanes in the county
> The no-stress air express

Does your product or service have any of these?

> On-site installation and/or service
> Quality design by old-world craftsmen
> The smoothest ride
> The fastest delivery
> The best flavor
> The most comfortable seating

Or, are you a professional who is any of these?

> The most experienced, caring, educated, or knowledgeable about something
> The busiest, oldest, friendliest, hardest working, youngest, wealthiest

Or are you . . .

The literary agent who placed the most novels with publishers

The attorney with the highest litigation success rate

The veterinarian loved most by cocker spaniels

The tree doctor who has saved the most trees

Defining Your Target Audience

The characteristic most common to a Web audience is that they have access to the Internet—at home, at work, or through a friend or relative. Much of this group still falls in a middle- to upper-income range, although school, library, and workplace access have broadened that range. Beyond their Internet access, your target audience is tied directly to your positioning (and vice versa). If, for example, your position is "The maker of the most durable industrial casters in the world," your target audience consists of prospective buyers and sellers of industrial casters.

How do you identify your target audience? And what do you do with the information about your audience once you have it? For the most part, the audience is the same one that you try to reach with your other marketing and advertising: the people who make decisions about buying a product, using a service, becoming a franchisee, donating to a nonprofit organization. What do you know about them? Make a list of reasons they need or want what you offer. Make a list of things you know about their demographics and psychographics. What is their income range? What age group? What size family? Where do they live? What entertainment do they enjoy? In other words, do your best to make your audience real to you. Why? So that your Web design can reflect the style, tone, and information that will appeal to them.

One more note: Some Web site planners and builders seem to forget that the visitors to Web sites are people. Some designers with a high level of creativity, design skill, and technological know-how create exciting, trendy, flashy sites that are more successful in showing off their abilities than in communicating with people about their needs and priorities.

Defining Your Internet Marketing Goals

The goals you set for your Internet marketing efforts influence or even dictate the content and design of your site(s) and pages. The following goals apply for most businesses Web sites:

1. Generate sales leads or prospects

2. Increase store sales, print catalog sales, or online sales

3. Convert prospects into buyers, and buyers into repeat buyers

4. Increase the loyalty and lifetime value of each customer or client

5. Provide online services that will save company time

6. Distribute marketing information to save direct mail costs or to reinforce and enhance effects of other advertising

In addition, goals can be set for site performance. These goals usually are related to the number of visitors to a site per day or hour, the number of automated forms submitted, the number of people who sign up for a newsletter or free information, the number of people who send e-mail inquiries from the site, or the level of direct requests or orders made from the site.

The most common mistakes that new-to-the-Web businesses make with their Web sites are:

Assuming that Web users will find the site on their own, just because it is there

Not defining clear goals for the Web site

Not providing a clear message or direction for visitors

Not budgeting some amount for promoting the Web site

Not providing sufficient opportunity for visitors to interact with the site and the business that it represents

BEYOND THE BASICS

Positioning: What Is It? Why Is It Important?

Say "Maytag" and people hear "reliable."

Say "Disney" and people hear "family."

Say "Rolls Royce" and people hear "luxury."

Positioning on the Internet and in marketing in general refers to how you (your company, products, or services) are perceived by customers. It is exactly that: a perception that people form.

Positioning is not something that you can touch. Positioning can be fragile and may require continuous tweaking. Your position refers to the place that your company, products, or services occupies in the minds of others. For practical business purposes, it is how people rank your products, your firm, and your services on a graduated good/bad perception scale against similar choices.

The name Maytag is a good example of positioning. For decades, this appliance manufacturer has put out a single message: *reliability*. As a result, when you ask people which washing machine is the most reliable, most will answer "Maytag." Is Maytag the most reliable washer? (See http://www.consumerreports.org.) Maybe, but not every model and not every year. But that doesn't matter in positioning. Maytag's goal, which it set for itself very early in its competitive history, was to gain and keep the position of number one in reliability in consumers' minds. As long as consumers keep thinking that way, Maytag maintains its positioning advantage over its competitors—even competitors who might make a more reliable washer.

Note that Maytag set out early to be positioned as number one in reliability. Being early is important because, once you gain the number one position in people's minds, it is very difficult to dislodge you from that position. So, if at all possible, capture your distinct position early, before someone else does. Fortunately, because the Internet is still a relatively young phenomenon, you may still have a good chance to distinguish yourself from competitors and capture your desired positioning. Maytag is also an excellent example of *branding*, or building a well-recognized brand identity. (See sidebar for additional information on branding.)

You and your Web site are, or perhaps should be, competing relentlessly with other firms that provide the same or similar services or products. Don't think that you can enjoy a friendly sharing of Web space. This is war. And on the Web, the speed with which a company gains market share may spell its success or failure over the next few years. Paying attention to positioning is crucial if a company hopes to get that market share on the Web.

STANDING OUT FROM THE CROWD: HOW DO YOU DISTINGUISH YOURSELF?

By the very nature of positioning, you must distinguish yourself in some way, ideally as something special. What could it be for you? What can you tell people about your firm, products, or service that will differentiate them from others in the minds of your Web site visitors?

Many firms on the Web today are not projecting any specific or distinct positioning whatsoever. Pages in their sites say and show basically the same things: a company logo, product photos, a list of services, a list of cities served, a general statement about "willingness to give 100%," a profound belief in real customer service and ethics. (Yawn.) Site reviewers for Web directories like Yahoo! categorize these sites as "lookie me" sites, that is, sites that appear to be most concerned with the company's ego. These sites could be called "epitaphs for living companies," and reviewers rank them lower than sites that demonstrate sincere concern for the interests and priorities of their visitors.

Your site must focus on creating and reinforcing a particular identity, ability, characteristic, feature, benefit, or service—a *position*. Emphasize a single theme and then let related points, information, graphics, and links to additional pages and/or sites support the position. Note that you need a *particular* position, one that separates you from other companies and Web sites that operate in your field (your competitors).

BRANDING

Branding, a well established marketing concept, became a huge concern for Internet marketers after the Web became a viable advertising medium around 1998. Thousands of firms began "banner wars," filling Web pages with small banner and tile ads (see Chapter 7) in an effort to "brand" their firm, through repeated impressions, at the expense of competitors. They strived to create brand identity and resultant share of market. The idea was that if you placed millions of tiny billboards to increase name recognition or brand awareness on the Web, you would make people remember your product or service or Web site and then do business with you.

Successful branding demands synergy from advertising, public relations, sales promotion, customer service, direct mail, newsletters, volume discounts, co-op programs, word of mouth, event sponsorship, POS, hospitality suites, and other communications tactics. Combinations of these tactics deliver a consistent message about a company and/or its products and services. Delivering that consistent message is especially important on the Web, where things happen fast and brands can be established or swept aside overnight. A small firm that provides local services may never become a national name—a brand name recognized in millions of households. You must, however, work to establish clear positioning in your target area.

According to Brand.com (http://www.brand.com),

Brand is the proprietary visual, emotional, rational, and cultural image that you associate with a company or a product. When you think Volvo, you might think safety. When you think Nike, you might think of Michael Jordan or "Just Do It." When you think IBM, you might think "Big Blue." The fact that you remember the brand name and have positive associations with that brand makes your product selection easier and enhances the value and satisfaction you get from the product.

While Brand X cola or even Pepsi-Cola may win blind taste tests over Coca Cola, the fact is that more people buy Coke than any other cola and, most importantly, they enjoy the experience of buying and drinking Coca Cola. The fond memories of childhood and refreshment that people have when they drink Coke is often more important than a little bit better cola taste. It is this emotional relationship with brands that make them so powerful."

About *brand identity*, Brand.com (http://www.brand.com) says:

Brand identity includes brand names, logos, positioning, brand associations, and brand personality. A good brand name gives a good first impression and evokes positive associations with the brand. A positioning statement tells, in one sentence, what business the company is in, what benefits it provides and why it is better than the competition. Brand personality adds emotion, culture and myth to the brand identity by the use of a famous spokesperson (Bill Cosby - Jello), a character (the Pink Panther), an animal (the Merrill Lynch bull) or an image (You're in good hands with Allstate).

Brand associations are the attributes that customers think of when they hear or see the brand name. McDonalds television commercials are a series of one brand association after another, starting with the yellow arches in the lower right corner of the screen and following with associations of Big Mac, Ronald McDonald, kids, Happy Meal, consistent food quality, etc.

Advertising legend David Oglivy said years ago that a brand is "the intangible sum of a product's attributes: its name, packaging, and price, its history, its reputation, and the way it's advertised."

Put whatever your company stands for behind your brand and carve out your chosen position in the marketplace. How will you know when you are getting close? You'll know when someone mentions your product or firm and immediately someone else says, "Oh, yes, they're the company that. . . ." And what they say next will dictate not only the online future of your firm, but the degree of its overall success at branding as well.

Following are examples of market position statements, taglines, or themes that make some firms or their products or services stand out.

Real Estate

Buyer's Agent, Exclusively—Buyers Need Representation, Too
Seller's Agent, Exclusively
The Beach (or Lake) Property Specialist
The Horse Property (or Ranch or Farm) Expert
The Internet Realtor® for Buyers (or Sellers, or both)
LuxuryHomesforCountryLiving.com
The Luxury Property Realtor®
The "Fixer-Upper" Specialist
The Realtor® for First-Time Buyers
Let the Neighbor Pay Your Mortgage (Income Property Agent)
Historical and Other Older Homes

Dental Professional

Spectacular Smiles Cosmetic Dentistry
Dr. Louis Smith, Pain-Free Orthodontics
Brighten and Whiten But Don't Lighten Your Wallet

Mr. Tooth, Children's Dentistry

Homer Marks D.D.S., Your Family Dental Health Center

Animal Doctor

Pets Are People Too (We treat your pets like they're members of *our* family.)

Country Veterinary Services, Specializing in Farm Animals

24/7 Emergency Animal Clinic

Wings and Feathers, Bird Rx

Soup

Just Like Homemade

The Creamiest

Ready to Eat in Less Than a Minute

All the Vitamins Your Kids Need for a Healthy Lunch

Soup in a Box—Just Add Hot Water!

Automobile

The Fastest Machine on the Road Today!

As Quiet as a Cloud

Easy to Park

More Miles to the Gallon

Choose from 100 Colors!

The Roomiest

The Cheapest Car on the Market

EXAMPLES FROM THE WEB

Enter the word "Purina" into the location box of your browser and you'll get Nestle Purina PetCare's main site. When we visited, the site was positioning Purina and its products as much more than pet food. The tagline reads "Advancing Life," and the site works to communicate the message that the company enhances people's lives by enhancing the lives of their pets. Purina says it and displays it in their images (Fig. 2.1).

The text and graphic from the Oliver Downing Real Estate Web site (Fig. 2.2) proclaim his specialty: "Historic & Other Special Homes."

Casters.com (Fig. 2.3) owns the most valuable URL (http://www.casters.com) in the caster industry. And while their corporation's name is Darnell-Rose, the title of their site, casters.com, takes advantage of and reinforces their wonderfully appropriate Web address. The top of the casters.com page clearly defines what the Web offers while listing several benefits, including a wide selection, durability, ease of use, and quality manufacturing.

When is pet food not just pet food? Screen capture from
http://www.purina.com, © 2000 Nestlé. All rights reserved.

Figure 2.1

Figure 2.2

Oliver Downing

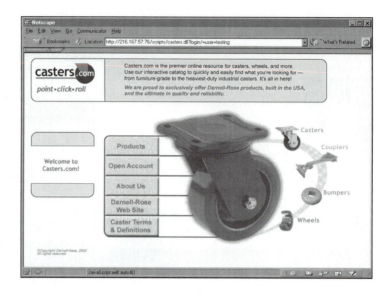

The Only Chocolate Chip Cookies Company unmistakably positions itself as exactly what it is: a company selling only chocolate chip cookies, which
they will ship to you or to someone else. The instant you see their home page,
shown in Figure 2.4, you know what they do. No guesswork required here.

TIP FOR SMALLER FIRMS

This cookie company is a client of a firm that offers turnkey online store services to small businesses. The firm is:

CCNow Incorporated,

706 Philadelphia Pike, Suite 5-B

Wilmington, Delaware 19809

(http://www.ccnow.com)

CCNow and firms like it provide a low-risk way for small and medium sized businesses to sell online.

The Professional Teeth Whitening Company at www.BriteWhite.com
has placed their positioning tag line, "Identical name brands & procedures
dentists use for 1/3 the cost," at the top of their home page, clearly defining
early what they offer a visitor (Fig. 2.5). The text on this page also helps position their product firmly in their Web visitors' minds. The first sentence
tells what they do, including a benefit (reasonable price). The rest of the
clear, concise copy convinces you that even clumsy *you* can *flawlessly* do
what only dentists did in the past. Precision targeting and clean wording
demonstrate this company's understanding of the value of positioning.

Consider how two head-to-head national consumer printing and office
services firms, Sir Speedy and Kinko's, were positioning themselves in the

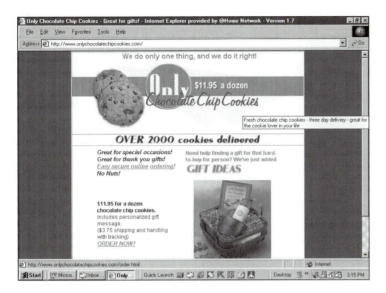

Figure 2.4

Onlychocolatechipcookies. com. Screen capture from http://www.onlychocolate chipcookies.com, © 1999–2002, Only Chocolate Chip Cookies.

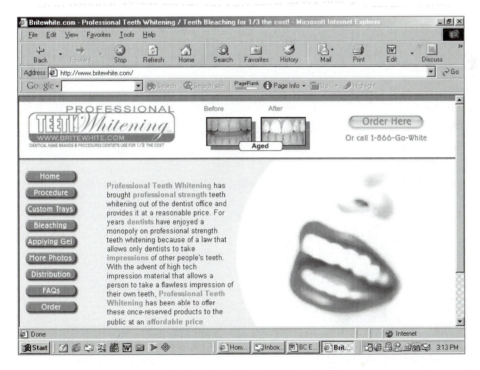

Professional Teeth Whitening. Screen capture from http://www.britewhite.com.

Figure 2.5

middle of 2002 and then in November of that year. The earlier statements positioned Kinko's clearly in consumers' perceptions, while Sir Speedy's claim required visitors to think about what it meant. By the end of 2002, the approaches had changed. Sir Speedy's main headline was clear. Visitors knew Sir Speedy's main service. Kinko's boldly told visitors to send their documents online—leaving it to visitors' assumptions and interpretations as to what Kinko's would do with them.

Web Site Headlines

	Mid-2002	November 2002
Sir Speedy	Get the efficiency of e-commerce and the comfort of local personal service when your document solutions come from the largest global digital network.	Your one source for printing solutions.
Kinko's	You can print, bind, and ship your documents online.	Send us your documents online.

Which of the four headlines do you think does the best job of communicating with consumers and businesses that have documents to be printed?

Analyze It

Which of the following phrases or statements do you think demonstrates the most effective positioning? Why?

1. (baby food) "You'd eat our baby food yourself!" or "for healthy, happy babies"
2. (toothpaste) "with the latest chemical discoveries to sanitize your mouth" or "when you want your mouth to feel fresh and clean"
3. (income tax service) "We attend 200 hours of training each year to master all the smallest details of changes in thousands of tax laws." or "You can trust our fast and accurate income tax preparation."

IDENTIFYING YOUR POSITION

How do you know what position to establish and capture through your Web site? Ask yourself several questions:

What are we best at?
What positions have other firms in our field not yet taken?
Whom do we want to attract? (See Audience section later in this chapter.)
What do we want to accomplish? (See Web Marketing Goals section.)

Select something in which you excel—whether it is "everything for everyone" or something more defined, such as, "We stock only the highest quality medical instrumentation in every category," and then stake out a position for yourself. The last question is especially important, because it must be a realistic assessment of what you can achieve.

Use the checklists below to think about the position you might want to claim. Place a check next to the items that best fit you, your work, your company, product, or service. Thousands upon thousands of descriptions can be created or considered, of course. Do not be limited by the few examples provided here.

CHECKLIST: IDENTIFYING A MARKET POSITION

PART 1: WHAT ARE WE? AT WHAT DO WE EXCEL? POSITIONING A COMPANY

- ❑ Getting new customers.
- ❑ Expanding our customer base.
- ❑ Retaining current customers.
- ❑ Getting referrals from current customers.
- ❑ Initiating frequent contact with customers.
- ❑ Ensuring on-time delivery.
- ❑ Advising buyers about which product best fits their specific needs.
- ❑ Explaining how to use each product so that buyers really "get" it.
- ❑ Helping buyers decide on the right price and the right time to buy a product.
- ❑ Getting business—actual sales—for our customers so that loyalty is developed.
- ❑ Helping customers expand their business.
- ❑ Helping buyers with a certain type of problem.
- ❑ Selling in large quantities. Selling in small quantities.
- ❑ Selling internationally or to a specific country or U.S. geographic region.
- ❑ Helping customers sell older, outdated versions of products they bought from us.
- ❑ Integrating customers into our customer relationship management programs.
- ❑ Assisting buyers with legalities of using our products.
- ❑ Helping customers obtain financing.
- ❑ Working with first-time buyers.
- ❑ Helping customers get maximum profits from using our products.
- ❑ Helping franchisees open new territories.
- ❑ Responding quickly to customer inquires, whether by phone, e-mail, or fax.
- ❑ Helping customers make presentations to *their* customers to help them close a sale.
- ❑ Negotiating unusual or creative transactions to help buyers.
- ❑ Understanding buyers' specific priorities.
- ❑ Educating clients about the latest selling tactics.
- ❑ Ensuring that our customers always have sufficient tools to help use or sell our products.
- ❑ Being supportive of nervous buyers.
- ❑ Having a terrific inside sales department that is very responsive to buyer needs.
- ❑ Giving customers access to our databases that might assist them.
- ❑ Providing exceptional content on our Web site to inform and educate buyers.
- ❑ Helping buyers with their product selections.
- ❑ Communicating complicated information.
- ❑ Dealing with difficult people.
- ❑ Shepherding complex transactions through to completion.

(continued)

- ❑ _____ .
- ❑ _____ .
- ❑ _____ .
- ❑ _____ .

- ❑ _____ .
- ❑ _____ .
- ❑ _____ .

Now write a position statement or "tagline" that fits your firm.

PART 2: WHAT AM I LIKE? WHAT IS MY FIRM LIKE?
POSITIONING AN INDIVIDUAL OR A COMPANY

- ❑ Smart
- ❑ Analytical
- ❑ Warm
- ❑ Energetic
- ❑ Thoughtful
- ❑ Efficient
- ❑ Calculating
- ❑ Creative
- ❑ Detail-oriented

- ❑ Persistent
- ❑ Mature
- ❑ Casual
- ❑ Formal
- ❑ Independent
- ❑ Team player
- ❑ Respectful
- ❑ Experienced
- ❑ Industry leader

- ❑ Dedicated
- ❑ Shy
- ❑ Businesslike
- ❑ Successful
- ❑ Assertive
- ❑ Outgoing
- ❑ R & D leader
- ❑ Customer-friendly
- ❑ Fast delivery

- ❑ _____ .
- ❑ _____ .
- ❑ _____ .

- ❑ _____ .
- ❑ _____ .

PART 3: WHAT IS MY PRODUCT (OR SERVICE) LIKE?
WHAT ARE ITS FEATURES AND BENEFITS?

- ❑ Fastest
- ❑ Smoothest
- ❑ Brightest
- ❑ Safest
- ❑ Environmentally friendly
- ❑ Easy to use (or open, apply, understand, prepare, etc.)
- ❑ Non-stick
- ❑ Odor free
- ❑ Biggest (smallest, tallest, widest, heaviest, lightest, etc.)

- ❑ Custom made (sizes, colors, decorated, etc.)
- ❑ Most efficient
- ❑ Brightest
- ❑ _____ .
- ❑ _____ .
- ❑ _____ .
- ❑ _____ .

PART 4: WHAT IS MY PRODUCT (OR SERVICE) SUPPORT LIKE?

- ❑ Free lifetime support
- ❑ Easy to find
- ❑ Available at your local hardware store (stationers, grocer, shoe repair, library, etc.)
- ❑ Friendly, helpful customer service
- ❑ Free replacement parts

- ❑ Lifetime guarantee
- ❑ Free (fast, overnight, reliable, etc.) delivery
- ❑ _____ .
- ❑ _____ .
- ❑ _____ .
- ❑ _____ .

IDENTIFYING COMPETITORS' POSITIONS

Don't overlook what your direct competitors are saying about themselves. Why? Primarily to avoid attempting to occupy a position that someone else has already claimed. Also, looking at competitors' positions may give you related ideas or refinements to use for your own position. Examine both their implicit messages (imagery, such as ad photos shot in upscale locales, using celebrity spokespeople who stand for something, etc.) and explicit positioning (what they say about themselves in print, radio, TV, and online).

UNIQUE MARKET POSITION STATEMENT

So we've agreed: A product should be perceived as unique or distinctive compared to similar products so that the target Web audience values and remembers it. After deciding on a position, communicate it by creating and using a memorable tagline or signature statement. We'll call this statement or phrase a *unique market position statement* (UMPS).

Martha J. Woodbury, developer of the real estate Web site Media Marketing—A Real Estate Super Site (http://www.nicheswork.com), discusses the idea of using a unique selling position in "The Competition Killer" (full text at http://www.nicheswork.com/usp.html). Although she speaks specifically about marketing real estate, the principles Woodbury outlines apply to any business: "You should include your [positioning] statement on everything you print, every talk you give, every article you write for the newspaper, every ad you place, every property sign or rider, in your voice mail message, on your Web site, your business cards, your fax cover sheet, your checks . . . everything you say and do."

Woodbury believes that an effective statement is one that communicates the unique services you provide, empathizes with your prospects' pain or desires, and provides a "guarantee." She suggests that you do this using 20 words or fewer in a phrase that is "unique, specific, and believable—but outrageous enough that your prospects will read it, stop in their tracks, and say, 'Really? How do they do that?'" She continues: "Connect emotionally with your prospects through fear of loss, greed, ego, desire, pain, frustration, to be better off than the Joneses, save more, make more, have more, spend less, get better service, etc."

How do you translate your marketing position into a unique marketing position statement or tagline? Start with the checklists on pages 37 and 38 and a dollop of imagination. Did you check "Communicating complicated information"? If so, consider taglines such as "You Like Straight Talk. So Do We." Did you check "Helping customers make presentations to *their* customers to help them make a sale"? Consider "The Service that Sells *Your* Customers." Did you mark "Helping buyers with a certain type of problem"? Try "Problems Solved Here."

Put your tagline with your company, product, or service name. "Peach-Grove SoftWare—Smart Solutions for Big Enterprise Needs!" Or "Buy the most house for your money—guaranteed! Jack Yost Real Estate." Or "The Canon DR-3080C Scanner—High Performance Color Scanning in a Compact Package."

Practice   Write a tagline for each of the following products or services. The name is provided, along with something important about the item.

1. Smith's Pills—_____. (Smith's sells vitamins for horses.)
2. Dandy Diapers—_____. (Dandy's diapers have lanolin to keep baby's skin soft.)
3. Walczyks' Windows—_____. (Walczyks' are designer windows featured in magazines such as *Architectural Digest.*)
4. Meyers' Maps—_____. (Meyers' creates high-detail maps based on aerial photos.)

CREATE A UNIQUE MARKET POSITION STATEMENT
Read the statements you wrote on page 38 or select three of the items you checked and write a tagline for each of them. Use your imagination. Don't worry about sounding silly. You can polish them up later. What's important is to find ways to communicate a position in a concise, memorable way.

Your Audience(s)

Your audiences, or target markets, are directly related to your positioning, and your Web marketing must address and serve these groups above all others. Such focus will bring more qualified, receptive visitors to your Web site, and it will save you money and time by avoiding audiences that are less receptive to your message.

Who are these audiences? Yes, of course they are buyers and information seekers who use the Internet. Just as important, they are the people who will respond to your positioning. If you position yourself as the "PVC Pipe Specialist for Big Commercial Projects," then your primary Web audience is contractors who specialize in large projects. If you are the "Upscale Realty Firm," then your Web audience is buyers and sellers of upscale homes.

Planning and developing your Internet marketing will require a little more information than this, however. You need to put your understanding of who these people are—their needs and wants, their backgrounds, lifestyles, and what motivates them—to work for you. That's why writing out a target audience description is an important step in your planning process.

Note that your site may have secondary audiences. These people are not the buyers of your products and services; rather, they are the people who refer buyers. For example, assume that yours is a national accounting firm that is very knowledgeable about the tax implications of selling off assets in the event of a bankruptcy or merger. A secondary audience for you might be corporate bankruptcy attorneys and commercial real estate firms.

Another example: Assume that you organize bicycle rides in which thousands of riders raise millions of dollars annually for charity. In addition to individual riders, secondary markets might include bicycle shops, online bicycling sites, and medical industry firms that relate to a recipient field such as breast cancer research. You might also find your audience among outdoor enthusiasts, exercise sites, gymnasiums, or YMCA and YWCA locations.

To clarify your thinking about your target Internet audience (or audiences, since you may want to reach more than one), write a description for each and every one. Why bother to write a description when you know these people so well? Writing an audience description will focus your attention on the specific characteristics of this group. You will improve your ability to create effective marketing statements, think of more helpful tools to place on your Web site, clarify your understanding of what motivates each audience, and be more likely to maintain focus.

What information should you include in an audience description? Based on your own experience with your customers or the clients you wish to attract, write a description of their markets, industries, lifestyle, education, approximate income, types of careers, leisure activities, reading habits, and so forth. Sometimes this information is called audience *psychographics*. Following is an example of a paragraph-style audience description for a firm with nationwide franchisees whose representatives visit homes and offices to sell and install window coverings. Remember that descriptions also vary by geographic region, area, or city. An upscale buyer or seller in Slippery Rock, Pennsylvania, may be very different from one in Beverly Hills, California, and your window blinds chain audience might be quite different from this one.

Sample Audience Description 1: Audience for a Window Blinds Buyer in South Orange County, California

Our target audience is a married couple, college educated, age 45–55, with no children at home, living in a 2,400 sq. ft. house with $90,000 to $140,000 in equity. They live in a major metropolitan area or nearby community. They are active, enjoy golfing and club memberships, are socially involved in the community, and take considerable pride in their home, in which they entertain often. Available market research indicates that they purchase window treatments every four to seven years and the average purchase is $800. Many will replace window coverings when they buy or sell their home.

Sample Audience Description 2: Audience for a Firm that Markets Industrial Casters Worldwide

Our target audience is an industrial buyer (of accessories and OEM components) for large aviation manufacturers (such as Boeing), airlines (American Airlines, Qantas, and others), and cruise and merchant marine shiplines. The audience is also a buyer of gurneys and other rolling carts for institutions, including hospitals, prisons, and schools. Our buyer is age 38 to 55, married or once-divorced, living in a suburb of a major city, earning $55,000 to $85,000 per year. Usually a male (data show 72 percent are male) who rose up through the ranks at his firm, is an empty nester with a net worth of about $300,000 who enjoys TV sitcoms, Monday night football, golf, and family activities. Fifty percent of our buyers are college graduates; virtually all completed at least two years of college.

Sample Audience Description 3: Audience for a Firm that Markets "Horse Property" for Real Estate Buyers and Sellers

Review this example of a list-style audience description for a realty chain that positions itself as a "horse property specialist." Remember, a horse property specialist's audience might be quite different depending on the geographic location of the audience being described.

- Family: Married couple with two or three children.
- Home goal: Property in semi-rural area with space and zoning for one to four horses.
- Education: Some college or college graduates.
- Career/Employment/Income: Sales, teaching, management; combined annual income range of $70,000–$110,000.
- Age: 36–50.
- Home size: 2,000 to 2,800 sq. ft.; 4 or 5 bedrooms.
- Home entertaining: Casual, patio, barbecue, etc.
- Current home equity: $40,000–$60,000.
- Cash-to-add: Usually none–$10,000.
- Credit: Varies. Often have significant credit card debt.
- Schools: Okay to take bus.
- Activities: Mostly family oriented. Horse training, riding events, school events, sports, etc.
- Cars: At least one van or five-passenger pickup, not new.
- Shopping: Standard and discount malls, tack shops, Western stores.
- Magazines: News, horse, home improvement, gardening, country.
- TV: Watch family programming, cable sports, animal and kid channels.
- Pets: Probably several dogs/cats in addition to the horse(s).

After reading these descriptions, you should feel that you know a little more about the three audiences. You have enough information to be able to ask a new customer a few questions to begin communication and the relationship-building process, and you have enough information to plan some of your Web site content.

CREATE A TARGET AUDIENCE DESCRIPTION

Now write an audience description for one of your target audiences. Use either paragraph or list format. To get started, imagine that a close friend has just said to you, "Tell me about most of the customers that you work with."

BOTTOMS-UP (VERSUS TOP-DOWN) GOAL SETTING

One way to discover goals for your Web site is to get as many people in the company as possible to contribute ideas. This is best done in a "bottoms-up" approach, starting with the lowest ranked company employees and working up to the CEO. The purpose is to avoid having top managers *dictate* the firm's Web approaches on their own (top-down management). Getting input "bottoms up" from "the trenches" can sometimes produce a better site; at least with more input from various perspectives on all facets of the site, its potential for success may increase.

Begin by having objective company staff poll workers in their departments about how the company Web site could help *them*—the individual employees—complete their job tasks. A bottom-up exercise asks employees "What can the Web site do to help *you* achieve *your* job goals in *your* department?"

In the next phase, the staffers condense the employee input by department and then pass it up the ladder for review. Often this review is done at different levels during brainstorming sessions. Sessions are repeated until clear approaches (to do lists) emerge that help the firm accomplish the following:

1. Serve the needs of site visitors, going beyond "bragging" about the company or its products or services. Examples of questions:
   - What kind of content do we need to make our site a valuable, enjoyable, interactive experience for our visitors?
   - How can we empower guests to buy from us, buy again, and refer others to us?
2. Serve the current and future needs of all departments
3. Minimize the cannibalization of current, non-Web, profitable operations
4. Allow for a transition period if current non-Web operations *will* be cannibalized, for example, switch from selling through manufacturer's representatives in certain regions to selling products directly from the Web site in those regions
5. Establish a budget sufficient to ensure creation and maintenance of a quality site
6. Establish a budget sufficient for effective initial rollout of the site

Web Marketing Goals

WHAT DO YOU WANT YOUR SITE TO DO FOR YOU?

Part of planning your Internet marketing must be determining what your Web site should offer visitors and what you want your site(s) to do for you. What will position the site in a particular way in the visitor's mind? What are your goals for your site? Why are you building this site? What is your practical business goal?

Goals are specific to your type of business. The goals for a firm that sells antique jewelry over the Web are far different from those of one that sells farm tractors through a nationwide network of dealerships. The goals for your Web site need to become extensions of your business plan and your marketing plan. Study those documents to find leads on setting your Web site goals.

When you think about your Web marketing goals, and in particular the goals for your Web site or one of your Web sites, decide at the outset whether you want this site to be a corporate identity site, a product or service information site, a transaction-oriented site, or a customer relationship management site. (These types of sites are discussed in Chapter 1.) Here are some reasons businesses give for establishing a Web site:

1. Our firm is losing sales to competitors because they have a site and we don't. We don't care if our site is great or not. We just need one to compete. (*Goal*: Minimal presence; probably not a customer relationship management site.)

2. When people see our print ads for our products, they phone and e-mail us with questions about the items we sell. The Web site makes doing that easier; it tells them about us and gives product and ordering information, too. (*Goal*: Answer the most common questions generated by our print ads to save considerable time on the part of our customer service staff; probably a product or service information site.)

3. Our firm's entire Web site relates to golf. We buy ads in all media to drive people to our site, which offers 1,500 links and 150 pages of helpful hints. Impressed with such content, many visitors sign up for my opt-in newsletter. We make money by selling ads both on the site and in our newsletter, which now reaches 200,000 golfers monthly (*Goal*: Increase advertising sales; increase number of site visitors and newsletter subscribers; could be a customer relationship management site. This example describes a vortal. See more on portals and vortals in Chapter 6.)

4. We are a major urban law firm specializing in corporate law. Our site tells our audience—midsized businesses—why an outside corporate law *specialist* is best and why ours offers them more. The site describes

the many extra services we provide—services that clients would not ordinarily get from other law firms. (*Goal*: Compete successfully with firms that offer more limited services; generate new client inquiries. Probably a service information site; possibly a corporate identity site or a combination of the two. The example does not describe sufficient interactivity to indicate an effective customer relationship management site.)

5. We specialize in selling gift products costing more than $5,000. Our site portrays us as the "prestige gift company." People who want to buy such items often select us over others in our market niche, and we want to keep it that way. (*Goal*: Maintain a position, or even leadership, in the upscale gift market. Could be any of the four types of sites described in Chapter 1.)

6. We call ourselves the "storage specialist" and target out-of-area home-buyers and corporations who want to relocate to any area of the country. Our site relates primarily to Web-savvy home seekers and corporate relocation firms and gives them many online tools to help with their moves and proper packing, storing, and shipping of goods. We partner with a national moving van line and several major relocation firms. (*Goal*: Empathize with out-of-area buyers and engage them as customers; attract relocation partners. Has potential for becoming a customer relationship management site.)

7. Our site helps people sell classic works of art, specifically sculptures. We use the latest Web technology available: 360° views and videos that zoom, plus classical music and jazz soundtracks. My sellers take great pride in telling friends that their art is shown in a video on the Internet, along with in-depth historical data about the work of art and about the owners, if they wish. To get people to visit my site and view such art, and to gain more contracts, I run ads in upscale magazines and on prestigious art Web sites. (*Goal*: Gain listings by appealing to pride of ownership and social status of upscale art sellers. The site is primarily transaction oriented.)

8. Our investment firm's site is designed to help existing clients learn more about establishing charitable remainder trusts to shelter certain property. Transactions always go more smoothly with clients who understand the process. Explaining the benefits in a Web site saves us a great deal of time that would otherwise be spent educating our clients. (*Goal*: Save time; educate clients. Has potential to be a customer relationship management site.)

These, of course, are just examples. There are thousands of specific reasons that companies create a Web presence. Now it's your turn. Write a statement of your Web site marketing goal(s).

Summary

Web sites that successfully market a company, product, or service have been built on careful, conscious positioning. They target specific, well understood audiences, and they are designed to achieve specific and, whenever possible, measurable goals.

Review Questions

1. Why should your business distinguish itself from competitors?
2. What are some ways in which your business is different from your competitors'?
3. In what ways are your products different from those of your competitors?
4. How are your competitors trying to position themselves in the marketplace?
5. How do your competitors portray their products or services as different or better?
6. How does your positioning relate to your target audiences?
7. How would you go about defining your target audiences?
8. What is the "human element" that you must always remember when dealing with customers and prospects?
9. List three common goals of most Web sites.
10. List three common Web site mistakes.
11. When planning a site, should people brainstorm together or by themselves?
12. Why is it important to budget adequately for Web site promotion?
13. What is *branding*?
14. What positioning has Maytag always sought (and achieved) for its products?
15. What is a "lookie-me" Web site?
16. What does a unique marketing position statement accomplish?
17. Why are secondary target audiences important?
18. Name your firm's secondary target audiences in order of importance.
19. How will your Web site attract secondary target audiences?
20. Why do you suppose Jello chose Bill Cosby as its ad spokesman?

Review Activities

1. Write three positioning statements for the following products or services:
   a. A new mouthwash
   b. A car repair shop for luxury autos
   c. A law firm specializing in personal injury cases
   d. A company that makes teddy bears
   e. A tax preparation service
   f. A zoo
   g. Tomato soup
   h. Office furniture

2. Imagine that you're in an elevator and you have 30 seconds to answer the question, "What business are you in?" What would you say?

3. Your company has asked you to create a bumper sticker that will communicate how it is special. Write three bumper stickers: one that positions the company, one for one of its products, and one for one of its services.

4. Write a title for your company Web site using no more than six words.

More Than a Pretty Face

Web Site Content

The content and design of a Web site must communicate the branding or unique market position *immediately*. As soon as the page displays on visitors' monitors, visitors should *know* that this site has the information, products, or Web functions they seek. Otherwise they may not stay long. If the content is *useful* to them, as well as interesting, informative, and (in many cases) fun, they'll stick around for a while. This chapter will help you identify the content that will be most effective for your market position, audience, and goals.

THE BASICS

The types and sizes of businesses using the Internet for marketing are extremely diverse, and their Web sites also look very different. Some Web sites are devoted entirely to a single product or service. Others are created specifically to provide follow-up on television, radio, or other media advertising. Some market the services of an individual; others market the services or products of a corporation with thousands of employees. Nonetheless, most Web sites do share some common features. For the most part, they include sections on the business and its history, its products and/or services, the employees, and information on how to contact the company. Depending on the business type and the size of the Web site it may also include sections on how to apply for a position within the company, industry or company news, or links to other sites with related information.

Having all these parts does not guarantee an effective Web site, however. A site could, for example, have information about a company without ever stating its branding or positioning. Or it could claim a particular position, say most customer friendly, and then fail to support that position by providing easy ways for customers to purchase, order, or inquire about products. Or it could provide an online order form "for fast and easy purchasing" that is so lengthy and complicated that visitors take one look at the information that is being requested and leave.

The content of your Web site depends on your positioning, audience, and goals. So, rather than providing a checklist of required Web pages or features, this chapter will address Web site content from the marketer's perspective. Regardless of the market position of a business, product, or service, the site must include content that accomplishes the following goals:

1. *Communicate the market positioning or branding.* Regardless of the size, look, complexity, or sophistication of your site, no visitor should ever leave it without knowing the marketing position. A company's unique market position statement (UMPS; see Chapter 2) or that of its product or service should be prominent and clear. Use a tagline together with the company or product name to help visitors recognize the intended market position immediately. A few (very few) companies are branded so strongly that they need no more than their name to communicate their position. Rolls Royce (expensive, luxurious), McDonald's (fast, consistent, kid-friendly), and Waldorf-Astoria (exclusive, attentive, elite) are examples of names that have become identified with their positioning. Their names convey their image quickly, clearly, and consistently to huge numbers of people.

2. *Prove or support the market positioning.* Stating that yours is the company that is or does something special is not enough. Support your market positioning with information about the company, product, or service. Include content, both written and visual, that clearly demonstrates that a product is the fastest, friendliest, healthiest, or whatever else characterizes its market position. Individuals who provide profes-

sional services, such as real estate agents, tax advisors, or artists, would support their position with information about their interests, experiences, and skills.

3. *Give visitors useful information related to the business, product, or service.* Such information may inform and educate visitors, give them reliable resources they need or will need, help them solve problems or make decisions related to a purchase, or entertain them. You know from experience or from market research what your clients and customers need. The Web site should help visitors resolve such questions, either with information contained in the site's pages or by linking to sites where that information is available.

4. *Provide content that is interesting to the target audience; that is, content that will attract them, hold their attention, and bring them back for repeat visits.* Content that is interesting to a target audience is probably also related to your market position. Are you a real estate agent for horse properties? Consider adding content or links to other sites with horse-related content, such as breeds of horses, feed and tack shops, horse grooming, equestrian competitions, working horses, horse breeding, horse riding, horse health and medicine, horse racing, and design of stables. This also helps position you as an authority in your chosen market position. Does your business sell books for kids? Your Web site's content should be interesting to a target age group, for example, ten-year-olds. Do you sell organic tomatoes? Add tomato recipes, a nutrition center, and links to sites that sell basil or pasta.

5. *Enable and encourage visitors to ask questions, place orders, make comments, and contact you.* Web sites that sell products or services directly to purchasers can and should include various easy-to-understand ways for Web visitors to purchase online and offline. The visitor to a Web site whose objective is to sell a software program should be able to pay for the program online and then download it immediately. The Web site of a nonprofit organization that survives by member gifts needs to give people various ways to make those gifts.

Most Web visitors like to communicate using their computers. If the only way they can reach you is by telephone, chances are they'll go elsewhere. (Be glad. Chances also are that it's 2:00 in the morning.) You need to provide ways for them to communicate with you from your Web site. A link that opens a visitor's e-mail program with a blank, pre-addressed message is still the most common and most used device that Internet visitors use to send questions and comments to Web site owners. Place such a link on *every* page. Explore other ways for visitors to communicate: online forms to complete, a guest book for comments, bulletin boards, and even scheduled live chats. You never know when, during a tour of your site, a visitor will be struck with an uncontrollable desire to contact you, so make it easy—from anywhere on your site. (The next chapter will discuss some of the more advanced functions for visitor communications.)

BEYOND THE BASICS

Communicate Market Positioning or Branding

Any visitor entering your site should know immediately what market positioning you are claiming or striving for. A statement of your unique market position (UMP; see Chapter 2) should be prominent and clear on the main entry page, and that positioning should be reinforced on subsequent pages. Such a statement, whether in text or graphics or both, will work to establish, reinforce, or build market positioning or brand identity.

A direct way to position a business or product at a glance is by using a tagline, headline, or visual element at the top of the page that communicates what it means for the Web site visitor. Examine the screen capture of Ford Motor Company's Web site for Lincolns (Fig. 3.1). Notice that the

Figure 3.1   "Luxury." Screen capture from http://www.lincolnvehicles.com.

word *luxury* is at the top of the screen. That part of the screen is also animated, drawing the visitor's attention to Lincoln's positioning—*luxury*.

Hormel Foods Corporation also places its positioning statement on its main Web page (Fig. 3.2). "For more than a century, Hormel Foods Corporation has promised and delivered a unique combination of quality and innovation, value, convenience, and wholesome goodness." The clear image of appealing food also helps complete the positioning. Is there any doubt that Hormel Foods is about food?

One more example: at http://www.hon.com, the HON company's office furniture site says, "HON offers an exceptionally broad selection of high-performance office chairs, durable and attractive desks, and the best selling files in the world." Its designer headline, "Define your space," tells visitors that HON sells more than furniture—it sells space!

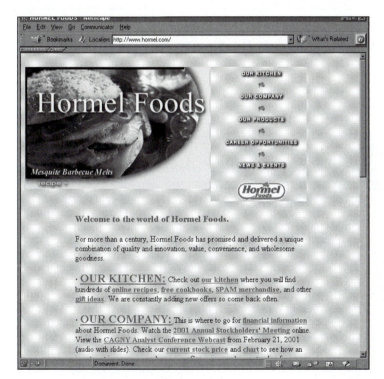

Figure 3.2

Hormel Foods Corporation screen capture from http://www.hormel.com.
© Hormel Foods Corporation

You Decide

1. Compare the screen captures shown in Figures 3.3 and 3.4, taken from two sites of ice cream companies. What positioning is each company claiming for its product? How does each company communicate that position?
2. Visit http://www.marbleslab.com and http://www.benjerry.com. How do these companies communicate their positions?

Figure 3.3

Yorkshire Dales.
Screen capture from http://
www.yorkshire-dales-ice-
cream.co.uk, © 2000.

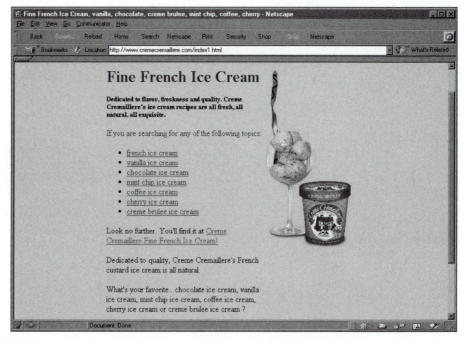

Figure 3.4   Cremaillere.Screen capture from http://www.cremecremaillere.com/
index1.html.

Support Your Market Positioning and Achieve Other Web Marketing Goals

By themselves, positioning statements may not be convincing, especially if the product, service, or business being presented is not already well known. One of the jobs of Web site content is to provide support for the position being claimed.

As with most things about the Internet, the ways in which Web sites support claimed positions varies widely. To some degree, however, similarities can be found among sites that are concerned primarily with a product or service, a specific line of branded products or services, a large number of related products, or an entire company. Table 3.1 shows some of the goals and types of content shared by these types of Web sites.

FOCUS ON A PRODUCT OR SERVICE

Web sites that focus on a single product are not necessarily small or simple. Remember, sites go well beyond what can be done with a product flyer or brochure. Sites work to position a product, increase visibility and/or recognition or brand awareness, create or improve product reputation or image, inform a particular Web audience, and encourage product sales or sell the product directly. Site content usually includes most or all

Table 3.1	AUDIENCE AND GOAL-RELATED CONTENT			
Focus	Examples	Web Audience(s)	Goals	Content
Product or service	Eggs; Vitamin A; Tabasco Sauce; Lipitor®; Lipton Green Tea; a particular book; a dentist, tax preparer, gardener; Realtor®	Potential purchasers (wholesale or direct) or people who influence purchasers; potential clients	Position product; increase visibility and/or recognition, increase brand awareness; improve product reputation or image; inform Web audience; encourage product sales or sell product directly	Features; benefits; testimonials; uses; advantages; sometimes product specifications or statistics; sometimes history of the discovery, development, testing, and sales of the product; often links to parent company Web site

(continued)

Table 3.1	AUDIENCE AND GOAL-RELATED CONTENT (*CONTINUED*)			
Line or brand of products	Minute Maid Juices; Ben & Jerry's; HON office furnishings; Pontiacs	Same	Position brand and/ or product line; inform Web audience about line and products; help potential customers/clients make decisions and choices; encourage product sales or sell product directly	Adds support for the identity of the entire line and information for the individual products in the line
Large number of related products or services, possibly from various sources	Books; camping equipment; computers and peripherals; camera equipment; antiques. Financial, legal, real estate firm; construction, repair services; portals/ vortals such as diabetesportal. com	Online purchasers; potential clients	Build *company* image; direct item sales. Amazon.com, fujitsu.com, tias. com . . . Sales of Web advertising. Realtor.com, ebay.com	Above plus information about the supplier or distributor or service provider. Site often set up as a catalog, storefront, or mall
Companies	SaraLee, Microsoft, IBM, Pfizer	Investors, jobseekers, potential franchisers, general public	Above plus investor relations, employee recruitment, franchise development. Build company image and encourage sales via distributors, offices, franchises, etc. May or may not offer direct sales	Above plus information about the company history, news, management, franchises, subsidiaries, divisions, etc.

of the following (although they might be named differently): product or service characteristics, features, benefits, advantages, uses, testimonials. Depending on the product or service, pages with detailed product specifications or statistics are included. Sometimes history of the discovery, development, testing, and sales of the product adds credibility and supports positioning, as well as engaging the personal interest of the Web visitor. If the product is part of a brand line marketed by a large company or if it has a parent corporation, links to the line, umbrella, or parent company Web site can also help position the product.

Examine the screen capture in Figure 3.5, the site for the cholesterol-reducing drug Lipitor®. This site uses various approaches to position Lipitor's makers, Pfizer, as the expert on cholesterol and Lipitor as the drug of choice for reducing cholesterol. The site itself is positioned as "your personal source for cholesterol information," which is saying that Pfizer is the authority, the expert, the holder of knowledge. Various features of the site demonstrate the expertise of Lipitor's makers. The site works to educate visitors about cholesterol, arterial sclerosis, and heart disease. The first four links, "My Cholesterol Control," "Risk Factor Survey," "Artery Gallery," and

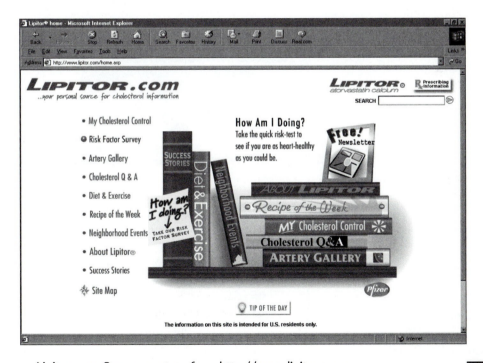

Lipitor.com. Screen capture from http://www.lipitor.com.
© 2000 Warner-Lambert Export, Ltd. LIPITOR is a registered trademark of Pfizer Ireland Pharmaceuticals, a Pfizer company.

Figure 3.5

"Cholesterol Q & A," all demonstrate that Pfizer is the expert, dispensing information about the serious concern over high cholesterol.

Further down the list are links to pages with information about Lipitor specifically—what it is and how it works—as well as to a variation on testimonials, "Success Stories." The pages also have links to the Pfizer Web site. And, as we'll discuss in the next section, this site has related useful information to engage visitors: quizzes, surveys, recipes, tips, and events information.

Pfizer does not sell Lipitor online, so how does the site help sell it? In four ways: (1) by increasing brand awareness; (2) by building the public's confidence in Pfizer and Lipitor; (3) by increasing the degree to which people are accustomed to the idea of taking a drug for cholesterol; (4) by repeatedly telling Web visitors to have their cholesterol levels checked and to ask their doctor about Lipitor.

Another site designed to inform consumers while positioning a product is the one by the American Egg Board (www.aeb.org, Fig. 3.6). Like the Lipitor site, a primary goal is to build a positive image. The site does not sell eggs online, but it does encourage visitors to use eggs (to eat as well as for decorating and other purposes). The Web site is an important component of the Board's work "to allow egg producers to fund and carry out

Figure 3.6

American Egg Board. Screen capture from www.aeb.org. Copyright © 2000 by American Egg Board.

proactive programs to increase markets for eggs, egg products and spent fowl products through promotion, research and education." The audience is not limited to egg eaters, but includes potential poultry ranchers, manufacturers of products that use eggs, wholesalers, and retailers. The site contains ample information for all these audiences, with information about eggs, chickens, and the egg industry. (The section called "retail area" contains information for retailers; it is not used to sell eggs directly.)

The site shown in Figure 3.7 is designed to sell a book, in this case, *A Boston's World*, written by—of course—a Boston Terrier. Visitors know immediately that the site is about this book, and the tagline, "Have a Ball!" does double-duty, referring to a benefit of the book as well as to the tennis-ball links on the page. Information about the book itself is found off the link "About My Book," and a copy can be ordered from the "Get Your Copy" link. Other links take visitors to related activities and pages about author Mickey, convincing visitors that Mickey and his book are worthy of their dollars.

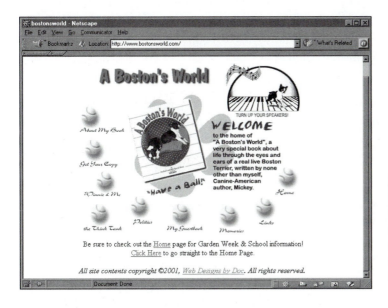

Figure 3.7

A Boston's World. Screen capture from www.bostonsworld.com. All site contents copyright © 2001, Web Designs by Doc.

FOCUS ON A BRAND, PRODUCT LINE, OR COMPANY

Is there any doubt in your mind that Pontiac is positioning its line of vehicles as exciting? If you could see the fire-engine red background (Fig. 3.8), any possible doubt would vanish. Although this Web site focuses on an entire line of vehicles, the types of information are similar to those we've examined earlier. The navigation bars across the top of the screen show that visitors can expect a lot of information about the various models and dealer locations, as well as testimonials, special offers, news, and

history (Fig. 3.9). Why a history of Pontiac? To demonstrate that Pontiac has always been exciting, and to make the point that a vehicle with this long and successful history must be a quality product.

From the main page, click into a model and you'll find the product features, specifications, and benefits. And each model has its own version of an "exciting" tagline. In the case of the Montana shown in Figure 3.10, the tag reads "Life is More Exciting in Montana."

Some company Web sites strike a balance between communicating with investors and communicating with customers or distributors. John Deere, positioned as an international, established, stable, successful, dependable farm- and other-equipment firm, uses a third of its USA/Canada home page for investor information and links. (See Figure 3.11.)

In the center of the page, John Deere places images and links that lead to content for its primary audiences: farmers/ranchers, homeowners/gardeners/estate owners, golf and turf professionals, ground care specialists, contractors, and loggers/forestry professionals.

When visitors click on the link to learn more about the company, the "About Us" text informs them of the company's growth, substance, and business philosophy in two short paragraphs:

> Deere & Company, founded in 1837, grew from a one-man blacksmith shop into a worldwide corporation that today does business in more than 160 countries and employs approximately 40,000 people worldwide.

The company is guided today, as it has been since 1837, by John Deere's original values: a commitment to product quality, customer service, business integrity, and a high regard for individual contribution. The company strives to create shareholder value through its pursuit of continuous improvement and profitable growth.

Deere provides copious information about its history and performance. The page on "Our Company" links to various sections about the history, John Deere the blacksmith, corporate contributions through the John Deere Foundation, annual reports, investor and stockholder information, and much more. (See Figure 3.12.)

Using a page or pages with information about a company should get visitors' attention and keep them reading. An interesting story with images will work much better than a list of statistics—although with eye-catching charts to bring them to life, statistics really can be arresting.

Figure 3.10

"Life is more exciting in Montana." Screen capture from http://www.
pontiac.com.
Copyright General Motors Corporation.

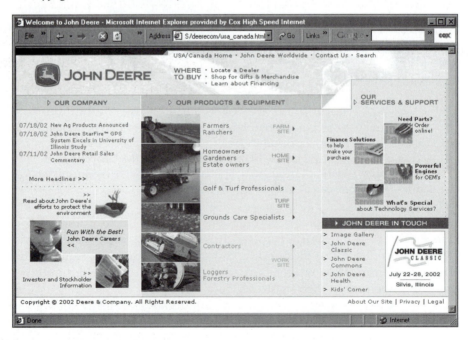

Figure 3.11

Screen capture from http://www.deere.com, July, 2002.

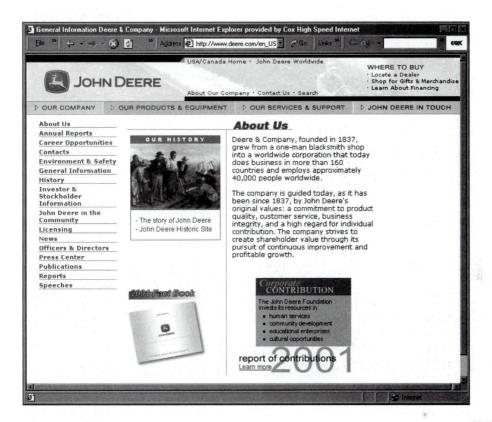

Screen capture from http://www.deere.com.

Figure 3.12

CKE Restaurants, Inc., owner of the Carl's Jr., Hardee's, and La Andra quick service food outlets, has an "About Us" page with three links that lead to: Financial Info, Press Releases, and Carl's Jr. History (Fig. 3.13).

Even if your firm does not date back to 1837 as does John Deere, offering some of your firm's history may add credibility and personality. Carl Karcher Enterprises, Inc. (CKE) tells an entrepreneurial super-story on its history page, along with a decade-by-decade illustrated summary of CKE milestones—a great rags-to-riches story from the 1940s.

Having left the family farm in Ohio, Carl moved to California with dreams of someday starting his own business. Carl and Margaret borrowed $311 on their Plymouth, added $15 of their own to buy the hot dog cart, and started their own business on July 17, 1941.

A few carts later . . . Carl and Margaret moved to Anaheim and opened their first full-service restaurant, Carl's Drive-In Barbecue, on January 16, 1945. Carl always enjoyed his work and always attempted to treat his customers as if they were in his own home. He believed that hard work and dedication would make him successful at whatever he tried to

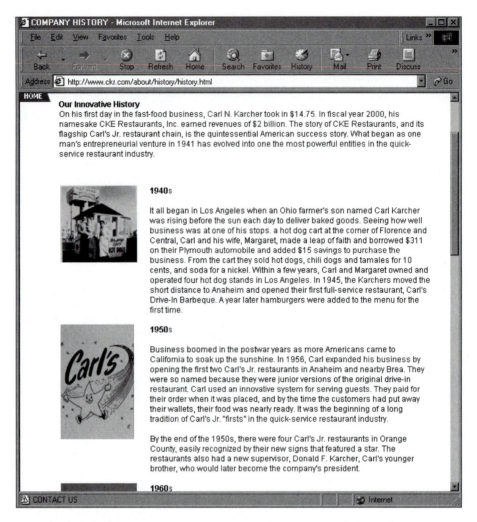

Figure 3.13 Carl Karcher Enterprises, Inc. Screen capture from http://www.ckr.com/
about/history/history.html.
© 2000 CKE Restaurants, Inc.

accomplish . . . and it did! In 1946, Carl introduced hamburgers to the
menu for the first time.

The Carl's Jr. story has been retold thousands of times by the media.
Thus, the story has gained the firm untold millions of dollars worth of
free media space over the years. So, if you have a terrific story to tell about
how your firm got started, tell it every chance you get! Do so especially on
your Web site's History page.

A COMPANY'S PEOPLE

Increasingly we see what we think is a positive addition to business Web sites: information about the people who own, operate, and work for the business. This people focus is actually a recognition of some of the earliest activities on the Web, which now hosts literally millions of personal Web pages that are largely "About Me." On business sites, pages about the history of the company, its accomplishments and news, and the people who make it happen all help to make a computer technology phenomenon more human. It recognizes that most people still want to deal with people. In addition, when people can send inquiries or other messages to a named individual, their confidence that the message will actually be read is significantly increased. Here are a few ways to include a company's people on its Web site.

INTRODUCE OWNERSHIP OR TOP MANAGEMENT

The executives of a firm are important assets—for customers, shareholders, and other investors—even for employees. Include a photo and a brief biography of each executive, emphasizing aspects of their experience that are most pertinent to the business. Include a quote from them related to their history or their belief in the company. Avoid posting a complete (and often impersonal) business resume. Advanced Access, a Web design and hosting firm in California, has presented biographical information very well (Fig. 3.14); it is especially important for a business in the technology arena where clients may still be intimidated by computers or the Internet.

TELL VISITORS ABOUT REGIONAL MANAGERS, LOCAL MANAGERS, SALESPEOPLE, AND CUSTOMER SERVICE REPRESENTATIVES

Firms with branch offices, dealers, or manufacturer's representatives around the country often add photos and introductions of the managers of these operations, too. Why? Such introductions increase the local connection with buyers or clients. A farmer in rural Grand Ledge, Michigan, for example, would rather know about the person she'll be meeting with or talking with when she's ready to buy a piece of farm equipment than she would about a firm's CEO in another state.

Some small businesses—a local printer with fewer than 20 employees, for example—post a personal Web page for each employee. Each person's responsibilities are listed, along with a photo of the person in the process of performing duties. This helps local customers get to know the people in the business and tends to increase loyalty to a firm's services.

Businesses with manufacturing or processing components should consider adding photos of the work being done and the people doing it. Turner Sculpture of Onley, Virginia, includes a handsome page showing

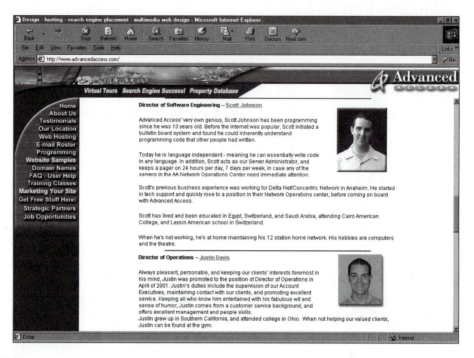

Figure 3.14   Advanced Access. Screen capture from http://www.advancedaccess.com.

and describing the process of creating a bronze sculpture (Fig. 3.15) to accompany its history, location and ordering information, and galleries of the Turners' works. Figure 3.16, "Works in Progress" at Turner Sculpture, includes a photo of William H. Turner applying his talent and skill in his creation of "Tiger."

WEB PAGES FOR LOCAL OFFICES, DEALERS, DISTRIBUTORS, OR OUTLETS

Many people search for products or services on search engines by adding the name of their city or county to their key words, as in "offset printing Ely Minnesota." Why? For many products, and especially for service businesses, people look for the nearest office or store location. Budget Blinds, Inc., is a good example.

A national franchiser with more than 290 franchisees in 37 states, Budget Blinds advertises a "We Come to You" approach to selling and installing window coverings. Dealers drive to a consumer's location to display, sell, and later install window coverings. Local information available on the Web is, therefore, important to these dealers. Local pages expand the corporate or parent reach into local markets, and the company serves visitors better by sending them *directly* to the nearest office or outlet.

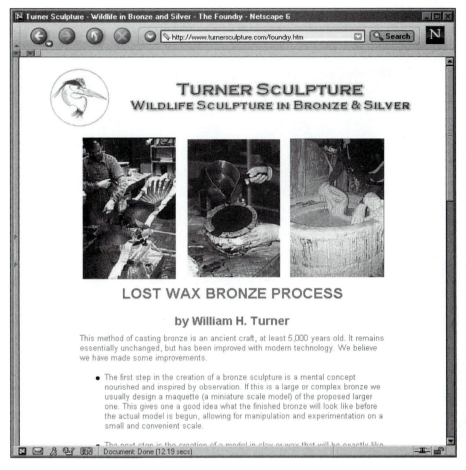

Turner Sculpture. Screen capture from http://www.turnersculpture.com/
foundry.htm.
All artwork, photographs, and web site design copyright © 1999–2002 Turner
Sculpture.

Budget Blinds created an individual Web page for each franchisee (Fig.
3.17), keyed to each franchisee's city, which helps search engines (see
Chapter 6) locate a dealer by city. The franchisee page gives local contact
information and links seamlessly to sections of the corporate Web site.
Thus, any single local franchisee page appears to be a much larger site—
barely distinguishable from the expansive corporate one at http://www.
budgetblinds.com. Visitors see the local franchisee's considerable content
actually located on the corporate site (Figure 3.18), which could influence
their decision about which window treatment company to call.

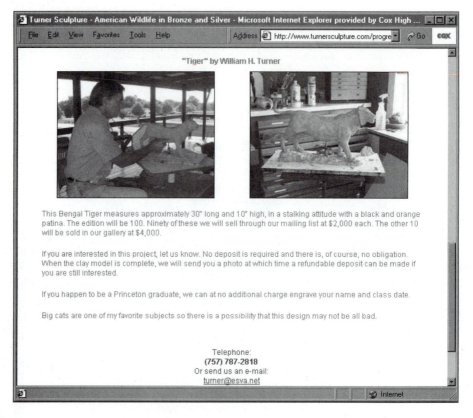

Figure 3.16   Sculptor at work. Screen capture from "Works in Progress,"
http://turnersculpture.com/progress.htm.
All artwork, photographs, and web site design copyright © 1999–2002 Turner
Sculpture.

Product or Service Information

Since the Web is such an intensely graphic environment, photos, drawings, diagrams, and other visual representations are key to the sale of many
products. Turner Sculptures' Web site, for example, displays clear individual photos of many of the bronze sculptures of the father and son artists (Fig. 3.19). John Deere uses schematic drawings, multi-situational
photos, zoomable and 360-degree rotating images (Fig. 3.20) to communicate the complexities of its equipment (along with miles and miles of
specifications).

Automobile Web sites are using the latest technologies in 360-degree
plus zoom product photography to demonstrate the high style and features

Figure 3.17

Budget Blinds local
franchisee Web page.
Screen capture from http://
www.budgetblinds.com/
sanclemente.

Figure 3.18

Budget Blinds, Inc.
corporate Web site.
Screen capture from
http://www.budgetblinds.
com. © 1999, Budget Blinds,
Inc. These pages display for
all the individual franchise
sites.

Figure 3.19

William Henry Turner's Fox and Rabbit III.
Screen capture from http://www.turnersculpture.com/gallery/537.htm.
All artwork, photographs, and web site design copyright © 2000–2002 Turner Sculpture.

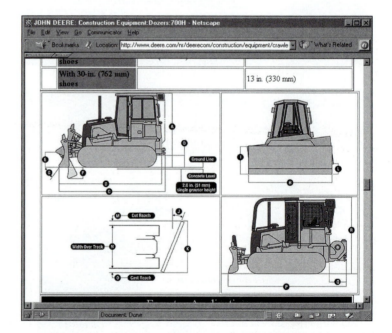

Figure 3.20

John Deere schematic.
Screen capture from http://www.deere.com/en_US/cfd/construction/deere_const/crawlers/700h_general.html? sidenavstate=11.

of their vehicles. Realtors® are using that technology to provide virtual tours of homes for sale. Golf courses, resorts, hotels, and other locations are adding virtual tours of their spaces and amenities.

What about services? How can services be shown on the Internet? In ways similar to brochures you find in banks or doctors' offices or print shops—but with a great deal more content and sophistication. Bank sites are excellent examples, particularly since banks provide similar services and are bound to follow some standard regulations. How do banks distinguish themselves? Generally speaking, the answer lies in the quality and range of the services they provide. The national Web site for Wells Fargo Bank (Fig. 3.21) is a large page packed with services.

Services available on the Wells Fargo site (wellsfargo.com) consist primarily of educating consumers regarding their options in many areas of their lives, including investing, home buying and selling, retirement planning, small business or student loans, taxes, online bill paying, online banking, news headlines, online stock brokerage, and much more. Best of all, this information is all in one place and is provided by a financial services company that has been around for more than 150 years. What could be more convenient or more credible? Banks can expand their Web marketing to include online banking, one of the earliest and most successful services offered on the Internet. Wells Fargo was the nation's first bank to offer it, in 1995.

Other examples of sites that provide services online include the U.S. Postal Service, FedEx, UPS, and other shipping companies that allow users to obtain quotes for transit time and cost. They also enable users to track the progress of a shipment from origin to destination and to check for

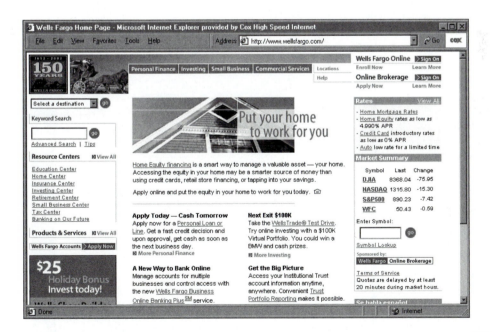

Screen capture from http://www.wellsfargo.com.

Figure 3.21

proof of delivery or signature by the recipient. DialPad and Net2Phone provide telephone services on the Internet, competing with long distance telephone services. Monster.com and other recruitment and job search sites allow users to upload a resume or job descriptions in real time. Magazines, newspapers, journals, and other print periodicals allow users to subscribe to their Web versions and read articles the minute they're ready to go to press.

EBay, "the world's online marketplace," provides an innovative, fascinating, and highly successful service on the Web by enabling users to place items for sale by auction, for which privilege they pay a fee to eBay. Literally millions of items are auctioned daily. Other entities have followed suit, attempting to garner some share of the public auction market, but none has been very successful in prying share away from the now-giant auction that was on the Web first.

TESTIMONIALS

Testimonials can contribute to building credibility for a product or service, especially for businesses that are one among many clone-like competitors or for sites that sell readily available items. U.S. Wings, for example, the site (Fig. 3.22) that bills itself as "the worlds leading authority on bomber jackets and aviation apparel" and "Official supplier to the U.S. Military," makes sure its visitors know that thousands of customers are happy with their products and service.

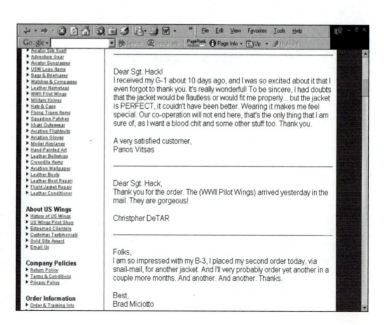

Figure 3.22

Screen capture from http://www.uswings.com/customers.html.

Realtors® and other service providers often rely on client testimonials to help communicate the quality of their services. The name, affiliation, and photo can add credibility to the testimonials. On the Web site (http://www.robingordon.com) for Robin Gordon of the Main Line, Pennsylvania, for example, are several comments from clients whose titles are impressive. Steve Burke, President of Comcast Cable Communications, Inc., writes: "Robin Gordon found us exactly the house we wanted. She did a wonderful job of determining what we were looking for; and actually found us a house not yet on the market."

STOREFRONTS, MALLS, CATALOGS

Businesses with various products to sell, either online or off, set up storefronts and catalogs on the Internet. The Web provides the perfect technology for catalog presentation and searching. Companies selling their own products exclusively, as well as those retailing the products of many other companies, are both easily found on the Net.

Catalog sites can be simple listings and descriptions of items or highly complex searchable sites. From the Peter's Row Publishing Web site (Fig. 3.23), users can click on a title to get more information about the book, price, and ordering. They can order books by e-mail, telephone, or mail.

Malls and some portals offer opportunities for small independent businesses to advertise and sell their wares or services fairly easily and together with other sellers. This increases the likelihood that Web users will find the small sellers. Antique and collectible dealers are using this approach very effectively at such malls as Tias (www.tias.com) and Ruby Lane

Figure 3.23

Peter's Row Publishing. Screen capture from http://www.petersrow. bookpub.net.

(www.rubylane.com). The search functions enable users to search all the items in all the shops, making the items for sale much more accessible.

Related Content of Great Interest to Your Target Audience: Get Sticky!

Arresting content and engaging functions make a site "sticky," a term that relates to how much time visitors spend in a site and how often they return. Amazon.com, for example, has several content enhancements designed to keep their visitors on the site for as long as possible. These features include editorial and reader reviews for each book, tables of contents, links to similar books, links to other books by the same author(s), links to related items in their Shopping and Auction sites, and links to other books that buyers of a particular book also purchased.

A few hours spent on the Internet exploring business-related sites will provide myriad examples of content that enhances the richness of a site, engages interest so that visitors spend time there, and earns repeat visits. Much of the information is not product specific, and it does not need to be. It is, however, best if the content has an obvious relationship to the subject matter of the site. Take another look at www.lipitor.com (Fig. 3.5). Quizzes, surveys, diets, exercises, recipes, and tips are all designed to engage visitors and keep them coming back. Although not all information is specific to Lipitor, it does relate to cholesterol. Table 3.2 shows examples of content that might be included for a lawn mower site and a scuba gear site.

Table 3.2	CONTENT EXAMPLES: LAWN MOWER SITE, SCUBA GEAR SITE
Lawn Mowers	Scuba Gear
Safety, sharpening blades, types of lawns, hitting objects, first aid, mowing edges, going over sidewalks, mowing wet grass, dry grass, engine maintenance, using oil, recommended fuel, pull cords, stalls, cleaning, storage, sizes and styles for particular needs and sizes of lawns, how frequently to mow, watering lawns, edging, mulch, etc.	History, inventors, Jacques Costeau, U.S. Navy dive tables, physics of diving, gases and how they affect the body, nitrogen narcosis, decompression, safety, underwater signals, boat entries, beach entries, night diving, photography, cave diving, reef diving, training, refresher courses, hotel/resort courses, snorkeling, spearing, drift diving, dive boats, storing gear, checking tanks, calculating the correct weights to use, wet suit cleaning and storage, zipper repair, fixing wet suit rips, dry suits, etc.

1. What related content would you include for a site that sells camping gear?
2. What related content would you include for a site that sells Vitamin E?
3. What related content would you include for a site that sells document reproduction services?

INTERNAL PAGES OR OUTSIDE LINKS?

Most large businesses prefer to have sticky content on their own site rather than linking to other sites (which sweeps visitors away, perhaps never to return). However, smaller businesses with fewer resources and limited budgets can increase visitor loyalty by posting a page of useful links that users can bookmark and then use as a mini-portal. Early in Web history, people thought that offering outside links was foolish because it took people out of a site. But the thousands of sites that succeed because of their many outside links have disproved that belief. So outside links aren't all bad, although linking to a *competitor's* site is not a good idea.

Most industries have one or more national (and/or state, county, or large city) associations that maintain Web sites with valuable articles, data, news, and other postings. Some offer excellent tutorials on doing business in their industry. One such site is that of the International Franchise Association at http://www.franchise.org. Another is that of Telebuild's site for architects at http://www.e-architect.com in conjunction with the American Institute of Architects (AIA). Do you sell something packaged in a steel container? The American Iron and Steel Institute at http://www.steel.org is a link you'll want to put on your site.

As an interesting departure from what most firms do, your links can be divided between business or industry-related links and links to information that virtually any consumer can use. Why both industry and consumer? Because, although your visitors may be potential buyers of your product or services, they are also human beings with the same basic information needs as anyone else. Creating several pages of consumer information links can enhance a site's stickiness; examples of such links include:

Art	Home & Garden
Autos	News
Business - Finance	Parenting
Careers	Pets
Cooking - Recipes - Wine	Seniors
Education - Reference	Shopping
Entertainment - Fun	U.S. Government
Health - Diet - Fitness	Travel - Airlines - Tickets

<u>Maps - Zip Codes</u>

<u>Weather</u>

Each link could lead directly to a site offering the information described by the link to a page of multiple related links. For example, the link to "Business - Finance" might lead to a single site such as Yahoo's investing page at http://finance.yahoo.com/?u or to a page with other links.

Tip!   **FINDING SITES TO RECOMMEND**

Make a list of all the topics that you would like to offer as links. If you sell lawnmowers, perhaps you'd offer a link called "mulch." To find sites to serve a link called "mulch," use a search engine, such as www.google.com, and search for "mulch" (without the quotation marks). You will get pages and pages of links to sites dealing with mulch. Compare a few and pick one that seems to have the best content. (Other firms will follow this same procedure when deciding whether to link to *you!*)

Enable and Encourage Visitors to Contact You

One of the easiest components to add to a Web page is a link to an e-mail address. An e-mail link or group of links should appear on every page of a site. (See the chapters in Part Four for more detail on communicating by e-mail.)

Forms that allow visitors to enter information and submit it to the site owner are also easy to create and easy to use. Most of them are called CGI (Common Gateway Interface) forms. Simple surveys, guest books, comment forms, and trouble reports are usually CGI forms. More sophisticated types of interactions are discussed in Chapter 4.

Telephone numbers and physical addresses on a site's pages continue to be important, especially for businesses that require appointments or verbal confirmations of orders.

Summary

Following are ten rules for Web site content.

1. Content must communicate and support the company, product, or service's market positioning or branding.
2. Content must be relevant, useful, and interesting to the target audience.
3. Content must be written and presented in language easily understood by the target audience.

4. Content must help achieve the goals established for the site.

5. Provide ways for visitors to communicate with marketing, sales, or customer service representatives in many easily found locations on the site.

6. Ask for the business. Asking is one of the first things taught to sales representatives and one of the most forgotten components of Web sites. Be sure that "Click here to order," "Call today for more information," "Please comment," and other ways of asking visitors to purchase items or connect with sales people are clearly visible.

7. Content must be sufficiently useful to bring visitors back for more. The corollary to this is to avoid having so much content that a visitor can become overwhelmed. Good organization (see Chapter 5) helps a lot.

8. Content must be up to date. Update a site by adding to it or changing it on a regular basis.

9. Avoid seas of small type. Most Web visitors absorb information in "bites" from headers and graphics. Put long articles, specifications, and reports on separate pages or in files that users can download to read later.

10. Spelling, grammar, and punctuation do count! Poorly written material will quickly convince a visitor that the site represents an unprofessional or sloppy business.

Review Questions

1. What features are common to many business Web sites?

2. Name a few companies or products whose branding is so strong that they probably do not need a tagline to communicate it.

3. Is it more important to talk about a firm's annual sales or about the visitors' interests?

4. How does the Web site for Lincoln automobiles communicate the product's positioning?

5. What is the primary function of the headline of a Web site?

6. What types of information should you expect to find on a corporate Web site?

7. How does the Lipitor® Web site help Pfizer sell the product with no online selling?

8. What does a hot red background communicate about a product?

9. What characteristics does including a company's 60-year history communicate to visitors?

10. What does including information about a firm's employees add to a Web site?

11. Why does a Budget Blinds franchisee's Web page appear to have more content than it really does?

12. Name three types of services or service-based companies that use Internet marketing extensively.

13. How can testimonials improve a Web site's effectiveness?

14. How do small antique and collectible dealers achieve some of the advantages of large businesses on the Web?

15. What does a site's *stickiness* refer to?

16. What factors help make a site more sticky?

17. What types of content would you consider adding to a site that sells collectible California pottery?

18. Why are some Web masters opposed to having links to outside sites?

The Key to Stickiness

Interactive Functions

Cluetrain.com:

A powerful global conversation has begun. Through the Internet, people are discovering and inventing new ways to share relevant knowledge with blinding speed. As a direct result, markets are getting smarter—and getting smarter faster than most companies.

The expectations of today's Web users are far greater than they were even a year ago. A static display of text and graphics, even good graphics, is not sufficient to engage most visitors or draw repeat visits. Web sites must *do* things. In particular, business sites must find ways to involve visitors with fast, useful, easy-to-use interactive tools. Online ordering, auctions (even live auctions), live chats, online banking, surveys and polls, and live events are among the functions that busy programmers have made possible, some of which have become commonplace.

THE BASICS

The most important function of a company's Web site is communication—not one-way telling and showing, not mission statements or public relations mantras or glossy brochure-like recitations—but encouraging and enabling visitors to communicate with you, the company's management and staff, with its clients or customers, and even with other visitors to its site. Communication power is the great strength of the Internet today—its highest potential. To the degree that a business can put that power to work on its behalf, it will be able to benefit from its investment in Internet marketing.

Doc Searls and David Weinberger, two of the "ringleaders" of the *Cluetrain Manifesto* (see http://www.cluetrain.com), put it this way:

The mass production of the industrial world led companies to engage in mass marketing, delivering "messages" to undifferentiated hordes who didn't want to receive them. Now the Web is enabling the market to converse again, as people tell one another the truth about products and companies and their own desires—learning faster than business. Companies have to figure out how to enter this global conversation rather than relying on the old marketing techniques of public relations, marketing communications, advertising, and other forms of propaganda. We, the market, don't want messages at all; we want to speak with your business in a human voice.

The Cluetrain Manifesto, p. viii

Internet communication requires some form or forms of interactivity and, in some cases, more than a bit of fun. The interactivity must allow visitors to interact with your product and services in ways that are informative, useful, easy, and engaging. These forms of communication may be catalogs shopping carts, auctions, downloads, product viewers, or other user-initiated functions that involve the visitor with you, your company, and your products.

The simplest types of interactivity are e-mail and contact forms. (See Part Four for more information on e-mail.) Beyond these, the key Web functions of Internet marketing are related to

1. Direct online selling and services

2. Online interactions that support selling or enhance Web statistics by keeping visitors returning for more

3. Direct communication among Web folk: Functions that enable and encourage the human voice of your site visitors, their friends, you,

your company, guests, observers, and a host of others to be heard (increasingly, literally heard) by one another. This function is thought by some to be most important of all.

Why isn't a bright, attractive, artful Web site proclaiming a company's grandeur and skill sufficient? Why does a site need more than good and plentiful information? The answer is a compelling one: The marketplace is demanding interactivity—or it will go somewhere else—fast.

In this chapter you will learn how various functions help your audiences interact with information on your company and its goods and services, with you, with each other. Remember that the interactivity must be useful, easy to use, service-oriented, and clearly related to your business.

BEYOND THE BASICS

Online Selling and Services

Interactive catalogs, order forms, shopping carts, auctions, and downloads are among the types of direct online selling that are becoming most familiar to Web users. Especially popular services include online banking, travel reservations, site- and Web-wide searching, educational course delivery and testing, and technology tutorials. In this section, we discuss key types of direct online selling and services used by businesses to involve, even captivate, their marketplace.

INTERACTIVE CATALOGS

Content is king, proclaim Web writers. Unless you have useful, informative content, all the gizmos and whirligigs in cyberspace won't help your site!

Functionality is king, proclaim Web programmers. Unless your site can do things in creative ways, all the content ever written or produced won't help your site!

What's the answer? You need both. Interactive catalogs marry content and function to benefit users and sell products and services. In their simplest form, online catalogs are lists of products or services, usually including a description and often illustrated with product images. Some catalogs may not be interactive at all. They require the user to find the item by reading through the list and then place an order by telephone, fax, or e-mail. Such pages may have been sufficient several years ago, but if your market is at all competitive, you'll need to improve on this scenario, big time.

Interactive catalogs use at least three basic components: (1) a "front end" that allows visitors to browse or search for an item; (2) a "back end" database that holds the product information; and (3) a means of ordering online through a shopping cart (see pp. 89–92 for more on shopping carts) or a reservation system. Many variations of interactive catalogs exist to suit specific products, services, and audiences. Catalogs vary in the appearance, size, content, and sophistication or creativity of the search/respond/order functions.

The front end, the part that users see and interact with, may present a list of categories of products/services for the user to select from. The user clicks on the name of a category and is shown a page with information on the items in that category.

A more interactive approach uses a search option that acts as the interface between the user and the database of product information. The search option may be fairly simple, such as one in which the user enters an item name or number and the Web site (the site's *system*) retrieves the information on matching item(s), along with related description, image(s), pricing information, and/or links to additional information. Some search options are very sophisticated. Some use "artificial intelligence" to ask visitors more questions about what they are looking for. Then the search engine narrows its focus and retrieves and displays the matching items. Here's a simple example of an exchange between a user and a sophisticated search function.[1]

> User enters: *computers*
> System displays: *laptop or desktop?*
> User enters: *laptop*
> System displays: *What will you use your computer for?*
> User enters: *computer-aided design (CAD)*
> System displays: *Many new CAD programs require speed, lots of memory, and a large display. We have 5 laptops that meet these criteria. What is your price range?*
> User enters: *less than $3,000*
> System displays: *We have two laptops in this price range.*
> . . .

The system then displays the descriptions, technical specifications, and images of the laptops that meet the user's criteria. And the user may choose to change the criteria during the process.

This interface is remarkable in the high degree of interaction between the Web site's system and the user, and particularly in the high degree of "humanness" of the function. In a five-month test of this type of search di-

---

[1]This example is based on Steinberg, Don, "The Man with the E-commerce Answer," *Smart Business for the New Economy*, Ziff Davis, February 2001, pp. 100 ff.

alogue using a program developed by Mark Lucente, Acer America's online notebook sales rose by 21 percent![2]

E-TAILERS AND MALLS
Web malls usually sell space to sellers of merchandise and visitors purchase goods directly from the "tenants." E-tailers, on the other hand, sell goods themselves, directly to consumers, from their own centralized catalog. Such firms include Crate and Barrel, Victoria's Secret, Lands' End, and Bloomingdales.

Another type of highly interactive front end allows users to select and/or change features of a product or products and view the results. Users can change the color and features of automobiles, for example (see http://www.chrysler.com). They can create a model of themselves and "try on" articles of clothing and then change the colors or accessories (see http://www.landsend.com). They can upload an image of their face and change their hair, makeup color, and style (see http://www.clairol.com). Once you've played with—and they are playful—some of these sites, clicking into a page of plain text is quite a letdown. These types of high interactivity between user and Web site (and the products they promote) are part of the process leading to online orders. Let's look at a few catalogs in more detail.

SIMPLE ONE-PAGE CATALOGS
Ragnar's Swedish Knife Catalog (http://www.ragweedforge.com/Swedish KnifeCatalog.html, Fig. 4.1) is a simple one-page collection of written product descriptions along with an image of each item. Clicking on a knife image in Ragnar's catalog takes the user to a larger image of that item. Ragnar's provides a list of additional product categories on each page. Clicking on the category takes the user to another page of catalog items.

HUGE CATALOGS WITH DATABASE SEARCH
The Library of Congress Web catalog (Fig. 4.2) is particularly notable for the size of its database. According to http://catalog.loc.gov, the database includes "approximately 12 million records representing books, serials, computer files, manuscripts, cartographic materials, music, sound recordings, and visual materials in the Library's collections. The Online Catalog also provides references, notes, circulation status, and information about materials still in the acquisitions stage."

Notice that the Library of Congress provides four distinct ways in which the user can search for items: Subject-Name-Title-Call Number,

---

[2]ibid.

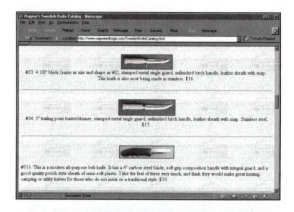

Figure 4.1

Ragnar's Swedish Knife
Catalog. Screen captures
from http://www.
ragweedforge.com/
SwedishKnifeCatalog.html.

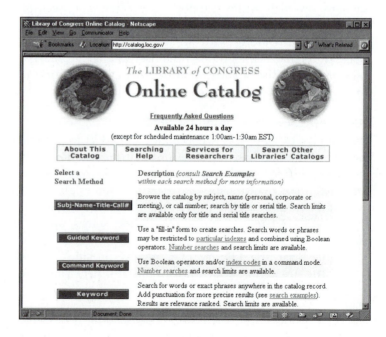

Figure 4.2

The Library of Congress.
Screen capture from http://
catalog.loc.gov.

Guided Keyword, Command Keyword, and Keyword. When the search function displays matches to the user, information about the item and its availability (for Library of Congress or Congressional staff, or for Interlibrary loan) is displayed.

CATALOGS WITH SEARCH FUNCTIONS AND CATEGORY LISTINGS

Some sites with very large catalogs give users some choices about how to find items. Many industrial firms offer an online catalog of products, especially firms that manufacture small parts or widgets of all kinds, such as electronics or nuts, bolts, washers, gears, screws, flanges, valves, and fittings. Figure 4.3 shows the entry Web catalog page for Allied Electronics, Inc. (http://www.alliedelec.com), whose database contains information on many thousands of parts. Notice that users can find items by using the site's search function (top right corner) or by browsing through sections of the catalog (center left).

CATALOGS WITH ITEMS KEYED TO PRINTED CATALOGS

Some catalogs offer sections in which users can find the products or services in the company's printed catalogs. (This function may be called "Shop From Print Catalog" or something similar.) Lands' End, one of the Web's busiest online stores, mails out millions of print catalogs annually (Fig. 4.4). The firm's site invites you to order products that you found in the catalog received at home online, using the product number from the catalog.

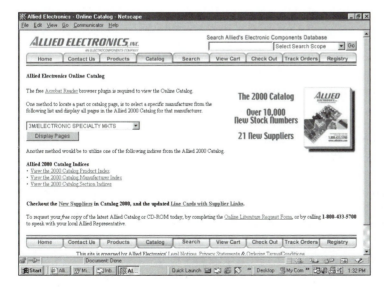

Figure 4.3

Allied Electronics, Inc. Screen capture from http://www.alliedelec.com/catalog/indices/indices.asp.

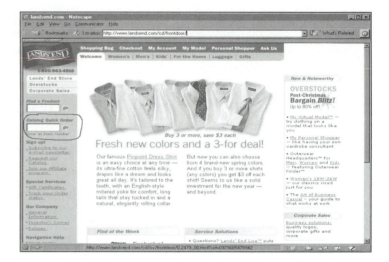

USER-CONTROLLED CATALOGS

Online catalogs make possible customer interactions with products not possible with print catalogs. Clairol's Web visitors can try out hair and makeup choices. Lands' End and other clothing catalogs let Web users put various items of apparel on body-type models, and then change the colors or patterns of the articles. Once visitors decide on the makeup or hair color or clothing they want to purchase, they proceed to the online ordering function.

Have a look at Figure 4.5, captured from the Try It On Studio. This page is reached through the main page of http://www.Clairol.com. This image is used for demonstrations, but users can join the site and upload their own photo to use as the basis of the makeover. From the window shown, the user can change the hairstyle and hair color.

MALLS AND OTHER SHOPPING SITES

One of the pioneers of the online mall concept is Choice Mall at http://www.choicemall.com. This huge site consists of many thousands of mini-stores, each with a "storefront" in the mall. Choice Mall sells pages to individuals who wish to have a store in the mall. The firm is allied with Guthy-Renker, one of the world's largest direct response television companies, with annual sales in excess of $350 million. Customers who buy something from an individual store in Choice Mall deal with the individual merchant/tenant who occupies a space there. Although the purchase is from the individual seller, the catalog itself is integrated. This means that users can search *all* the inventory of *all* the shops with a single search.

One popular mall for antiques is Tias.com Antiques and Collectibles, at http://www.tias.com (Fig. 4.6), which offers more than 1,300 categories with over 300,000 items. Antiques and collectibles dealers are especially

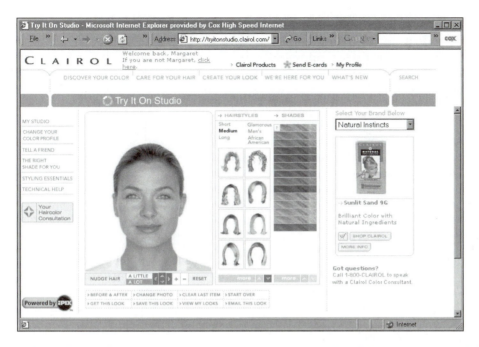

Try It On Studio. Screen capture from http://tryitonstudio.clairol.com.
© 2002 Clairol, A Division of Proctor and Gamble, Stamford, CT 06922.

Figure 4.5

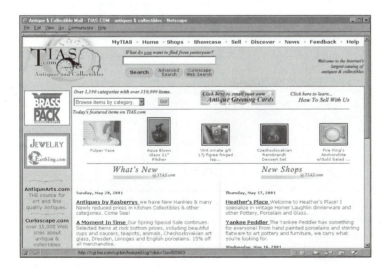

Figure 4.6

Tias.com. Screen capture
from http://www.tias.com.

pleased with the ability to have hundreds or thousands of visitors each day view their items, a huge audience compared to the small percentage of that traffic possible in their physical shop. Tia's also offers tools for inventory management, distribution, and other functions, along with training and customer support. See http://www.tias.com/other/aboutSoftware.html.

Web users who want to find "more than 20 million used and rare books, periodicals and ephemera offered for sale by thousands of booksellers around the world" (or who want to sell them) use sites like Bibliofind. com (http://www.bibliofind.com, Fig. 4.7), now owned by Amazon.com; half.com; powells.com; abe.com; or several others. All of these large sites sell products from a catalog that is called up by visitors from a database.

If you think your business could benefit from an online catalog with search functions and ordering systems, be sure to seek counsel from specialists in catalog software before moving ahead. Good catalog navigation is an art form and it is worthwhile to get the best you can afford. For information and a glossary on electronic catalogs, visit the National Electronic Commerce Resource Center online at http://www.tda.ecrc.ctc.com/kbase/doc/brief/ecat2.htm.

ORDERING ONLINE

Sites that intend to sell products must do more than provide information, even if it is delivered in a very sophisticated way. In traditional marketing terminology, they must ask for the order. Simple ways to ask for the order

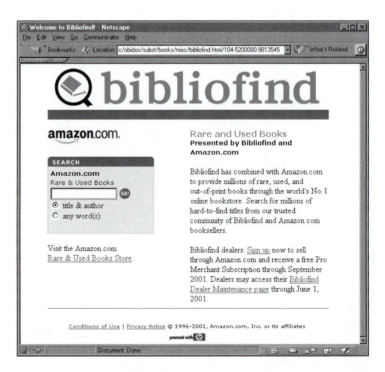

Figure 4.7

Bibliofind. Screen capture from http://www.bibliofind.com.
© 1996–2001, Amazon.com, Inc. or its affiliates.

include displaying a phone number for telephone orders or a printable order form that can be completed online or by hand and faxed to the order department. Providing even the minimal command for users to send an e-mail to a linked e-mail address to request the product is better than providing no order function at all. Increasingly, however, business sites are using "shopping carts."

Shopping carts are highly interactive. Users identify items they want to purchase, and the shopping cart keeps track of them. At their convenience, users "proceed to check out." They confirm their purchases, the prices, and tax or shipping costs, and then charge the total to their credit card. Shopping carts typically work in conjunction with a financial institution's real-time credit card processing system to check the validity and balance of the credit card owner's account. Various forms of security to prevent credit card theft or breach of confidentiality protect shopping cart transactions.

Part of the reason that shopping carts have become so popular is their ease of use and their interactive novelty. With a shopping cart, a user can complete a transaction in a matter of seconds. Shopping carts have become popular with vendors because customers use them and because the programs that operate the shopping carts are relatively inexpensive and easy to install.

The steps required for an online purchase are: (1) The user selects an item and adds it to his or her order form or shopping cart. (2) The site calculates the charge, and enters the customer shipping and credit card information. (3) The customer gives final okay. (4) The order is processed and forwarded to the fulfillment department or warehouse for shipping. Figure 4.8 shows a step-by-step online transaction from the user's side, in this case an Amazon.com purchase.

Usually a final confirmation of the online order is followed by display of a form that can be saved or printed out as a receipt for the purchase. Many sites also send an e-mail to the purchaser to confirm the order. The funds from the customer's approved credit card are deposited into the merchant's account electronically.

Many buyers wonder, after a sale, if they made the desired choices for color, size, amount, or any other number of parameters. This is a valid concern, because in B2B selling, a slight mistake could cost thousands of dollars. Thus, online marketers typically provide some means of after-the-sale checking of an order. Amazon.com, which offers B2B, B2C, and C2C selling, offers many means of checking an order after a purchase (Figure 4.9).

An online shopping cart needs to work flawlessly from day one, so select a firm and software with great care. Test a number of shopping carts from the front end—that is, as a purchaser—to see how they work from all perspectives. Talk with several customers of any finalists being considered as a potential shopping cart source; ask about their experiences, both good and bad, with the company, and about installation, setup, reports, and so forth.

Figure 4.8

Steps in an online transaction. All screen captures from http://www.amazon.com.

1. The visitor searches the site and selects an item to purchase. The visitor clicks on "Add to shopping cart."

2. The item(s) being purchased is (are) added to the shopping cart and kept there as successive purchases are made. Items in a shopping cart can be deleted at any time prior to final purchase. When a user has made all choices, he or she proceeds to "Check Out."

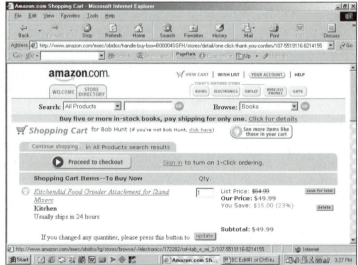

Complete shopping cart programs can be purchased for less than $500 a year, not including a real-time credit card processing account. Online real-time credit card processing accounts (or merchant accounts, which require that you have good credit) typically add 2.3% or more to each transaction, an additional $0.20 to $0.30+ per transaction, and charge about $10 for a monthly statement. Merchant accounts are reasonable, but the cost is variable and is often based on your credit record.

One of the many firms that sell shopping cart programs is Easycart. com. It offers a system for as low as $399 with instant installation. See

3. Customer fills in desired shipping method.

4. Credit card information is gathered. The shopping cart delivers the customer identification and the charge amount to a credit card network over a secure server for approval of the charge. The consumer's credit card is verified online for the intended purchase.

http://www.casycart.com for more information. For custom shopping cart programs, EMK Design at http://www.emkdesign.com has done pioneering work in this field. A provider of powerful applications in this field is Mercantec, a leader in products and services that enable Internet commerce, at http://www.mercantec.com. For up-to-date information on shopping carts and to identify more firms, use your favorite search engine, such as Yahoo! or Alta Vista, to search for online shopping carts. Also, a number of free shopping carts are available. See an example at http://www.cowtown.net/stores.htm or search for "free online shopping carts."

Figure 4.9

Screen capture from
http://www.amazon.com

AUCTIONS

Use auctions to sell your merchandise? Definitely! One approach, if your company is big enough, is to set up your own auction site. This could save you the expense of paying fees and commissions to auction sites such as eBay. Alternatively, some small businesses regularly list goods for auction on existing auction sites and link their auction pages to their product or company Web site. In other words, they use auctions as an inexpensive way to gain visibility for their company and their products (Fig. 4.10). Large auction sites draw hundreds of thousands of visitors each day, and visitors who look at auctions are, essentially, self-selecting themselves as potential customers or clients. This is a proven way to advertise to a targeted market!

The success of eBay, the first famous auction site, demonstrated dramatically that millions of Web users would use an auction site to buy and sell items. Much of the appeal is the direct contact with other eBay members, creating a sense of community. However, eBay has added restrictions to contacts among members in an attempt to reduce the conduct of business off eBay, which was reducing eBay's commission opportunities. We think the change is not a good one for users, although it may make sense for eBay's executives and stockholders. Founded in September 1995, eBay includes 18.9 million registered users and claims to be the most popular shopping site on the Internet as measured by total user minutes. In 2000, eBay members transacted over $5 billion in annualized gross merchandise sales (value of goods traded on the eBay site). (See http://pages.ebay.com/community/aboutebay/overview/index.html.)

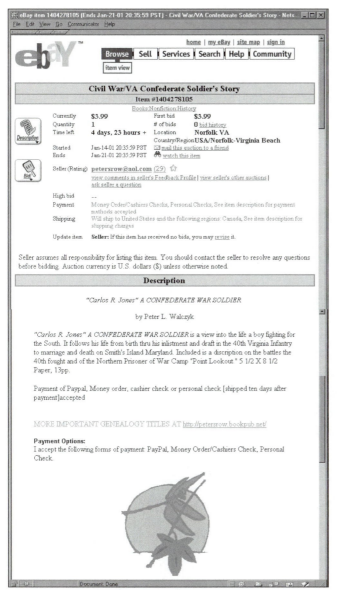

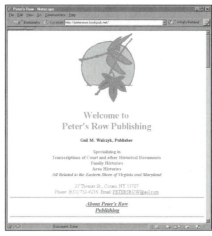

Figure 4.10

Connect auction pages to business Web pages. Notice how this small publisher of history and genealogy titles uses the eBay auction site to gain visibility for its site, which contains a complete catalog. The dragonfly logo also links to the site. Screen capture on left from http://www.ebay.com. Reproduced by permission of eBay Inc. Copyright © EBAY INC. All rights reserved. Screen capture on right from http://www.petersrow.bookpub.net.

What volume will auction sales generate? On the day we checked, eBay *alone* was displaying approximately 5.77 million listings. The majority of listings are displayed for seven days, although some displays last three, five, or ten days (and some real estate listings may stay online until sold). Presuming that an average of approximately 824,000 listings close each day, and that 65 percent of them are actually sold, eBay alone would account for more than half a million individual sales each day. We could not learn the average sales price per item sold for eBay, but even an extremely low estimate yields millions of dollars sold every day on that auction site. Using $10 as an average sale amount, half a million sales daily at $10/sale times 365 days/year gives us $1.825 *billion* in sales for eBay alone. eMarketer predicted that auction sales would reach $9.2 billion for year 2001 and $12.1 billion for 2002. (See http://www.techtv.com/money/story/0.23158,2436426,00.html.)

Many sites provide advice about selling on online auctions. One good source of information is http://www.beaconnet.com/help/basics/ebay. htm. Buyers of items at auctions can pay by check, money order, cashiers check, or credit card, depending on the seller's preferences. They can also make use of online money transfer services such as PayPal.com or eBay's Billpoint, which enables person-to-person and individual-to-business payments over the Web. With tools like Paypal.com, transfers of auction payment funds can be made quickly and securely.

TIP!   CUSTOMERS SPEND REAL MONEY, VIRTUALLY

Is a restricted, secure payment collection or credit card charge system beyond your company's budget for Web marketing? Open a business account with PayPal. Your customers can transfer money from their bank account, credit card account, or PayPal account quickly and easily. PayPal (http://www. paypal.com) is the number one finance site on the Internet, according to PC Data Online, and one of the fastest growing Web sites, according to Media Metrix. PayPal constitutes over 10 percent of all Internet traffic in the financial services category—more than Citibank, Wells Fargo, and Bank of America combined. Why? Because PayPal is user-friendly, has set itself up to benefit from virtual marketing by giving users a $5 referral bonus for each new account, and because it got there first. (And a big part of gaining strong online marketing position—or strong position in any marketplace—is being first.)

Web users frequent auction sites of various types, including sites for B2B, B2C, and C2C transactions (see Chapter 1). Here are a few of the more popular ones.

Auction Type	Sample Sites
B2B	Adauction.com, Manheim Auctions (Cox Interactive)
B2C	Egghead.com, Bid.com, FirstAuction.com, Ubid.com
C2C	eBay.com, Auctiongate.com

Visit one site in each of the three categories listed above. Identify their strengths and appealing features. What are the most obvious similarities among the three types of sites? The differences?

SELLING DOWNLOADABLE PRODUCTS

Businesses that sell data, images, music, books, or software should consider distribution of their product via downloadable files. Companies that use this mode of distribution benefit from customers' impulse purchasing and their desire to obtain the product in the fastest, easiest way possible. No-hassle instant gratification means many rewards for sellers. Explore some of the sites listed below. If you produce or market similar products, you should consider download delivery of your merchandise.

Software

Internet.com	http://www.internet.com/sections/downloads.html
MSN.com	http://www.computingcentral.msn.com/FDL/
C/Net.com	http://www.download.cnet.com
ZDNet.com	http://www.zdnet.com/downloads/powertools
ZDNet.com	http://www.zdnet.com/downloads/specials/free.html
About.com	http://www.about.com
Downloadmall.com	http://www.downloadmall.com
Softdisk.com	http://www.softdisk.com
Shop.Tucows.com	http://www.shop.tucows.com
Microsoft.com	http://www.microsoft.com
Netscape.com	http://www.netscape.com

High-Resolution Stock Photos

Stock Photo Warehouse	http://www.stockphotowarehouse.com
Stock Photography Online	http://www.stockphotographyonline.com
E-Film Group	http://www.efilmgroup.com/stock.html

AUDIO

Most recording and marketing of music is done by "the music industry," so the number of small companies engaged in this business is negligible. Furthermore, hundreds of sites offer music for free downloading. Nonetheless, if you are a producer of music, pursuing this delivery option is probably a matter of survival. One option would be to contract with one of the existing large music download sites in return for a commission or a licensing fee.

At its peak, Napster, a directory that enabled users to locate other music lovers and swap songs, boasted 60 million users. In 2000, it became the subject of major court battles over its "shareware" approach to delivering music and was forced to discontinue the sharing of songs by millions of users without the permission of the copyright owners.[3] Napster may come back online in 2002, but it needs to negotiate agreements with more major record labels before it can make such a move effectively. Meanwhile, other companies are working to create similar deals and offer online music. Listen.com, for example, plans to launch an application called Rhapsody that will enable users to pay a subscription fee to store and play songs.

Another well-known site for music is MP3.com (http://www.mp3.com), which has signed an agreement with top music labels to distribute their titles. MP3 makes available for free more than 700,000 songs from more than 100,000 digital artists.

Although music dominates, audio downloads are not limited to music. Audio books can be purchased and downloaded from various sites as well—http://audible.com and http://www.blackstoneaudio.com/html/main.html being two of the best. Thousands of books have been recorded and made available for download, an extension of the books-on-tape concept. Businesses in the publishing field should consider creating audio versions of their titles.

E-BOOKS

Virtually unheard of a few years ago, e-books now inhabit the Web in the offerings of hundreds of online publishers and distributors. At these sites, users can purchase and download a book to read from a computer monitor, a printout, or an e-book reading device. (E-books are for reading rather than listening.) Visitors can download e-books or request that they be e-mailed.

Both Amazon.com (http://www.amazon.com) and Barnes&Noble.com (http://www.bn.com, Fig. 4.11.) have large offerings of e-books. Companies manufacturing e-book reading devices also sell e-books (see http://www.adobe.com, for example; Fig. 4.12). Adobe manufactures the free Adobe Acrobat eBook Reader for use on personal computers. (In this case, the reader is free and the e-books are the revenue-producing items.) Learn more about e-books at http://www.epublishingconnections.com or http://www.ebookconnections.com/ReadersPrimer.

PROMOTIONAL USES OF DOWNLOADS

In addition to being offered for sale, e-books, audio files, and other downloadable products can serve various promotional purposes. Use them, for example, as an incentive to build your opt-in magazine or newsletter

---

[3]See http://www.cnn.com/2001/TECH/internet/10/30/napster.ap/index.html.

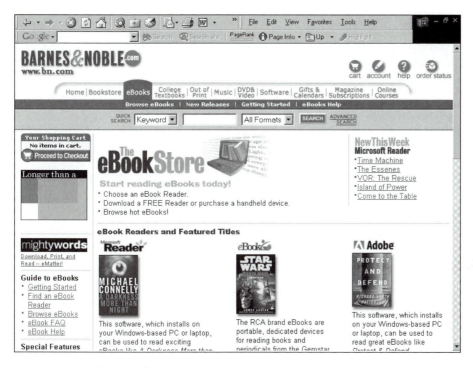

Barnes & Noble.com's eBookStore. Screen capture from
http://www.bn.com.

Figure 4.11

e-mailing list (for further discussion of opt-in mailings and permission marketing, see Part Four). Offer your e-book, screen saver, or other downloadable product as an incentive to get people to complete your online survey, or as a free bonus to purchasers of your product, or to users who make an online reservation for one of your fishing trips, or simply as a free gift for visiting your site. Preferably the downloadable item should be related to your business, to your market position. If your business deals with homes, offer an e-book of hints on home fire safety, burglar proofing, family first aid, or some other related topic. If you sell educational software, offer limited versions of some educational games. If you sell weight-loss products, offer a downloadable program for users to track their calories or weight or activity levels (with your advertising clearly displayed and with links to your online store) as an incentive to buy.

ONLINE SERVICES

Early leaders among online services are providers of online banking and online investing. Competition in the online financial services arena is especially rigorous among companies that saw the benefit of online portfolio management early on. Some of these companies advertise heavily on

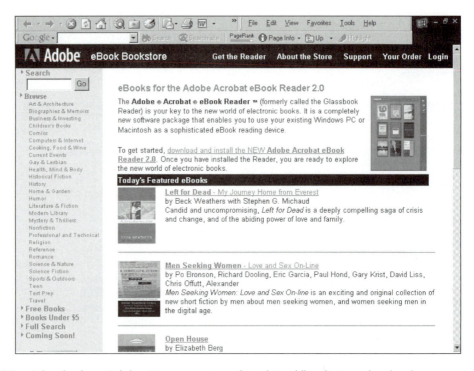

Figure 4.12   E-books from Adobe. Screen capture from http://bookstore.glassbook
.com/store/default.asp.

television and elsewhere. Some of the larger firms in the online trading
field include:

E-Trade	http://www.etrade.com
Charles Schwab Online	http://www.schwab.com
Swiftrade.com	http://www.swiftrade.com
Suretrade.com	http://www.suretrade.com
Ameritrade.com	http://www.ameritrade.com

Companies in this arena should consider adding human voice to their
Web sites as one means of differentiation. (For more on adding human
voice, see the section on Live Customer Service.)

Online Interactions That Support Selling

In some ways, online interactions that do not actually sell products or services are an extension of the site's "look'n'feel." Although they may not be
as critical as the interpersonal interactions described in other sections,

they are certainly worth consideration. The goal is to attract visitors and get them to spend some time on your Web site and then to return to your Web site.

SEARCH ENGINES

Search engines provide a fast, interactive means for users to scour the Internet for information, products, and services. Search engines can also be customized for a site. Such custom engines search only the database of keywords for a particular site or group of pages within a site. Dozens of firms offer engines to search a single Web site, among them Excite.com at http://www.excite.com; Atomz.com, at http://www.atomz.com; and WhatYouSeek at http://www.whatyouseek.com.

FREE SAMPLES

If your product or service is downloadable, make free samples available for users to download. One song from an album, a chapter of an e-book, or a 30-day free trial of a software program offers the same potential benefits as free samples given out at a department or grocery store or through the mail. Users test the samples and then, sellers hope, come back for more. Photo and clip art sites are good sources for ideas about samples. Here's a selection to help you get started:

Webshots.com	http://www.Webshots.com
Photosphere.com	http://www.photosphere.com
ClipArtWarehouse.com	http://www.clipartwarehouse.com
Clip-Art.com	http://www.clip-art.com
Free-Animal-Clip-Art.com	http://www.Free-Animal-Clip-Art.com
Real Estate Clip Art	http://www.realestateclipart.com
Fresher Image	http://www.free-clip-images.com
Clipart.com	http://www.clipart.com
ClipArtConnection.com	http://www.clipartconnection.com
AllFreeClipArt.com	http://www.allfreeclipart.com

If your product or service is not downloadable, offer printable coupons for discounts or samples that users can send in or take to their local retailer.

SCREEN SAVERS

Screen savers are easy to create and distribute as downloadable executable files. Hundreds of firms create professional screen savers for many different markets and needs. We like the simplicity of the home page of

Figure 4.13

Screen Savers from
cassdesign.com. Screen
capture from http://www.
cassdesign.com.

CassDesign.com (http://www.cassdesign.com), and especially their solid positioning line, "Screen Savers that Motivate and Inspire" (Fig. 4.13).

Downloadable free screen savers may be particularly effective if your company deals in a brand name product that has a following. Are you a motorcycle parts dealer? Offer a Harley screen saver. Are you a videotape distributor? Offer screen savers of cult films or current popular actors. Do you sell fishing gear? How about a screen saver showing a huge large-mouth bass standing on its tail with one of your lures hooking him in the jaw?

Dozens of firms, including CassDesign.com (http://www.cassdesign.com), offer hundreds of screen savers related to various business types that can be modified easily.

Whatever the screen saver, the business name and/or logo and Web address should be visible.

GAMES AND PUZZLES

Almost any product or service can serve as the basis for a game or puzzle. Many firms add the firm's logo and imagery to a wide variety of toys, games, puzzles, and magic tricks. ImageBuilder Software, Inc. (http://www.imagebuilder.com) is a major player in creating branded games and puzzles. Its subsidiary, Active Arts Software, offers many technologies and software tools for cobranding and licensing, with new ones coming soon for WAP (Wireless Application Protocol) and PDAs (personal digital assistant). (See http://www.activearts.com/licensing.)

OTHER INTERACTIVE FUNCTIONS

The possibilities for interactive functions on business sites seem limited only by one's imagination. Here are a few ideas.

- Do you provide accounting services? Is tax preparation your specialty? Offer a free tax information booklet distributed using a downloadable Adobe Acrobat file or e-book (with your contact information displayed throughout, of course).

- Do you sell containers of various sorts? Add a calculator to your site to help visitors estimate the size container they need. (See one for fish tanks at http://www.actwin.com/fish/faq/tanksize.html.)

- Do you sell items that require custom measurements, such as drapes, blinds, or closet organizers? Add a slide presentation that shows your clients exactly how to measure windows or other areas.

- Is your business related to pet health or pet supplies? Show visitors how to administer medicine to their pet, or to clip their pet's claws, or take their pet's temperature.

- Does your company deal in home improvement? Host how-to home improvement seminars with live streaming through your Web site.

- Do you make or sell wine? Host a free streaming video showing your site visitors how to host a wine tasting party, such as the one at http://www.waganer.com/enjoywine.htm. (And for live videostreaming projects, be sure to offer the tape of the program on the site for later visitors.)

Check out the following sites for ideas for free gifts:

http://www.ilovefreebies.com
http://www.totallyfreestuff.com
http://www.freestuffcenter.com
http://www.allnewspapers.com/freestuff
http://www.411freestuff.com
http://www.freestuffcentral.com
http://www.thefreespot.com
http://www.virtualfreesites.com/free.html

Functions that Enable Visitor Communication

Every day developers add new functions to the array of tools that enable Web visitors to communicate with companies and with each other. Increasingly, business sites are adding bulletin boards, chat rooms, online meetings, online seminars, video conferencing, teleconferencing, and live customer service via individual chat. E-mail and contact forms are now so universal and indispensable that a site without them will soon be lonely.

Use of these conversational functions or tools is increasing not simply because the developers enjoy creating them (which, of course, they do). Nor does their real significance lie in their novelty. Rather, these tools are filling a key purpose for Web use, the underlying reason for its global expansion: people's natural need and desire to communicate with people. These are the tools that allow Web visitors to communicate with you—a very different function from your telling and showing your products and touting your greatness.

These tools also let people get to know you—the you that is the people who make your company what it is. This is the Internet operating at its subversive best. Imagine letting employees spend an hour a week in the company's Web site chat room talking with clients and potential clients. Unanticipated consequences might include increased loyalty, appreciation, and creativity . . . for both customers and employees.

What is wonderful about many of these functions, especially those among and between the visitors themselves, is that the conversations often tend to be unvarnished statements of opinion—market research at its cost-effective best.

LIVE CUSTOMER SERVICE

Think about shopping. You finally find the product you seek at the price you want, but you have just one critical question before you are ready to purchase. In a bricks and mortar store, you could ask a clerk; online, you might have to wait hours (or days) before your e-mailed question is answered. Or consider consumers who need help with their new digital camera or personal digital assistant or above-ground swimming pool or car stereo. Just the thought of calling the store or the manufacturer is daunting.

No longer. Now live customer service gives Web users immediate access to your customer service or sales representative. It works very much like AOL's Instant Messaging, but requires no downloading of a program or plug-in. Users simply click on your "Talk to us Now" Web button. This function connects real people in real time—the cement of the Internet. This live customer service feature allows visitors to interact one-on-one with a real live human who (we hope) knows all the answers. Live customer service tools, some of which are free or inexpensive, include a Web

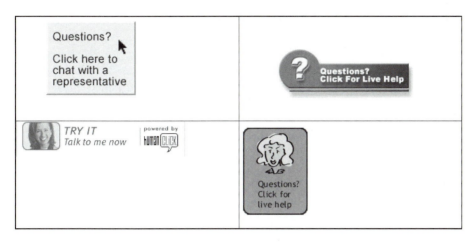

Buttons are screen captures from http://www.humanclick.com.

Figure 4.14

button with text inviting visitors to ask for your help. Figure 4.14 shows sample buttons provided at http://www.humanclick.com.

Using the services of HumanClick (http://www.humanclick.com), an early leader in this field (or similar services), you download and install a free software program that lets you operate the chat-room-like split-screen white board. The program signals you with an audio or a visual alert when visitors enter your site or when they ask to chat.

The software also provides you with considerable data about what a visitor is doing in your site. For example, using your operator window you will receive a real-time view of a visitor's profile, including such information as the name of the visitor's Internet service provider, the Web pages viewed, and the length of the visit. At any point during a visit to your site you may, with one click, open a chat request on the *visitor's* screen and offer assistance. You can send "canned" answers to the most common questions or you can create an answer on the spot. You can even take the visitor to other pages on the Web by sending the Web page addresses, which are clickable.

OTHER COMMUNICATIONS

CHAT ROOMS

Chat rooms are proliferating rapidly on the Internet, probably because of the ease of installation and use. The primary difference between a chat room and the live interactions described above is the number of people involved. Chat rooms can accommodate large numbers of users at one time.

Web visitors can join in a live chat on a Web site with a single click. Customers can discuss industry information or talk with each other about your service. Users may sound off about product problems, try to help each other solve some of those problems, and discuss needs for certain product features . . . all of which can help you improve products and services. Such conversations can also help your customers get to know you and your company—with the possible outcome of enhanced product or company loyalty. Why? Because that's what happens when people converse freely with other people, even in this written fashion, rather than simply interacting with an impersonal Web page.

Most successful chats follow a schedule so that visitors show up when others are online. Visitors often prefer to do the scheduling themselves. Without scheduled times—unless your site has many thousands of visitors a day—chat rooms may be unused, like desert islands. Schedule and promote a monthly (or more frequent) chat session with the CEO or the customer service manager or a product marketing director. Promote these chat times in opt-in newsletters as well as on your Web site.

BULLETIN BOARDS

Bulletin boards enable visitors to log in and ask questions or post statements. Their comments provide insight on ways to improve your company or Web site. To maintain decorum, many firms opt for a bulletin board that either screens out provocative language or can be edited by a manager before the posting is displayed publicly. Never change a negative comment into a positive one; you will be found out and the situation will only deteriorate. Rather, if possible, acknowledge the criticism and comment on how the problem might be corrected.

POLLING

Polls convey power. Users have the power to give you their opinion. Those opinions give you power to improve—your company, your products, your Web site. In addition, many Web visitors *like* to answer polls, especially if the Web page provides instant feedback about the responses. If the topic is of particular interest, users will return to the site to see results at a later time. Web page polls can be added easily and without sophisticated (and expensive) software. Use them to evaluate new product ideas, to determine the importance of various product or service features, or to get feedback on your customer service efficiency or friendliness. You'll be limited only by your ability to think of questions. Firms that offer free polling applications can be found at http://directory.google.com/Top/Computers/ Internet/Web_Design_and_Development/Authoring/Free_Services/Polls_ and_Surveys/.

Sites with large numbers of daily visitors can even conduct and post results of "quick polls" within minutes. These quick polls are the type used on TV network Web sites during political campaigns. OpinionPower.com (http://www.opinionpower.com) suggests the following uses for quick polls:

- Increase audience interaction

- Increase time audience uses your site

- Increase page views

- Increase advertising space

- Learn about your audience as a group, not as individuals

- Use information to serve your audience more effectively

- Provide audience with information about its preferences

ONLINE MEETINGS

TELECONFERENCING

Most telephone users are familiar with, or at least understand the concept of, teleconferencing. Uncle Harry in Minneapolis, Cousin Sue in Marshville, and Grandma Bess in Kiowa can all talk to each other on the phone at the same time. Computer networking has expanded the scope of the concept, since conferencing can take place using a network connection. Once the network teleconference is set up, users can talk using a microphone and speakers connected to their computers. Importantly, they can also share computer applications and use a whiteboard that all the participants in the teleconference can see and write or draw on. Your customer service representatives and sales representatives can actually draw pictures to help explain product elements.

One of the earliest Internet teleconferencing programs was Microsoft's NetMeeting. The "new and improved" NetMeeting includes audio and video conferencing features, whiteboard functions that allow users to share and edit graphical information, text-based chat, and other functions. For additional information, get details at http://www.microsoft.com/windows/netmeeting.

VIDEOCONFERENCING

Videoconferencing is among the fastest-growing segments of the computer industry. Videoconferencing differs from teleconferencing in that it allows transmission of video. Participants can use this tool as a one-to-one (two-person) conference, in which case the system is similar to using a video telephone. Small video cameras transmit the participants' pictures to each other's computer monitors, and participants use their computer's microphone and speakers for audio.

Videoconferencing can also be used to connect several people at once. Participants communicate in a "virtual conference room," as though they were all at the same table. Reductions in the once-exorbitant costs have increased the use of videoconferencing for both internal and external communications. Still, these systems generally require special network arrangements with an outside provider that outsources the service to the company (and networks its various locations). As in Hollywood movies, participants sometimes gather in a conference or seminar room, looking at jumbo screens as they participate in the meetings.

In addition to Microsoft's NetMeeting, Webex.com (http://www. Webex.com) provides software that allows users to hold interactive Web meetings with real-time data, voice, and video communications through a standard browser.

OTHER ADVANCED TOOLS

WEBCASTING AND NET EVENTS

Internet Events are often distributed through Webcasting, which is also often called *netcasting* or *Internet broadcasting*. Webcasting is the process of transmitting live or prerecorded audio or video to personal computers that are connected to the Internet. Webcasting is very much like TV or radio in that it delivers one-to-many communications. The software that enables Webcasting is known as *streaming media*.

ONLINE SEMINARS

To bring your firm's staff up to speed on a new procedure or sales approach, consider Webcasting a seminar on the subject. The cost of a Webcast—compared with that of travel, lodging, food and expenses to bring employees (or customers, vendors, dealers, franchisees, etc.) to a central location—can frequently make Web conferencing a viable alternative. As travel risks and restrictions increase, Webcast may become more common. Employee productivity is also a factor in online seminars, product demonstrations, or training. Employees can view online presentations from their own computers, saving the time and expense of off-site training. To view an online video presentation, go to http://play.rbn.com/?url=rn/rnc/g2demand/0524keynote1_100.rm&proto=rtsp.

BROADCASTING A COMPANY MESSAGE AS AN EVENT

Companies can Webcast the announcements of new products, shareholder meetings, major seminars, breakthroughs in technology—or they can introduce their next Hollywood blockbuster movie. Webcasts are frequently advertised to a specific audience or to a national consumer or business audience as a Webcasting event. Webcasting enables a CEO or other executive to deliver messages worldwide to employees of a large firm. Webcasts can be delivered live, but are usually made available from a Web page, viewable at the user's convenience. Company messages can be Webcast to specific audiences by providing password-protected access at a specified Web page. Your audience goes to a particular Web page to log in and view the full sound and video presentation.

Generally, streaming messages can be broadcast to anyone who "tunes in" on the Internet. Such broadcasts should be well publicized ahead of their release, especially if the release is a one-time-only transmission. If the broadcast will be available online for a prolonged time, as most Webcasts are, be sure to list it in directories of events, such as the Yahoo! Events for Business directory at http://www.broadcast.yahoo.com/Business.

STREAMING MEDIA
How does streaming media work? Streaming media technologies transmit audio and video from a centralized source, known as a *server,* to a software client on a PC. The software is called a *media player.* When the user requests a streaming media file such as a video, the server sends a stream of data to the media player, which plays the data (audio and/or video) as it is received.

The Yahoo! broadcast site offers a large and comprehensive selection of streaming media programming, including live and on-demand corporate and special events from their business services customers and live and on-demand special interest shows and Internet-only Webcasts. Yahoo! provides the Webcasting and audio-visual production services listed below, plus Web and multimedia development, consulting, and other services.

Webcasting Services

- Live audio and video broadcasting

- On-demand audio and video hosting

- 24/7 audio and video broadcasting

- Internet and Intranet broadcasting

- "Self-service" audio and video hosting

- Pay-per-view broadcasting

- Secured broadcasting

- Multicasting services

A/V Production Services

- Live Webcast engineering

- Audio/video production

- Audio/video satellite uplinking and downlinking

DOCUMENTS SENT BY AUTORESPONDERS

An autoresponder is a program that automatically answers any or some e-mail messages or specific commands issued from a Web site. For example, a Web site might have a list of free reports of interest to that site's target audience. The user can click a checkbox next to the desired reports, enter an e-mail address, and click on Send or Submit. The autoresponder automatically sends the selected reports to the e-mail address entered by the user. The answers can be long and can carry attachments. These tools are useful for sending large files—even catalogs with thousands of items—to customers or prospects.

Even the simplest autoresponder functions generate two positive results: (1) you obtain the user's e-mail address, which you can add to your database for possible future communications; and (2) your company has sent a message, by request, directly into the user's in box. This means that, after these users have left your Web site, they will see the name of your company, your e-mail address, and information from your site in their own e-mail. Indeed, this is the advantage of placing such information or reports in autoresponder format rather than directly in the pages of the site. A variation would be to put part of the report on the site, with links for users to "Request the full report by e-mail." Autoresponders work best when they are clearly described for the user. For example: "To have our 300-product catalog e-mailed to you instantly, send an e-mail to sales@superduperfirm.com."

One familiar form used routinely on thousands of sites is the confirmation notice sent to a user after filling out and submitting forms, either to register as a member or subscriber, or to order a product or make a reservation. Autoresponders are also useful for sending samples to potential e-magazine or newsletter subscribers, welcome and thank-you letters, ad rates, and price lists.

MORE INTERACTIVITY FOR YOUR WEB SITE

FREE E-MAIL

Users who sign up for free Web-based e-mail at your site will return every time they want to retrieve or send e-mail. Most of these programs use the name of the host site in the e-mail address or add advertising or a slogan to each message sent. This means that users are helping to advertise the host site to their e-mail correspondents.

FREE CALENDARS

Calendar programs allow visitors to create and maintain their schedules. Members can check their schedules from any computer connected to the Web, and they must visit your Web site to do it.

OPT-IN NEWSLETTERS

Offer to send visitors timely news of your industry or a regularly scheduled newsletter packed with useful information, tools, or offers. Since visitors sign up for (opt in for) the newsletters, these mailings are not considered spam, even if the mailings contain links that lead the recipient back to pages in your site. The newsletters or the links can include coupons, special limited-time discounts, used equipment sales, deals on blemished products, and so forth. However, if the mailings are limited to promotional content, recipients will soon view them as spam. More effective newsletters include content that is rich, unique, succinct, and clearly valuable to the recipient.

Summary

Interactive functioning has changed the ways people use the Internet. No longer content with looking up definitions, finding phone numbers, or sending e-mail, users communicate with each other live, make things happen on the Web, and control and change things. Effective Internet marketing recognizes these functions and their impact on the marketplace—and uses them to its advantage.

Important types of interactive functioning include interactive catalogs and other selling purchasing tools, product delivery by download, live communications with real people in real time, teleconferencing and video-conferencing, surveys, polls, autoresponders, and free Web-based tools.

Review Questions

1. Name three types of interactive Internet functions related to marketing and/or selling.
2. What are the three primary components of an interactive Web catalog?
3. Why would industrial firms making many, many products benefit from having an interactive Web catalog?
4. What does the "front end" of a shopping cart generally refer to?
5. What does the "back end" of a shopping cart generally refer to?
6. What steps are involved in purchasing an item using an online shopping cart?
7. How can publishing an online e-book and offering it as a free download help achieve a firm's marketing goals? ·
8. What is the function of PayPal.com?
9. How can a small shop benefit from selling in an online catalog, without incurring the cost of an entire shopping cart system and all its programming?
10. How can offering an item on an auction site such as eBay be used as a promotional activity?
11. What dollar volume did eMarketer project for online auctions in year 2002?
12. Why would you want to add Human Click to a Web site?
13. List some costs that can be saved by using Webcasting rather than in-person meetings.
14. What is an *opt-in newsletter?*

Look 'n' Feel

Site Appearance and Organization

In previous chapters, you identified a distinctive market position, targeted audiences, established Web site goals, and created or found mountains of interesting information for specific Web audiences. Now it's time to put all that information together in an attractive and logical (or at least easy-to-navigate) format. How do you decide what will be attractive to visitors? How do you ensure that they will be able to find the information they want quickly and easily? Answer these questions and you'll have all the pieces for directing your Web site design and construction.

THE BASICS

Appearance

What should a Web site look like for a particular product, service, or company? What will appeal most to specific audiences? What color or style or size typeface will do the most to reinforce a positioning? The following five general criteria are key to using the appearance of a site to accomplish a site's goals.

1. REFLECTIVE OF YOUR POSITIONING

The appearance—the colors, graphics, fonts, and other visual elements—of a site should be appropriate for the market positioning of the product or firm. The graphics and visual style should reflect and even build positioning—reinforcing visitors' perceptions of the company, product, or service.

For example, does the company sell valuable art or luxury automobiles? The look needs to be elegant and sophisticated. Does the site advertise candy or toys or games for children? It needs to use bright colors, clean and simple graphics, and a typeface that lets the visitor know the site is related to kids. If the product is positioned as the "softest fabric in the world" or "the dishwashing liquid that is gentle on your hands," neon orange and green flashing banners won't communicate the correct message.

2. DISTINCTIVE

The appearance of a site should help it stand out from the sites of competitors. Do competitors' sites display their headline directly at the top center of the home page and their product or service photos on the top left? Do they always place their logo on the top right with their links to content in green?

Yes, we exaggerate, but after a while many business sites begin to look achingly familiar. Strive to make your site memorable. Distinctiveness is a key consideration when planning a site. What different (yet appropriate) things can be done to a site to make it more noticeable and memorable to visitors?

3. CONSISTENT FROM PAGE TO PAGE

Your visitors should always know which site they are visiting. This does not mean that every page of a Web site should look exactly like every other page. It does mean that each page should have some recognizable element that is the same . . . the same navigation bar, a small logo, a blue line across the top, a distinctive typeface.

4. CLEAR

If a Web site is confusing to read or to navigate, visitors will leave quickly, without learning what content is being offered. They'll find a competitor's site—one that is easier to navigate. Make sure that each page of your site is:

(a) Easy to read.

(b) Clear about where to click.

(c) Not too busy or crowded with too much information or too many graphics, animations, links, or other elements.

(d) Not distracting from the main goal or focus of the page.

5. INTERESTING AND COLORFUL.

And to all of these characteristics we add that, whatever the appearance of the site, the graphics *must* display quickly. No matter how wonderful those images are, slow-loading pages will make visitors scram.

Organization

Visitors to a Web site do not start on page 1 and work their way through to page 45. Web pages are linked together, and each page has links, or shortcuts, to other sections or pages, or even to other Web sites.

Think of the organization of a site as an org chart, similar to one depicting a company's reporting structure. Then realize that each box needs to link to some of the side boxes and to some of the boxes two levels down or up, not only the boxes directly above and below. Assuring that visitors can find their way from one part of a site to another quickly and easily requires clear organization and directions. Following are three general guidelines to apply to the organization of your site:

1. *Put first things first.* A home page, the main entry to a Web site, must present the positioning and communicate the content and personality of the site. It must provide the navigational links to help visitors start to explore the site's information and use its tools.

2. *Be directive.* A Web site must clearly point the way to information, benefits, and actions for visitors. Simple, straightforward navigational tools, such as statements ("Click Here," "Enter Catalog"), buttons, or navigation bars should help visitors find their way. Label each link with a distinctive and easy-to-understand name that indicates what awaits the visitor who clicks there. Avoid vague, unmodified terms like "Resources" or "Information."

3. *Use only a few layers.* Effective sites must be easy to navigate and renavigate. Visitors should be able to remember where things are. A Web site that is very complex and convoluted, with many layers and crossing connections, will soon confuse and frustrate users trying to find their way. Users should be able to get to the desired information with as few clicks as possible, preferably fewer than four or five. Group pages logically. Use sub-index pages to link to various pages of each group, rather than trying to link to all the pages from the main page.

BEYOND THE BASICS

Appearance

Some people think of a Web site's home page as similar to the front of a printed sales brochure. We have all heard that the purpose of a sales brochure's front page is to intrigue you enough to open the brochure and read more. But when a Web site's home page is designed well, it does much more than a brochure cover ever could.

The entry page to a Web site should capture the interest, so often fleeting, of people who impatiently seek information, education, and entertainment. Within a few seconds, the page must deliver something the visitor is looking for in a way that glues fickle mouse pointers to the site. The page must grab the visitor's attention immediately. It should get that "Okay! This is the place!" reaction. The site's appearance and organization are critical to getting this recognition.

You want to make a good first impression, one that communicates professionalism and helpfulness and is warm and inviting. You wouldn't conduct business wearing a fluorescent orange spandex bodysuit crammed with a dozen buttons that flash different colors and a lapel pin that plays a rock music standard while a beanie on your head whirls a day-glow propeller . . . would you? (Okay, maybe if you work on the boardwalk. . . .) Upon meeting a potential client, you wouldn't immediately lay out all your own baby pictures or shots of your bathroom or your overfilled garage, or photos of you at age ten on a Ferris wheel . . . would you? If you did, your credibility as a businessperson might be in questionable territory right away. Yet such inappropriate elements are proudly displayed to first-time visitors on home pages of many smaller firms.

In this section you will learn the basic criteria of Web site appearance and see how these criteria can be achieved in various ways.

THE FRONT DOOR

A home page must look *inviting* and *interesting*, two attributes that must be *experienced*. If the home page *looks* inviting, it is. Web designers tend to refer to this aspect of a site as its "look 'n' feel." Some features that can lead to a desirable look 'n' feel include:

- Good use of white or open space to separate graphic and text elements and avoid a cluttered look.

- A clearly visible headline that tells what the site is about instantly and communicates purpose and positioning.

- Subheads or button links that offer additional categories or features.

- Smaller, rather than larger, graphics for fast downloading.

■ Carefully selected use of special functions such as those requiring un-common plug-ins or Shockwave, Flash, RealPlayer, QuickTime Movie, or similar programs.

Many new Web users don't know how to download or use such plug-ins. They may have old versions of browsers. Many sites built around Java script or plug-ins can't be searched or indexed by search engines. And gaudy, full-media splash pages sometimes crash visitors' browsers, too. So use technology that is readily available to everyone in your intended audience, even if they use older browsers.

TIP!   **USE CAUTION WITH "SPLASH" PAGES**

Dramatic and captivating splash pages are sported to introduce large sites and sites of designers who are delighted to try new ideas. These pages appear before the main entry page of a site. They often feature impressive animation and sound. Very high-end (expensive) corporate sites often have *spectacular* splash pages. See http://www.cocacola.com for an outstanding example.

Splash pages, however, can be slow to load, especially for users with older equipment. Also, search engines cannot find much to index on such splash pages. (See Chapter 6 for more details on search engines.) If being found on search engines is an important goal, which it is to many small to medium business Web sites, why use a page that engines have difficulty adding to their index or directory? Web sites should be designed first for function, then for splash. Smaller businesses will reap more value for their Internet budgets by focusing on top quality content and overall appeal, saving costly animations for later.

If, however, you believe your particular audience (say, a high-tech group that is likely to have high-speed connections) will appreciate such extras, include them off a special link. Visitors with older programs will be able to avoid going to a page they can't see (and be irritated with you as a result).

APPEARANCE CAN CHANGE

Many new Web creation tools enable designers to create sites that change. Some of the changes include graphics that display at random or in some predetermined rotation sequence each time the page is accessed. This encourages visitors to return to the site to see what's new or what's different. Other sites place *cookies* (small pieces of code) on a visitor's Web browser so that they can recognize a repeat visitor and give that visitor different images or text on subsequent visits. Amazon.com, for example, greets customers with a personalized statement such as "Welcome back, George Smith," and then displays recommended books, CDs, and videos based on George's previous searches and/or purchases. This type of personalization can be an especially powerful marketing tool—and the cost for such features is coming down.

DOWNLOAD TIME

Most Web users will not wait for a slow or "fat" home page to download. A very rough rule of thumb is to allow a half-second per kb for a page to download at typical modem dial-up speeds, especially during peak Internet usage times. Following this rule, a 30 kb Web page takes 15 seconds to download. A 60 kb home page takes a half minute. Text items load almost instantly into a visitor's browser, so placing the positioning headline and subheads at the top of a page in text format helps assure that those key elements are displayed immediately. Such headlines keep viewers interested in reading text while the remainder of the page loads.

Some designers who routinely work with broadband high-speed Internet access forget that many consumers with home computers do not have such fast access. These designers may create stunning pages that people never see because the pages take too long to load. Check the speed of a page or site at WebSiteGarage.com (http://www.Websitegarage.com) using the free, multi-featured diagnostic center.

Table 5.1 shows loading speed results for two Web pages. Since loading speed depends on *both* the speed of the Web site and the speed of the user's connection to the Internet, this table shows the load time for various connection speeds. Page A is a typical image-intensive home page of an individual. Page B is the entry page of Microsoft's MSN.com at http://www.msn.com. As you would expect of Microsoft, the page loads very quickly. And don't imagine that MSN.com is just a scrawny site with little content or interesting design on its home page. It is one of the best designed and most complete portals (see Chapter 6 for more on portals) on the Web. The message? It is possible to have a terrific home page that also downloads quickly.

Table 5.1	LOADING SPEEDS	
Connect Rate	Load Time for Page A, in Seconds	Load Time for Page B, in Seconds
14.4K	142.28	3.71
28.8K	78.08	2.24
33.6K	66.86	2.00
56K	52.24	2.00
ISDN 128K	18.27	1.00
T1 1.44Mbps	4.38	1.00

KEEP IMAGE FILES SMALL

The key nonuser factors in download time are the images and special programs on a Web page, and sometimes the speed or amount of traffic on the server hosting the site. How fast an image loads is related to the size of the image—the image's *file size*, that is. Two images can have the same apparent dimensions but display on a visitor's monitor at very different speeds. As a general rule, the larger the file size, the longer the loading time. Images with higher resolutions and with more colors have larger file size and take longer to display. (Most files with music and/or animations also take longer to load, so use these features—tempting as they might seem—guardedly.)

Notice how Turner Sculture (Fig. 5.1) has used open space, headlines, links, and small images on this page of its Web site, informing visitors immediately that the studio specializes in "Wildlife Sculpture in Bronze and Silver."

Screen capture from http://www.turnersculpture.com/categories/birds_01.htm.

Figure 5.1

All artwork, photographs, and web site design copyright Turner Sculpture.

DRESS CODE

Following are the five criteria listed at the beginning of this chapter. We have added suggestions to help you implement each guideline.

REFLECTIVE OF YOUR POSITIONING

Is your position related to a specific type of industry segment? Do you specialize in selling wholesale to businesses, selling retail to consumers, selling retail to other firms, or offering bargains to anyone who wants to buy? The Grass Masters site (Fig. 5.2) uses a lot of bright and dark green. The image showing a home and lawn tells us that the equipment is for residential use, and the mower itself is bright yellow so that it stands out. The positioning statement is bright and large: "Quality Equipment for Great American Homes and Gardens." The text that overlays the image works to help Grass Masters position itself further: "Innovation," "Quality," "Love of Home," "Joy of Gardening." The name Grass Masters shows up clearly on the logo (although it doesn't show up here in print as clearly as on the monitor). The logo itself, the cartoonish male face, may not be your personal favorite, but market research may have told Grass Masters that this logo appealed more to their target audience than did other choices. (See Chapter 1 for more examples of communicating market positioning.)

Analyze It   Visit Slot Machines USA at http://www.slotmachinesusa.com. Notice that the graphics and headline tell visitors *immediately* that the firm's specialty is slot machines.

Now visit JMJ Products at http://www.totallycatholic.com. Here the graphics and headline tell visitors that JMJ Products specializes in religious items for Catholics.

Compare the look of the two sites. What differences do you see?

Figure 5.2

Grass Masters. Screen capture from http://www.grassmasters.com.
© 2001 Grassmasters, Inc.

DISTINCTIVE

The appearance of a Web page or site must distinguish it from competitors. The Godiva Chocolatier site (Fig. 5.3) communicates elegance and clearly targets upscale purchasers. The box is gold-foil wrapped with silk/gauze ribbon and frosted fruit decorations. The top bar uses a black background detailed with gold. The positioning? "Chocolatier." This word communicates something far different from "candy maker" or "chocolate candy." It says "privilege, expensive, rich, and fine"—in addition to rich chocolates.

Take a look at the Hershey Foods Corporation Web site (http://www.hersheys.com, Fig. 5.4). Does this site have the look 'n' feel you would *expect* Hershey's Web site to have? Note that this site lets the Hershey's signature font and colors (brown and white) do most of the positioning work. Such use of color and font is acceptable for Hershey's because Hershey's is sufficiently well known to be considered a *brand*. The Hershey's site appears to be targeting a much broader consumer audience than Godiva. Does this match your perceptions of Hershey's?

Small companies with nowhere near the resources of a Hershey's or Godiva can still make their Web sites stand out from the competition. One tactic is to purchase a site from a company that uses custom templates. The companies that build and maintain template-based sites are improving continuously and offer many more variations than in the past.

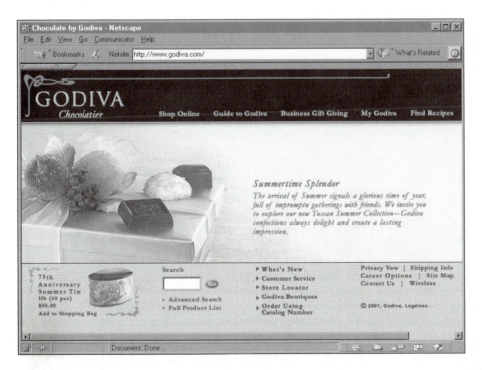

Godiva Chocolatier. Screen capture from http://www.godiva.com.

Figure 5.3

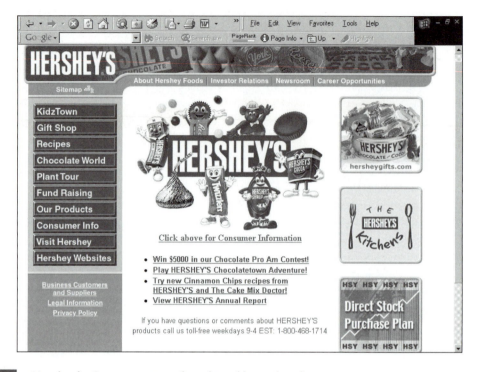

Figure 5.4 Hershey's. Screen capture from http://www.hersheys.com.

Furthermore, by talking with the Web site developer or paying a little extra, a company can add its own custom graphics or photos to a template site to help distinguish it from others. Look at the two real estate sites shown in Figures 5.5 and 5.6. Although you may not realize it immediately, these two sites are based on the *same* template.

Analyze It Compare the two real estate sites shown in Figures 5.5 and 5.6.

The two Web sites, which were created by Advanced Access in Anaheim, CA (http://www.advancedaccess.com), are based on the same template. The designers, however, have applied different text, colors, and graphics to customize them. The look and feel of the two sites are very different.

List the elements of each site that tell you the purpose and/or positioning of each. Be specific. Write five adjectives or phrases to describe each site. For example, do any of the following adjectives describe the site? casual, formal, fun, boring, sedate, bright, serious, cute, elegant, sporty, official, elegant, clever, gloomy, funny, mysterious, plain, chock full, splashy, fancy, heavy, or smooth. Use some of these words or think of others that describe the sites.

Screen capture from http://www.imperialbeachhomes.com.

Figure 5.5

CONSISTENT FROM PAGE TO PAGE

A Web site needs some consistency of appearance from page to page in order to "hold together." Consistency also helps assure that visitors always know whose site they are using and who has provided all the useful or entertaining information and tools.

Consistency does not require that every page of a site look like every other page. It does mean, however, that the site should have some recognizable element that is the same on each page: a small logo, a photo, a colored line across the top (or side), a distinctive typeface, or some other unifying element.

The continuity element should be visible in the portion of the page that is displayed when the visitor arrives at the site, that is, not lower on the page where it cannot be seen until the visitor scrolls down. (Borrowing from an old newspaper term, this is often called presenting the important information "above the fold.")

Many sites use a menu or navigation bar, either vertical (usually down the left) or horizontal (usually across the top) that is the same on each page. This not only facilitates user navigation, but also shows visitors that they are still viewing the same site. "Framed" sites also help achieve a de-

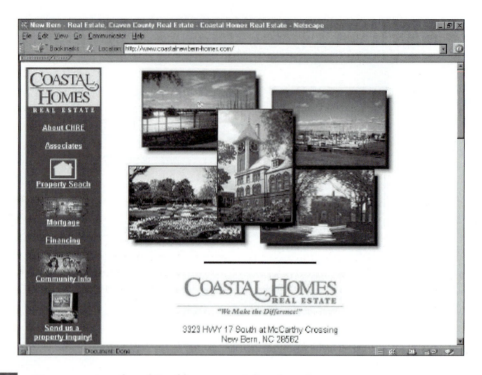

Figure 5.6   Screen capture from http://www.coastalnewbern-homes.com.

sired level of consistency, although controversy about using frames arises every now and again. Frames are discussed in greater depth in the Organization section of this chapter.

CLEAR

A Web site must be easy to read and to navigate; otherwise, visitors will tire of it and leave, perhaps never to return. Here are some guidelines for clarity:

1. **Easy to read.** Use of an average size typeface with plenty of leading (white space) so the type and graphics are not crowded makes reading easier. The size of the typeface should make emphasis clear. Readers will focus on a heading or the phrase that stands out.

   For text that consists of a sentence or more, or if a small size is used to save space, use a *serif* font—one with thick and thin strokes and "feet" at the ends of the letters. (A *sans serif* font lacks the "feet" on the letters. See Table 5.2). Why? Because a serif font is easier to read.

Table 5.2	SERIF VERSUS SANS-SERIF FONTS

Serif	Sans-Serif
These letters are easier for readers to distinguish and recognize because each letter has some thicker parts or "feet" or other features that facilitate the reading process. Times, Garamond, and Palatino are common examples of serif fonts. The font used in this paragraph is Garamond.	These letters are somewhat more difficult for readers to distinguish and recognize because the letters have so few distinguishing features. They are plain and there is no variation in line weights. Sans-serif fonts are best used for headers or short pieces of text. Helvetica, Arial, and Avante Garde are common examples of sans-serif fonts. The font used for the text in this paragraph is Arial.
These letters are easier for readers to distinguish and recognize because each letter has some thicker parts or "feet" or other features that help with the reading process. Times, Garamond, and Palatino are common examples of serif fonts. The font used in this paragraph is Palatino.	These letters are somewhat more difficult for readers to distinguish and recognize because the letters have so few distinguishing features. They are plain. Sans-serif fonts are best used for headers or short pieces of text. Helvetica, Arial, and Avante Garde are common examples of sans-serif fonts. The font used for the text in this paragraph is Helvetica.

> AVOID THE OVERUSE OF UPPER-CASE (CAPITAL) LETTERS. INFORMATION PRESENTED IN ALL CAPITAL LETTERS IS ACTUALLY HARDER TO READ (FEWER VISUAL CUES FOR YOUR BRAIN TO DISTINGUISH) THAN TEXT USING BOTH UPPER- AND LOWER-CASE LETTERS.

The variations in line weights and the serifs give the brain more cues for faster recognition of letters and words.

Avoid the overuse of capital letters. Information presented in all caps is actually harder to read (fewer visual cues for your brain to distinguish) than text using both upper- and lower-case letters. Furthermore, when everything is capitalized, the most important information loses its emphasis. In place of capital letters for emphasis, use italics, bold, and color.

To be sure that a phrase, tagline, or header is perceived consistently from user to user, browser to browser, use an image. Browser settings—usually those of Netscape Navigator or Microsoft's Internet Explorer—control the appearance of regular text to a great degree. You might specify 14 point Avant Garde Bold, but if the visitor's browser cannot find or recognize that type, it will substitute something else, such as 12 point Helvetica. For regular headers, this substitution may not matter. But if the size or style of type is part of your positioning image or relates to a font used in your trademarked graphics or logo, it could be very important.

Present text in fairly short paragraphs or bulleted lists. Both strategies make your text easier for the visitor to read and comprehend. Keep line length to no more than 5 or 6 inches. Text that runs *all the way* across the screen from left to right may be difficult for some people to read.

Far easier to read is text presented in a line length that approximates the width of a newspaper or magazine column, which we have all grown accustomed to reading.

Use caution when placing text on a colored background. That lime green text on a marine blue background may look great in your browser and on your computer, but your visitor's monitor might display the image in colors so similar to each other that reading the text is difficult. Text on pages using a colored background must be of a highly contrasting color and large or bold enough to assure readability.

2. **Clear about where to click.** Pages that promise to deliver key information or benefits but fail to make the links to those items easy to see only frustrate visitors. The navigation bar, buttons, and text that link to other pages must be obvious and clearly worded. (See pp. 127–137 for a detailed discussion of navigation.)

On franchise.com's site example (Fig. 5.7), subheads that may be difficult to understand—with short labels, such as "Franchise TV"—are made clearer by the addition of a line of description. Some Web sites use this one-two punch consistently. This style may call for reducing the type size for the descriptions, but avoid using a type size smaller than 8 point, which many people have difficulty reading.

3. **Not too busy or crowded.** Avoid crowding information, graphics, animations, links, and other elements on a page. Crowded elements draw attention away from the main goal or focus of the page. A page that overwhelms the visitor is just as big a problem as a boring page. Crowded pages can actually bury the key messages they are trying to communicate. Keep pages open and clean. Avoid gratuitous animations or other elements on the page just because your Webmaster says he or she can create "this really, really incredible special effect right on the home page."

TIP!   **MAKE ALL ELEMENTS USEFUL**

One rule of thumb is to make sure that everything on your site is "doing work": giving target audiences information and solutions, building market position, and providing ways for visitors to communicate.

Franchise.com. Screen capture from http://www.franchise.com.

Figure 5.7

INTERESTING AND COLORFUL

What's the most boring site design you can think of? It's a page with paragraph after paragraph of text, without images, mouseovers, links, borders, backgrounds, color, heads, or subheads. In the early years of the Internet, this is exactly what most pages looked like. For the most part, they were academic or government articles and reports. The Internet is a very different world today, and the expectations of Internet users have changed considerably. Web sites that do not take advantage of appropriate design tools are a waste of time and money.

The Internet is a colorful place. Virtually no one using the Internet has a monochrome monitor. Colors develop emphasis and interest. Colors can help with a site's clarity by delineating various areas of a page or making some features, links, or text more obvious. Include graphics and photos that tell the visitor more about your products, company, and market positioning.

The colors, graphics, fonts, and other visual elements of a site should reflect and enhance the unique market position—the way visitors perceive the company, product, or service. Color can convey weight, warmth, coldness, mood, and personality. A Web site advertising Tyvek Happy Birthday balloons generally does not contain large amounts of black. Black and navy blue are heavy colors. Because Tyvek doesn't want to convey that their floating balloons are heavy, they use light and cheery colors such as sky-blue and "happy" yellow.

Yellows and light reddish-blues are warm colors, and are thus often used on travel sites promoting warm-weather destinations. Conversely, yellows may not be appropriate on a state police site. But use care: yellow may also convey envy, sickness, cowardly behavior, and backstabbing.

Red and orange are also warm colors. They strike emotional chords. Red tends to be a favorite color of fast-paced, action-oriented, devil-may-care people, which may explain why red cars get more traffic tickets than others. But using too much red and orange may result in tension.

Violets, blues, and greens are cool, peaceful, calming colors. Blues and light greens soothe the soul just as music does and invite images of pastoral, outdoor settings.

Color selection should be part of the overall look of the site. Like the other aspects of the visual character of a site, color should work to communicate the site's intended purpose or message. Find more references on color usage at:

http://www.pantone.com/allaboutcolor/allaboutcolor.asp?ID=34
http://www.pantone.com/allaboutcolor/allaboutcolor.asp?ID=43
http://www.pantone.com

Properly used, and with care exercised to assure that the type is clear and readable, background shading can help visitors recognize page sections more easily. The page shown in Figure 5.7 uses background shading for the headers of the main topics to set them apart and make the sections easier to find.

Analyze It

Which two colors would you choose as the primary ones for each of the following Web sites? Why?

Site that advertises:	Colors	Reason(s)
1. Tomato juice		
2. Bottled water		
3. An amusement park		
4. Accounting services		
5. A dental office		

Organization

The primary measure of a site's organization is *ease of navigation*. Visitors should be able to find their way around the site, moving easily from one page to another and *back*, without having to ask themselves, "Where did I see that?" Visitors seeking specific information should be able to find it easily and quickly, without having to drill down through many layers of pages, hunting for the right place to click on each page, scrolling and squinting.

Employ these general strategies to build a site that is easy to navigate:

1. Organize the information and pages so that important data or functions are no more than two or three mouse clicks away.

2. Include easy-to-see navigation bars or lists with links to the major pages of the site at the top, side, or bottom of *each* page.

3. Provide clear directions to visitors so they know what they need to do next.

Figure 5.8 shows a basic Web site anatomy for marketing *services*. In this example, as with other effective Web sites, *all* pages have a link back to HOME and a separate link to each of the MAIN LINKS. These links may be part of a navigation bar at the top or side of your page, or at the bottom—maybe both. *All* Web pages should have an active e-mail link or a "contact us" link so that visitors may request information or place an order.

FRAMES

Some sites use a design called a *frame* to keep one part of the page visible while another part changes. In the examples shown in Figure 5.9, the user could click on a link in Part A or B and the intended page would be displayed in Part C. Moreover, the page that appears in Part C could actually be from *another site*.

Compare the Dacor screen captures shown in Figure 5.10. Notice that the appearance of the navigation bar on the top stays constant. Click on a link in the navigation bars at the top or left side and the display in the main frame changes, while the navigation bar information still shows.

Not everyone is a fan of framed sites. Two factors make the use of framed sites somewhat more difficult than nonframed sites. Jerra Morris, owner/principal at Web design firm Advanced Access (http://www.advancedaccess.com) points out that some clients prefer nonframed sites

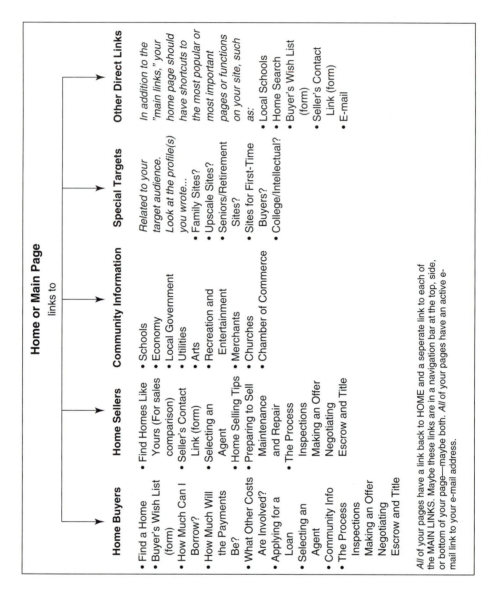

Home or Main Page

links to

Home Buyers
- Find a Home
- Buyer's Wish List (form)
- How Much Can I Borrow?
- How Much Will the Payments Be?
- What Other Costs Are Involved?
- Applying for a Loan
- Selecting an Agent
- Community Info
- The Process
  Inspections
  Making an Offer
  Negotiating
  Escrow and Title

Home Sellers
- Find Homes Like Yours (For sales comparison)
- Seller's Contact Link (form)
- Selecting an Agent
- Home Selling Tips
- Preparing to Sell
  Maintenance and Repair
- The Process
  Inspections
  Making an Offer
  Negotiating
  Escrow and Title

Community Information
- Schools
- Economy
- Local Government
- Utilities
- Arts
- Recreation and Entertainment
- Merchants
- Churches
- Chamber of Commerce

Special Targets
Related to your target audience. Look at the profile(s) you wrote...
- Family Sites?
- Upscale Sites?
- Seniors/Retirement Sites?
- Sites for First-Time Buyers?
- College/Intellectual?

Other Direct Links
In addition to the "main links," your home page should have shortcuts to the most popular or most important pages or functions on your site, such as:
- Local Schools
- Home Search
- Buyer's Wish List (form)
- Seller's Contact Link (form)
- E-mail

All of your pages have a link back to HOME and a seperate link to each of the MAIN LINKS. Maybe these links are in a navigation bar at the top, side, or bottom of your page—maybe both. All of your pages have an active e-mail link to your e-mail address.

Figure 5.8   A basic site anatomy, using a real estate example.

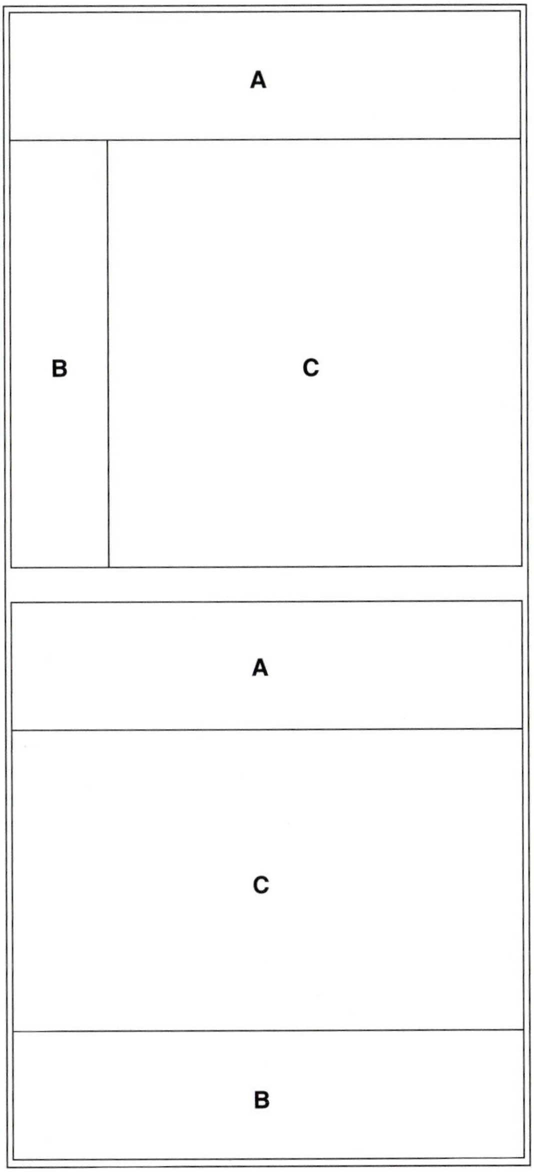

Figure 5.9

Two layouts for framed pages.

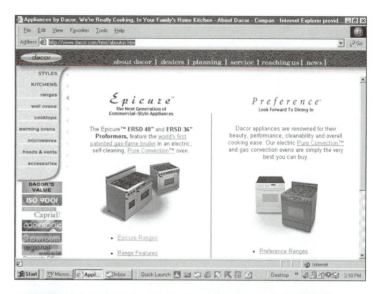

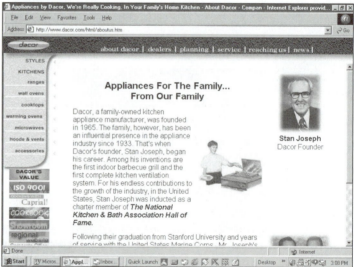

Figure 5.10

Dacor. Screen captures
from http://www.dacor.com.

to avoid the extra scrolling that frames usually require. Also, without extra
code to link visitors to a printable page, printing pages from a framed site
is often either not possible or requires extra steps.

Some search engines (see Part Two for a detailed discussion) may not
search some or most of a framed site. However, framed sites have a "nonframes" page, which sets the sizes and names of the frames and which
search engines *do* read. The nonframes page may have its own metatags

and text and links. Knowledgeable site builders construct this page so that it contains all the necessary components to be read by the search engines.

TIP!	VIEWING FRAMED PAGES

To view a page that has been framed, simply place your cursor on a blank part of the framed page and right-click. This will open a drop-down menu from which you will select "Open Frame in New Window" in Netscape, or "Properties" in the MSIE browser. Click on "Properties" and you'll see a "General" page and "Address (URL):" The address shown there (http://www.whatever.com) is the true address of the framed page. Copy that address and paste it into your browser's location/address box and you will go to the true, unframed version of that page.

Some firms worry that owners of sites that show up framed in the main window may object, since their URL does not show in the address box of a framed page. Displaying a framed page may imply that the outside framed page is actually on the displaying firm's site rather than on a separate site—possibly owned and maintained by a completely separate individual or entity. Some analysts have expressed concern about copyright infractions. This issue remains to be resolved; meanwhile, millions of sites use the technique.

NAVIGATION BARS AND LISTS

The navigation route through a site to desired functions or information should be obvious to visitors. The easiest way to assure that visitors can navigate is to include *clearly labeled* navigation bars or lists of links to the interior pages of the site. Figure 5.11 shows the main page of Kent Paint and Decorating. A navigation bar appears at the top of the screen as well as down the left side. Users can get to an intended page by using the links at the top or at the side. They can also click on the images of products at the right side of the screen to go directly to information on that product.

Furthermore, when a user clicks on one of the links, such as "Art supply," the top and left side navigation bars remain in place while the much larger bottom section changes to display the "Art supply" page (similarly to framed sites, discussed above). So, regardless of which page is displayed, visitors can find their way easily to a different page.

Figure 5.12 shows what happens when a user clicks on the down arrow next to the label "Product Quick Find" near the top of the page. A drop-down list appears with a list of product categories. The user clicks on the desired category and then on the "Go" button.

The pages on www.kentpage.com are rather long, and visitors may scroll quite a distance toward the bottom of a page. Once a visitor has scrolled down, the top navigation bar and some or all of the left naviga-

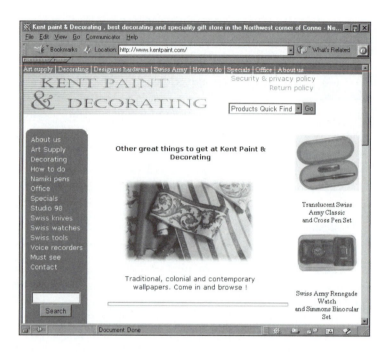

Figure 5.11

Kent Paint and Decorating.
Screen capture from
http://www.kentpaint.com.

tion bar disappear. This site has included a navigation bar at the *bottom* of each page as well, so visitors do not have to scroll back to the top before they can click to go to another page.

Another way to provide navigation is to use a navigation list. This tool is particularly useful for a site that has many pages to be accessed from the front page or a subindex page. Shepherds Garden Seeds, for example, chose to use a combination of graphic link navigation bars on the left side of its page and a text list of its categories on the right side (Fig. 5.13).

One advantage of using text links, either in a navigation bar or in a list, is that text links can be added, deleted, or reworded in just a few seconds. Buttons, however, are small images, and creating new buttons is more time consuming. Furthermore, search engines can read text links but not images. To gain additional search engine value from buttons, site developers add text *mouseovers* to the graphics that are readable. Text links and mouseovers add key words to a page to make it more findable by search engines. (See Part Three, Getting Found.)

NAVIGATION VARIATIONS AND COMBINATIONS

IMAGE LINKS AND MAPS

Images are often used as links, and they can be very inviting and informative. Usually, however, they occupy more space on the screen than do lists and bars. Images of tabs like those on manila folders are used on some

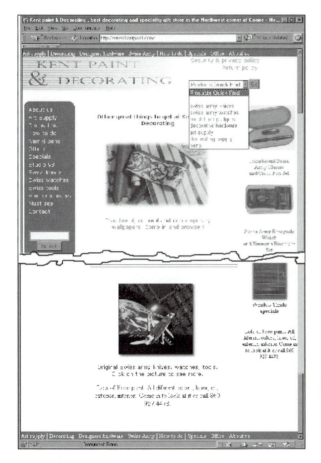

Figure 5.12

"Product Quick Find."
Screen capture from
http://www.kentpaint.com.

sites to communicate to the user that certain information will be found in
that folder. Dana Crandall, the designer of the home page for Mickey
Nock's book *A Boston's World,* used tennis balls, a Boston terrier favorite, for
the navigation buttons (Fig. 5.14). When the user points the mouse at a
tennis ball, the "click-me" hand appears on the ball and the image at the
center of the page changes to give the user more information about the
page at the end of that link.

The tennis balls on *A Boston's World* are individual images, but links
can be mapped to larger images as well. An image of the parts of a plant
could have links connected to the various parts of the plant, with each
link going to information about that part, its name, properties, and function. An image of a file cabinet with labels on the drawers could have
links attached to each drawer. An image of a state map could have links to
demographics, businesses, parks, or other place infomation. The possibilities are endless.

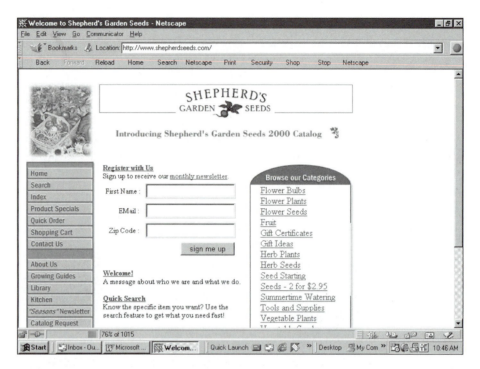

 Figure 5.13   Shepherd's Garden Seeds. Screen capture from
http://www.shepherdseeds.com.

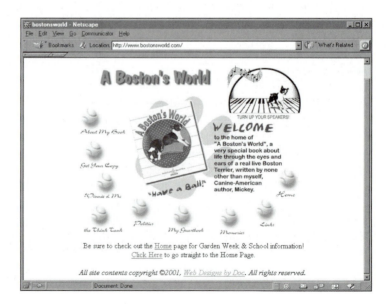

Figure 5.14

A Boston's World. Screen
capture from http://www.
bostonsworld.com. All site
contents copyright © 2001,
Web Designs by Doc.

DROP-DOWN MENUS

Figure 5.15 shows Godiva.com's drop-down menus on the navigation bar at the top of their page. Such a design gives users many more options without having to click (or drill) through many pages to find the information they seek. This design is also easy for visitors to use because it works in a way similar to the way menus work in most Windows applications. The Godiva drop-down menus differ from the one in Figure 5.11 for Kent Paint and Decorating in that they actually drop from the navigation bar, allowing for as many drop-down menus as there are items on the navigation bar.

SITE SEARCHES

Yet another way that Godiva Chocolatier has provided for users to find what they seek is a site-only search engine (Figure 5.15). This search engine searches *only* the pages on www.godiva.com. Users type in a word or phrase related to what they want to find, click on the Go button, and a list of choices appears from which to select. When we entered the word "almond" and clicked on Go, godiva.com returned the page shown in Figure

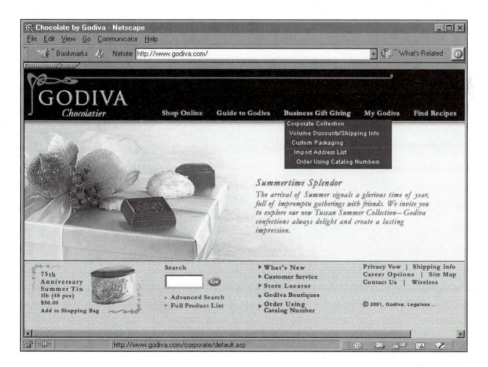

Godiva Chocolatier. Screen capture from http://www.godiva.com.

Figure 5.15

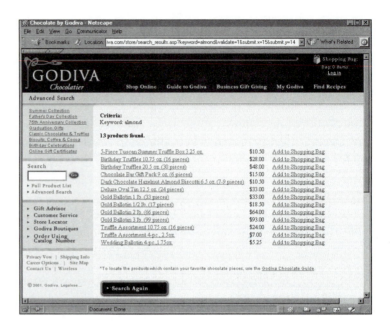

Godiva Chocolatier. Screen capture from search results for "almond" on http://www. godiva.com.

5.16, which gives a list of 13 choices, each with a link to more information about that item.

Small businesses without means to create customized search engines can use some developed by Excite (http://www.excite.com). Also, many companies that host business Web sites provide search engine programming; it's worth asking about.

GETTING BACK FROM ANOTHER SITE

ASK FOR A BOOKMARK

Pages that link to information located on a different site risk losing visitors forever. Some pages remind visitors to use the Back button of their browser, but people who get more than four or five Web pages (or clicks) away from where they started may not return. One way to help them return to a site is to suggest that they *bookmark* the page in their browser. The Internet Explorer browser calls this a *favorite*. Some programmers take the extra step to make a clickable favorite. In other words, when the visitor clicks on the reminder, it automatically creates the bookmark in their browser.

Although the bookmark function does not help a user navigate within a site, it does enable them to find their way back. Bookmarks are important: using bookmarks and typing in URLs account for more than one-third of all the ways that people access Web pages (see Part Three for details).

STAY IN THE BACKGROUND

Another way to avoid losing visitors is to code each outside link so that a new browser window opens each time a visitor clicks to go to a page outside the site. The original browser window (with the earlier site) remains in the background. Operating in the new browser window, the visitor can wander all over the Web, but sooner or later they notice the background and return to it. Maybe they'll even look through the site further. The downside is that from the *new* window, the user cannot use the Back button to return to the original site.

Burpee Seeds. Screen capture from http://www.burpee.com/main.asp.

Figure 5.17

Here is an example of the HTML code for a regular link to an outside site: <a href="http://www.prenhall.com">An informative site</a>

But using the *following* code for the link opens a new browser window and keeps the originating site in the background:

<a href="http://www.prenhall.com" target="new">An informative site</a>

In both cases, the link itself looks like this: *An informative site*

One school of thought holds that you should never offer outside links: all of your links should connect within your site. The determining factor is the purpose and scope of the site. Vortals and other sites intended to provide links to useful information all over the Web *must* have many outside links.

Analyze It

How many links do you see on the page from Burpee Seeds' site (Fig. 5.17)? See if you can identify 50 or more.

How many *types* of links do you see? Name them.

Summary

For many small and medium size businesses, the Web is a major marketing tool, perhaps the *only* one. The impression of that firm's worth may be dictated by what visitors see when they first enter the site. A Web site has about six magical seconds to make its impact, for good or ill. The most effective entry page is one that communicates its message quickly, is not too busy or cluttered, and uses color and images to build its positioning. Likewise, interior pages must reinforce that positioning, be consistent in appearance, and be easy to read.

Once visitors become engaged with a site, its content and organization must keep them there. The key to effective organization is logical and easy navigation. Critical factors to an engaging Web site are use of only a limited number of layers and clear, directive navigation.

For other businesses, a Web site is simply an adjunct or supplement to other marketing and sales efforts. Such is the case for large national firms with strong brand awareness, loyalty, and repeat customers who know their products and services well and see them on shelves or use them daily. Yet, even for these companies, effective use of Web marketing can add to or detract from sales. Web users can compare products, services, and companies much more easily using the Web than ever before, so even large companies can be hurt by poor Web design and functioning.

Every element of a site's look 'n' feel is important in the quest for positioning and sales: every image, every section of white space, every color, every link.

Review Questions

1. What is the most important criterion for Web site organization?

2. What five general criteria are key to a Web site's accomplishment of its goals?

3. List three rules of effective Web site organization?

4. Name three features that can help make a site's entry page look inviting.

5. What sort of look 'n' feel would you expect a site selling expensive tropical fish and related equipment to have?

6. Why is an attractive site less important than one that addresses a firm's goals?

7. Why is it useful for a site to be different from those of competitors?

8. Why should all pages in a Web site have some element that is consistent?

9. Is it better to guide visitors carefully from page 1 through page 45 of a site or to let them go wherever they wish? Why?

10. Why does a Web page need to be *directive*?

11. Why is it better to use smaller images than larger ones?

12. Why does a Web page need white space?

13. What is the purpose of a site's headline?

14. Why is it good to avoid gaudy *splash pages* and rich media effects on home pages?

15. What are the dangers of a cluttered Web page?

16. Why should lines of text not fill the entire width of the screen?

17. Why is it important to ask visitors to *bookmark* a site?

18. What is one advantage of using *framed* Web sites?

19. What do the colors yellow, red, and orange usually communicate?

20. Give an example of mapping links to a graphic.

Part Three

Getting Found

Your Internet presence is worthless if no one can find you.

As the Internet has grown to hold billions of pages, the task of assuring that clients, customers, and potential clients and customers are able to find the Web site for your business or product or service has become more artful. No longer can simple registration with a search engine or listing of a site in a directory, or even purchasing banner or tile ads on portals secure a given site's continuous, reliable findability. Using Web directories and search engine results, not only do people need to find the link to your site, they also have to decide to *click* on that link to get to your information.

With the dot-com visibility, even notoriety, of the past several years, the general public has grown accustomed to hearing and/or seeing the now-familiar "www" dot-this or dot-that on television and radio and in all forms of print media. Businesses on the Web have adjusted to the idea that they need to "advertise their advertising." Web addresses now appear on everything from the wrapper on lettuce to skyline towers, billboards to skywriters, pencils to 747s.

The chapters in Part Three will help ensure that your target audiences will find your Web presence by using on-the-Web tools and links or off-the-Web labels, sales collaterals, advertising, or promotion.

The chapters in this part are:

Chapter 6: Portals, Vortals, Search Engines, and Directories
Chapter 7: Internet Advertising of Your Web Site: Links, Banners, Tiles, and More
Chapter 8: Promotion (On and Off the Net and Print Advertising)

LEARNING THE LANGUAGE

The following terms are used in Part Three. Familiarize yourself with them by reading the plain language definitions provided.

alternative text   Sometimes called *mouseovers* or *alt tags.* Words that display while an image is loading and when the user places the mouse/pointer over an image. Unless the Web site owner/creator changes the alternative text, the name of the graphic file, such as house.gif, will show. However, any text may be used, such as: "Sam Brown agent for first-time home buyers in Bowling Green, Kentucky." Some search engines read this alternative text along with visible text to help determine a site's relevance to specific keywords.

banner ad   A small, rectangular, usually horizontal ad that appears on Internet pages. Banner ads usually link the visitor to the Web site or page of the banner owner (advertiser).

banner exchange   Reciprocal banner display, characterized by the statement: "I'll put your banner on my site if you'll put my banner on yours." Banners often, but not always, include an active link to the target site, becoming link exchanges.

bridge page   A Web page that leads visitors to another site, hence, a bridge. Several sites offer free pages; tripod.com and geocities.com are among the better known sources. Often, but not always, these pages carry their own metatags and their URLs can be registered with search engines. Because some search engines penalize such pages in their rankings, the Web savvy put at least some new or different information on each bridge page, rather than simply a list of links to pages in the target site.

dealership   Display of a graphic and link to an e-commerce site in return for a commission on items sold to visitors using that particular link. Sites with large inventories sold in a catalog format are the most frequent offerors of dealerships.

directory   A list similar to your familiar Yellow Pages, with links and Web site information organized according to categories. General directories, like Yahoo!, are broadbased and include thousands of topics. Some directories focus on a given topic, and may be considered vertical portals, or *vortals.*

domain name   The main part of an Internet address, including its extension. In the address http://www.disney.com/news/pocahontas.htm, for example, "disney.com" is the domain name. Until late 1999, domain names were limited to 26 characters; now they may include as many as 76 characters.

Domain name extensions (suffixes) indicate the *top-level domain* (TLD) to which the name belongs. For example: .com indicates a commercial business; .net indicates a company that specializes in networks; .gov is used by government sites, local, state, or national; .org indicates an organization, usually nonprofit; .edu is used by educational institutions, school districts, and schools; .mil stands for "military." Some extensions indicate the country where the site is based: .mx for Mexico or .ca for Canada, for example. Early in the year 2000, .md was added for use by physicians, hospitals, and other medical-related entities. In 2001, more extensions were added, such as .name, .biz, .pers, and .ent.

hidden text Text written in the coding of an Internet page that does not display on the site. Common examples are the METAtags with title, keywords, site description, and other information that some search engines read and store in their databases.

home search site Web sites that enable consumers to search for and view text and photos of homes for sale that match their criteria. Examples: Homeseekers.com, Realtor.com.

keywords Words people enter into search engines to find information on the Web. Most search engines match words being searched for with Web pages that have them. A typical consumer keyword search might be "Manhattan, NY real estate" (no quotes). Keywords are also listed in the METAtags (hidden text) of Web site pages for reading by search engines.

link exchange Reciprocal linking between or among sites, usually without exchange of fee or other consideration.

metatag Sometimes written METAtag. Coding with information about an Internet page or site. These tags tell what the page is about (META Title and META Description) and provide keywords (META Keywords) that represent the page or site content and more. Many search engines use metatag information to determine ranking of a site in displayed search results.

portal An Internet site offering a selection of resources and services, such as e-mail, links to popular sites, search engines, shopping malls, promotions, chat rooms, or free Web pages. Many major search engines, such as Excite and Infoseek, are now portals.

robot A program that runs automatically. Some Web pages contain hidden text telling robots what to do; for example, "return every 7 days" or "do not catalog this page." See also *spider*.

search engine An Internet site, function, or program that maintains databases of Internet pages, with their keywords and URLs, and retrieves the information according to keywords entered by users, displaying a list of Internet sites and/or pages. Examples include Excite, Infoseek, Google, and Webcrawler.

signature link Text, graphics, and/or links added automatically at the end of outgoing e-mail messages.

specialty site Any site that deals almost entirely with one topic; for example, http://www.gardening.com is a gardening specialty site.

spider A program that automatically retrieves Web page information for use by search engines; a type of robot.

sponsor A site, individual, or company that receives highly visible credit for supporting a section of a Web site. For example, Goodyear Tires might sponsor a section in AOL called Tires & Auto Accessories.

tile ad A small, usually square ad that appears on Internet pages and usually links the visitor to the Web site of the advertiser.

URL registration Reservation of a main Internet site address (domain name). Internic, more recently called Network Solutions, is an entity officially authorized to regulate assignment of domain names.

vortal A vertical portal; a web site that serves as an Internet gateway to pages and sites related to a particular topic or interest.

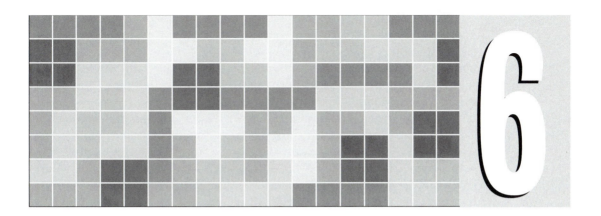

Portals, Vortals, Search Engines, and Directories

Of all the ways that people find information on the Internet, the most common are the links and searching tools on a portal site—a "gateway" to the Internet. Most of the links on a portal are part of the portal's *directory*, a list of categories not unlike those in the familiar Yellow Pages. Categories link to subcategories and lists of links to Web sites. Other links, however, are advertisers or content partners. For example, a portal might partner with ABC News and provide links to the day's top news stories on ABC's Web site. Or the portal might partner with fnn, the Financial News Network, and provide links to the latest financial stories, stock quotes, and other updates on the fnn Web site.

Portals also have a search engine or a selection of search engines for visitors to use by entering words or phrases related to what they are looking for. When someone searches for a product or service you offer, you want the search engines to find *you*. When someone uses a directory, you want to be sure your site is listed.

Portals that focus on a particular topic or audience are called vertical portals, or *vortals.* Vortals are especially useful for finding or advertising *related* products and services. A vortal might have links to Web sites whose content is related to scuba diving, for example, and might include scuba equipment, scuba history, scuba travel, scuba jobs, and scuba experts. One for landscape architecture might have links to sites with content on plant types, diseases, tolerances, landscape design tools, professionals, soils, hardscapes, or yard art. Vortals often have search engines that search only their theme-relevant database. Some have search engines that search the entire Web. The Web is home to vortals for a multitude of subjects. And if you don't find one to advertise your particular wares, building your own vortal may not be a bad idea.

This chapter provides information on search engines and general directories found at portal and vortal sites and other locations on the Internet. Search engines and directories undergo significant changes without warning; technological advances spur new tools and techniques and seem to do so with speed unparalleled in history. We've updated these pages just before printing, so you will find the most recent information available.

THE BASICS

Search Engines

When a visitor enters words into a search engine, the engine looks into its database of words and phrases and site addresses and responds with a list of links to sites that it "thinks" fit the search criteria. How does it get the words, phrases, and Web site addresses? Basically in one of two ways: (1) Web site owners register their sites with the search engines and (2) search engines send out programs (spiders and robots) to wander around the Internet reading the text and/or the hidden text (especially the metatags) on Web sites and then cataloging what they find.

More often than not, these two processes work together in this way. You register your site address, or *URL* (Uniform Resource Locator), with the search engine (easy to do as well as free) and then the search engine sends out the spider to find *keywords* on your site. If you have the keywords in your visible text and hidden text that match the words that someone enters in the search engine, your site will come up higher in the search engine's results.

REGISTER YOUR SITE WITH THE MAJOR SEARCH ENGINES

Registering your site with a search engine is easily done. Go to the main page of the search engine and look for a link labeled "Add URL" or "Add Your Site." Follow the link to the "Add URL" page. Once there, enter the main URL of your site(s), and, if prompted, your e-mail address. Most engines also permit registration of internal pages. Some request a short description. Write carefully! This description is often the one shown when the engine lists your site.

To add your URL to search engines, go to their home pages and click on "Add URL" or "Add Your Site." Some major portal and/or search engine home pages include:

http://www.altavista.com
http://www.aol.com/netfind
http://www.directhit.com
http://www.dmoz.org
http://www.excite.com
http://www.go.com
http://www.google.com
http://www.overture.com
http://www.hotbot.com
http://www.infoseek.com
http://www.lycos.com
http://www.magellan.com
http://home.netscape.com
http://www.nbci.com (formerly snap.com)
http://www.msn.com
http://www.webcrawler.com
http://www.yahoo.com
http://www.fastsearch.com
http://www.search.com
http://www.askjeeves.com
http://www.alltheweb.com/
http://www.northernlight.com/

Some search engines clean their databases of addresses on a regular basis. This means that you need to re-register your site with the engines every few weeks. If you have hired a company to maintain your site, be sure to require that they do this for you.

USE PERTINENT, EFFECTIVE KEYWORDS, TITLES, HEADINGS, AND TEXT

Various search engines use different formulas, programs, and strategies for reading a Web site or page in order to catalog it. They might read any of the following or any combination of the following parts of a site or page:

Site title
Major headings

Minor headings

First line of first paragraph

First line of all paragraphs

All text on the site

Photo and graphics captions

Alternate text for graphics

Keywords provided in metatags

Note: By far the most important of these is the metatag for a site's title. An effective title in the source code of a site can be difficult to compose because it must serve two distinct purposes: (1) announcing your site and (2) providing the words that many search engines use to rank one site over another. Make sure that the words and phrases that you think people will use to find you are included in the components listed above as often as possible without sounding forced or repetitive.

The most common keywords that users enter into search engines when searching for a product or service are generally not specific enough. They might key in "window tinting" and get lists of firms all over America. A better search would be, say, "window tinting Atlanta," assuming that the searcher lives in Atlanta. To discover the keywords used most often to locate a given topic, go to the suggestion page of Overture.com (formerly GoTo.com) a top-ten search engine. At this writing, that page was found at: http://inventory.overture.com/d/searchinventory/suggestion/.

TEST YOUR POSITION IN THE SEARCH ENGINES FREQUENTLY

Even if you hire a company to submit your site address to the search engines, check on them yourself. Go to the engine and enter the keywords that you hope will bring up your site. Are you in the top ten? Perfect! Top twenty to thirty? That can be okay, too, but check your site's keywords and text to see if there's room for improvement. Not in the top thirty? Then you need help fast, because more than three-fourths of search engine users do not look beyond the first two pages of search engine results. If you have hired a service to maintain your site and to register your site with the search engines, then it's time to wake up the service!

Directories

An Internet directory is an index of links that lead users to information. The index is organized into categories, not unlike your local Yellow Pages. Users look for the categories that are most likely to contain the information they seek and then "drill down" through levels of information until they find what they are looking for. Like Yellow Pages, most directories will allow you to advertise on their pages (for a price); some will add a plain link to your site for free, with additional charges for enhancements.

Major directories you should be listed in include:

Yahoo.com
Looksmart.com
dmoz.com
Galaxy.com

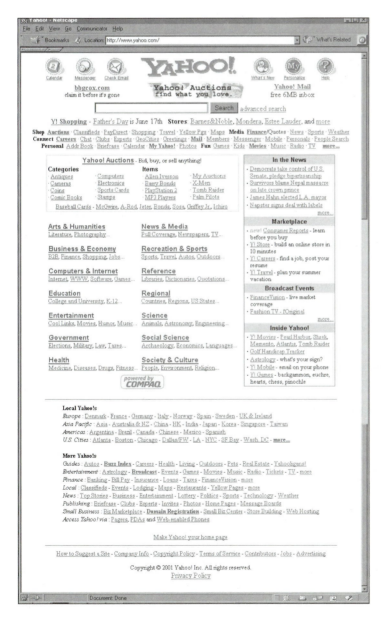

Figure 6.1

Yahoo! portal showing a
search engine field
(immediately below the
Yahoo! logo) and the
categories of the directory.
Screen capture from
http://www.yahoo.com, June,
2001.
Reproduced with permission of
Yahoo! Inc. © 2000 by Yahoo!
Inc. YAHOO! and the YAHOO!
logo are trademarks of Yahoo!
Inc.

And there are dozens more directories, especially regional ones and specialty ones relevant to your industry, in which you should be listed. For example, if your business relates primarily to tourism or entertainment, you'll want to be in a site that lists such businesses by city, such as CitySearch.com (http://www.citysearch.com).

How do you identify the directories for your city, county, state, or region? Begin finding them by using a search engine to look for the name of the geographic element (city, county, state, region, etc.) along with the words: Directory Add URL. Read the instructions for adding your site to the directory.

Yahoo! is a frequently used directory (Fig. 6.1). Estimates vary but generally indicate that Yahoo! does about half of all Internet searches. Listing your site *correctly* with Yahoo! is, therefore, an important step. Do not even think about adding your site listing to Yahoo! until you have read all the instructions that Yahoo! and other sites provide about adding a listing. Find information about adding your site listing to Yahoo! at http://docs.yahoo.com/info/suggest. Read the information and follow the directions very carefully. If you make a mistake and Yahoo! indexes you in the wrong area of its directory, correcting the error could take months or even years. You will lose all the people who could have visited your site, but didn't.

List your site in industry-specific directories and vortals as well as in general directories. The key directories for your industry can be found by searching for the name of your industry (construction material-pipes) or its primary product (PVC pipe).

Because people find information on the Internet primarily by using search engines, when someone searches for key words representative of products or services that you offer, you want the search engines to find you.

BEYOND THE BASICS

Search Engines

How do search engines find a particular site? In a combination of ways: (1) Web site owners register their sites with the search engines, which is both easy and free and (2) search engines send out programs (spiders and robots) to read the text and/or the hidden text (specifically, the metatags) used on sites and catalog it.

More often than not, these two processes work together. You register your site address, or URL, with the search engine, which sends out a spider or other robot to find keywords on your site. If your text and hidden text contain the correct keywords your site will come up higher in the rankings when the search engine displays the results of a search.

Search engines do not all work in the same way, which is why the job of keeping your site high on the results pages can be such a challenge. Search engines' spiders are programmed in different ways to look for, store, and then report information from the sites they visit.

HOW SEARCH ENGINES WORK

The primary goal of search engines, such as Excite, Infoseek, Webcrawler, and AltaVista, is to help people find information on the Internet. They stay in business by selling advertising; the rates are related to how many visitors use their site to search. Search engine services need to be comprehensive, quick, and useful to their users. Your concern is that they help prospective clients find you.

Using a search engine to find information is free—to the user. Advertisers, on the other hand, pay handsomely to have their banners, buttons, and other graphics and links splashed around on the pages that users see. How do search engines work? Basically, the user enters a few words or a phrase in the search engine's page, and the search engine responds with a list of links that connect to Web pages. If the words entered are very general, the search engine will return thousands, hundreds of thousands, even millions of links. Fortunately, they show you only about ten at a time. Even more fortunately, the search engine shows them to you in order of relevance—most relevant to least relevant—according to the search engine's own criteria.

The search engine also provides a short description of the pages it found. Often the appropriateness of the description depends on the page itself, not on the search engine. A search engine works best when the keywords entered are specific. "PVC pipe Miami Florida," for example, will yield more specific results than will "plastic pipe."

WHAT INFORMATION SEARCH ENGINES PROVIDE

Figure 6.2 shows the list of Internet sites that feature air compressors in Miami and nationwide that was displayed by Google. The results are based on the keywords typed in and the criteria of the Google search engine. The air compressor sites most likely to serve Miami are shown highest, in most cases, because the words "Miami" and "air compressors" were included somewhere on the site.

In addition to the site title and description, the search engine shows the Web site address (URL) of each site listed. Some engines assign a ranking or relevancy number next to each listing. For example, "82%" shown next to a site description means that the search engine is "82 percent sure that this site is what you are seeking," based, of course, on the keywords entered. Some search engines provide a link to "similar pages" or "more sites like this one." Clicking on such links displays more top-rated sites based on the keywords entered.

Figure 6.2

Google search response page of results for keywords "air compressors miami." See links to "similar pages."

Most people who use search engines read the information for several sites listed in the search results and then click on a link to go to a site that seems to be the best fit or sounds interesting. If the site grabs them immediately, they might explore it for a while and bookmark it (or make it a favorite) to return to later. Otherwise, chances are they'll use their browser's Back button to return to the search results and try another site.

SEARCH ENGINE TIP! META-SEARCH ENGINES

Meta-search engines search the top-ranked results of other search engines and deliver those summaries or the summaries for the top ten.

Remember, you can't "add your URL" to the meta-search engines. If your site is being found by regular search engines, it will come up in the meta-search engines too. Here are six popular meta-search engines and their URLs.
Metacrawler
http://www.metacrawler.com

Megacrawler
http://www.megacrawler.com

Dogpile
http://www.dogpile.com

Ixquick
http://ixquick.com

37.com
http://37.com

Megaspider
http://megaspider.com

Very few searchers look at results beyond the first two results pages. So tell your Webmaster how important it is that your firm appear, ideally, on page one for as many logical keyword phrases relating to your company as possible.

Knowing just this much about search engines tells you:

- You want your site to be displayed on page one, or at least in the top 20 sites listed, in search engine results when your target words or phrases are sought.

- The description of your site that shows in the search results needs to be stated clearly and must get the user's immediate attention.

- The main (or home) page of your site needs to convince visitors immediately that they've come to the right place!

REGISTER YOUR SITE WITH SEARCH ENGINES

The process of registering your site with a search engine is fairly simple, and in most instances it's free. Most search engines have a link on their search page or on their results page that lets you "Add URL." Sometimes the link says "Add a Site" or "Suggest a Site." Clicking on that link takes you to a form where you enter the address of your site and your e-mail address.

Some engines send their robots or spiders to your site to read and store keywords and descriptions in the engine's database. Other engines ask you to enter a short description and/or keywords that apply to your site. For these engines, write carefully! The description will be used in the listing of your site that is displayed in search results, and the keywords that you write may be the only ones that will be used to call up your site. So be sure those keywords match words and phrases people would use when searching for a company like yours.

Check and double check whatever you enter for perfect accuracy when adding your URL. Some engines will inform you that a URL has a mistake in form, such as a comma instead of a period, a missing colon, or a slash going the wrong direction. However, engines cannot check the spelling of your URL or your e-mail address. If an engine tries to find a Web address that does not exist because it was misspelled, the engine will ignore or delete the submission.

Some search engines clean their databases of URLs on a regular basis so that their data is current. This means that you need to register your site with the engines repeatedly—every few weeks. If you have hired a company to maintain your site, be sure they do so for you, regularly. Otherwise, mark your calendar so you don't overlook this important task.

Can't someone else do all this URL work for you? Sure. Finding a service on the Internet to register your URL with search engines is not difficult. Often you'll see such services advertised on the search engines themselves, and sometimes they'll even add your site for free. Usually, however, they will charge you a set fee for the service or offer to sell you the related services that they provide, such as Web site maintenance or hosting. Do they actually perform the work that they promise and repeatedly enter your URL as they say? Most do, but beware. Better to get from them the names and numbers of their customers in your area who have used their service and call those customers to discuss their satisfaction levels.

Make registration of your site address with search engines part of your Webmaster's job! If you decide to pay an individual or a company to create a site and host it for you, remember to ask how they will ensure that the search engines find your site and list it in the top 10 to 20 links on the results pages. Many Web site designers know how to make a site functional and visually attractive, but are out of touch with the latest search engine technologies and aren't aware of how to make a site more findable. (If you suspect this to be the case with your Webmaster, consider showing that person this chapter.)

How long after adding your URL will it be until your site shows up on a search engine? You won't see the results immediately. It will take anywhere from a few days to many weeks. The same is true for any change that you make to your site that might influence its rank with search engines. The automated robots and spiders that check sites for changes visit only periodically. As the number of sites on the Internet increases, the time between registering and showing up on an engine seems to get longer.

Table 6.1 shows the average amount of time that it takes key engines to show a site after its URL has been submitted. All search engine sizes and submission times are approximate and may be inaccurate. These figures are compiled by an excellent search engine information site, SubmitCorner.com (http://www.submitcorner.com) on its page at: http://www.submitcorner.com/Guide/SE/comparison.shtml. Estimates are from November 1, 2000.

SEARCH ENGINE TIP! STAY TUNED!

Search engines change their programs without notice. Stay up to date on search engines and how to make them work for you by subscribing to the free e-mail newsletters from Web Position offered at http://www.webposition.com or from Search Engine Watch at http://www.searchenginewatch.com.

Registering your site does not ensure that a link to it will show up in the top 20 or 30 sites listed in the results of a search, however. That part of the picture is related to the content of the site itself, including the "hidden" keywords that most search engines read.

Table 6.1	SEARCH ENGINE COMPARISON				
Search Engine	Approx. Size	META Tags Support	Spider Support	Popularity Increases Rankings	Submit Time
Alexa	Unknown	None	No	No	4 weeks
Altavista	350 million	Yes	Yes	Yes	2–5 days
AOL Netfind & Excite	250 million	Description Only	No	Yes	2–4 weeks
FAST Search	340 million	No	Yes	Yes	1 week
Google	560 million	Yes	Yes	Yes	2–6 weeks
GoTo (now Overture)	110 million	No	No	No	< 3 days
HotBot	110 million	Yes	Yes	Yes	2–4 weeks
Infoseek	50 million	Yes	No	Yes	1–2 weeks
Lycos	Unknown	No	No	No	3–4 weeks
Northern Light	265 million	No	Yes	Yes	2–4 weeks
Snap	Unknown	No	No	No	2–6 weeks
Webcrawler	50 million	Yes	No	No	2–3 weeks
Yahoo!	Unknown	No	No	No	4–8 weeks

Note: The research and findings above are independent reviews and should be used only for informational purposes.

USE PERTINENT, EFFECTIVE KEYWORDS, TITLES, HEADINGS, CAPTIONS, AND TEXT

Make your site come up high in search engine results. When someone enters keywords or phrases into the search engine's entry box and then clicks on Go or Search Now, the engine checks its database for matches of keywords or keyword phrases. It then reports back with a list of sites. The more matches that a site has in the engine's database, the higher the engine will place it in the results list.

Now the question becomes one of ensuring that the engine's spiders and robots find those keywords and phrases on your site. Caution: If you use the same term too often, some search engines will delete your URL from their database. Why? Because if a site has used a term repeatedly, solely for improvement of search engine ranking, it may not actually be representative of the amount of keyword-related content on the site. Besides, it's not "playing fair."

What keywords do people use when they are looking for information about your products or services? To find out, use the search word suggestion tool at Overture.com at http://inventory.overture.com/d/searchinventory/suggestion. Enter the name of your product or service. If you manufacture, wholesale, or retail PVC pipe, enter that term into the Overture.com suggestion box. The search engine will show you how many times that term was searched on during the preceding month and the number of associated searches that made use of that term. If you market your PVC pipe solely in a city or county or state, be sure to add that word to "PVC pipe" in one of your searches. Your results for PVC pipe will look similar to Table 6.2.

Be certain, therefore, that your site contains keywords naming the cities you serve, as well as the phrase "pvc pipe." Your keywords should also include the name of your county and any nicknames for your area, such as "the big apple" for New York City or "twin cities" for Minneapolis/St. Paul. If you are in a city or region that is frequently misspelled, include the common *mis*spellings—such as Misissipi—and *mistaken* state abbreviations—such as Michigan's MI for Mississippi (MS) or Missouri (MO), or Alaska's AK for Arkansas (AR). To see the frequency of geographical terms (cities, states, counties) used in keyword search strings, use Overture.com (see below).

Include general product, service, or industry terms among your keywords and text; people often combine such terms with the geographical words, resulting in search strings such as "Dubuque Iowa furnaces," "Missoula Montana carpets," or "Tampa Florida houses for sale."

WHAT SEARCH ENGINES READ WHEN THEY VISIT YOUR SITE: VISIBLE TEXT AND HIDDEN TEXT

Each search engine uses its own programming and formulas to read and catalog the information it finds on Web pages. The engines may read both visible and "invisible" or "hidden" text. *'Visible' text* is what you see when you look at a page in your browser. *'Hidden' text* is the programming code that you see only if you select Source from the View menu of your browser.

VISIBLE TEXT

Following are the most common visible Web page elements that search engines' readers, robots, and spiders read. The engines might read only one of the pieces in this list, or they might read several of them. You need to be sure that you have used target terms in all of these pieces.

1. Major headings and subheadings

2. The first line of text on the first page of the site

Table 6.2	SEARCHES DONE IN SEPTEMBER 2002*

Count	Search Term
9,738	pvc pipe**
1,103	pvc pipe fitting
336	pvc pipe
334	pvc pipe manufacturer
306	clear pvc pipe
300	pvc water pipe
298	pvc pipe price
254	pvc pipe furniture
250	pipe pvc recall
185	pvc sewer pipe
184	lawsuit pipe pvc
182	pipe project pvc
154	dimension pipe pvc
150	manufacture pipe pvc
132	pipe pvc size
125	40 pipe pvc schedule
111	plastic pvc pipe
108	flexible pvc pipe
107	pipe pvc repair
106	pipe pvc specification

Source: http://inventory.overture.com/d/searchinventory/suggestion/

* Only top twenty shown here.

** When the same report was done for September, 2000, the number of searches for "pvc pipe" was 1,012, a dramatic two-year change!

3. The first line of text on every page

4. The first line of every paragraph

5. Every word of every page

If your site includes the content we discussed in Chapter 3, it has the key terms related to your positioning. The list of the ways different spiders read your site has important implications for the wording and organization of your headings and paragraphs.

Some search engines give more weight to the keywords used in *headlines* when calculating a site ranking. Also, some engines include the presence of complete sentences that contain keywords as a ranking factor. So, whenever appropriate, put a period or question mark at the end of lines of text because that's how spiders often decide what makes a sentence.

HIDDEN TEXT

Your site has hidden words, or *metatags*, that search engines read.[1] Search engines read the title of your site, a list of keywords that are supposed to describe the content of the site, and other information contained in these metatags. The metatags that search engines read most often for ranking purposes are those for the site or page title and those for your description. Most engines rank a site higher if the keywords searched for are repeated several times among the words in the title and the description. And many engines also compare the words there to the words actually in the site to be sure that Web masters are not just "packing" the metatags with extra keywords. Here's an example of a firm's metatags (http://www.searchenginewatch.com):

```
<head>
<meta http-equiv="Content-Type" content="text/html; charset=windows-
1252">
<meta http-equiv="Content-Language" content="en-us">
<meta http-equiv="PICS-Label" content='(PICS-1.1
"http://www.rsac.org/ratingsv01.html" l gen true comment "RSACi North
America Server" by "danny@calafia.com" for
"http://searchenginewatch.com/" on "1997.07.27T10:07-0800" r (n 0 s 0
v 0 l 1))'>
<meta name="description" content="Search Engine Watch is the
authoritative guide to searching at Internet search engines and search
engine registration and ranking issues. Learn to submit URLs, use
HTML meta tags and boost placement.">
```

---

[1]Metatags, also written METAtags: META is short for "metadata," which essentially means a summary of data or data about data found in your site. Metatags are a form of HTML code, the underlying code for the World Wide Web. Excellent explanations of metatags and HTML can be found at http://www.stars.com/Search/Meta/Tag.html and at http://www.searchenginewatch.com/webmasters/meta.html.

To see the metatags on a site, select "View" from the menu bar of your Web browser and then select "View Source" from the dropdown menu. The metatags, plus the coding that tells your Web page where to display images and text, will appear.

```
<meta name="keywords" content="listings search engine watch Web
site, danny sullivan editor internet.com using meta tags improving
placement, how to submit urls to major internet search engines
Webmaster's guide, rankings search engine registration tips for
searching better reviews, tutorials technology report free newsletter,
news articles placement engine submission online help
www.searchenginewatch.com">
<title>Search Engine Watch: Tips About Internet Search Engines &
Search Engine Submission</title>
<base target="_top">
</head>
```

And here's one more example of metatags (http://www.hatterasyachts
.com):

```
</head>
<TITLE>HatterasYachts</TITLE>
<META NAME="DESCRIPTION" CONTENT="Hatteras Yachts -
Manufacturers of luxury fiberglass sportfishing and motor yachts">
<META NAME="KEYWORDS" CONTENT="hatteras yachts
hatterasyachts yacht marine boat boats sportfish motor yachts motor
yacht marlin fishing">
</head>
```

Another type of hidden text is referred to as *alternate text* for photos
and graphics (Fig. 6.3). Search engines cannot read pictures or graphics, so
a photo of your team showing one of your products will not improve your
ranking with search engines. But many search engines do read the hidden
alternate text for your images. To see the alternate text for images, hover

Figure 6.3

Mouseover text, "News for You," appears when users point their mouse at the dog. It also appears if the dog image fails to display for some reason. The extra text with the word "news" is read by some search engines, which might help the site come up higher in search results.

your mouse pointer over an image; you will see either a file name, such as "photo.gif," or some words, such as "Engineers and designers constantly quality check our Blippo products." This alternate text is displayed only briefly. If you don't specify alternate text, the file name of the image is used.

You or your Web master can add target words to these hidden areas. Why bother? Because some people still choose to view Web pages without the images showing—with only text showing. And because some search engines read and catalog these *alt text* words, increasing the likelihood that the site will be found by users of the engine.

Some new search engines and directories do not rely entirely on automated spiders and robots. These engines use human assistance to evaluate the relevance of Web sites and add them to the database. See the section on the Open Directory Project, later in this chapter.

HOW DOES YOUR SITE RANK? TEST IT WITH VARIOUS KEYWORDS

One way to determine whether search engines are finding your site and to see if your URL appears in the top 20 links on the results pages is to check each search engine yourself. Go to each engine, enter the keywords you think visitors might use, and then look for your site listing.

Remember, too, that you can tell which keywords are used most frequently to search for sites like yours by using Overture.com's key word suggestion tool at http://inventory.overture.com/d/searchinventory/suggestion/. The process may be somewhat time consuming, but it is also very instructive. If your site is not represented to your satisfaction, it's time to talk with your Web master.

Some software programs check your ranking in the search engines for you. Such programs are available at http://www.jimtools.com, http://www.positionagent.com and other sites. You can also check your site's ranking on various search engines automatically by using the free limited edition of the rank-checking product available at http://positionagent.linkexchange.com. After you enter your Web site's URL and the keyword or keyword phrase that you believe most consumers will enter to find your product or service, the program gives you a page showing how your site ranked on various search engines. The results show which engines listed your site and where it was positioned in the results list. Shown in Figure 6.4 are partial results for rankings of http://www.hatterasyachts.com using the keywords "yachts," "motor," and "hatteras."

If all this business about metatags and invisible codes sounds too difficult, don't worry about it. Most managers don't do this work themselves. Instead, they hire someone—a Web site design firm, a technician, an in-house or outside Web master, or a technician at a local Internet Service Provider (ISP) firm—to construct a Web site, add or delete pages, and make updates and changes. Do, however, be sure to communicate to your Web

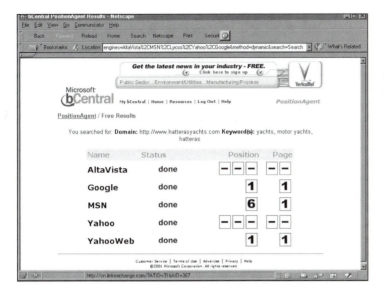

Figure 6.4

The free ranking tool at http://positionagent. linkexchange.com shows results for a Web site according to selected keywords. The results show the position (ranking) of the site and the page of results on which the listing appears. Here we searched for http://www.hatterasyachts. com using keywords "yachts," "motor," and "hatteras."

master that you want your site to be kept current—*including* its metatags, which must stay consistent with the keywords your target audience visitors use. (You could give this book to your Web master to read. . . .)

SEARCH ENGINE TIP! | **WATCH SEARCHES IN PROGRESS**

You might gain some insights into the terms that people use to search the Internet by viewing the keywords people are searching for—live. Go to any of the sites listed below and watch the search entries. (Caution: Words are not typically censored for you.

However, some of the sites listed will give you the option of filtering out "adult" terms.) You will notice that most people do not use very specific keywords for searches.

http://voyeur.mckinley.com/cgi-bin/voyeur.cgi
http://www.metaspy.com

Another way to check a site's rankings is to use top-10.com (http://www.top-10.com/free.html). (This site may not function well with older browsers.) Follow the instructions and then fill out the form, paying special attention to the keywords the form requests. These keywords can be ones currently on your site, or you can enter other combinations to see how well your site does with those keywords. Or you can check on your competitors.

After you fill out the form and submit it, Top-10 will send your report immediately or in a few hours, depending on how busy the site is. The report will help you evaluate how well the keywords on your site are working for you. Remember, your goal is to do all you can to have your site listed on page one if at all possible, or on page two (typically within the top 10 to 20 positions) of every search engine's summary pages.

SEARCH ENGINES RANK SITES BY POPULARITY

Every time you add your URL to another site, your site becomes easier to find on the Web. Major search engine information site WebPromote.com (http://www.webpromote.com) says:

> If you have more sites that link to your page than your competitor does, your page will rank more highly on the engines. Numerous links will not only improve your rankings, but you will also improve your traffic (following links is the second most popular way people find new sites). Furthermore, on Excite, HotBot, and Lycos, link popularity also determines whether the engine will crawl deep into your site and index more pages or not. Do not ignore this step, no matter how hard it sounds.[2]

Want to see how many sites have links that point to your site? Just go to AltaVista (http://www.altavista.com) and enter your query this way: link:yourdomainname.com. (So, a firm with the URL http://www. AceBuckets.com would enter "link:acebuckets.com.") Your search results would show how many sites Alta Vista found that contained links that pointed to your site. Searching for "link:marthastewart.com" reveals about 5,400 pages pointing to Martha Stewart's site.

HOW MANY LINKS POINT TO YOUR SITE?

Another method of determining links is found at LinksToYou (http://www.linkstoyou.com). There, enter your URL in the Links To You counter. Searching for the URL http://www.booksonrealestate.com you learn the following:

WWW.BOOKSONREALESTATE.COM

<u>AltaVista</u> found **2** links to you.

<u>AltaVista</u> found **2** links to you *excluding* your own links.

<u>Infoseek</u> found **39** links to you.

<u>Infoseek</u> found **38** links to you *excluding* your own links.

<u>Hotbot</u> found **9 matches** links to you.

<u>Fast</u> found **8** links to you.

These totals are, surprisingly, quite good compared to more than 90 percent of sites on the Web. But if you want to see really huge numbers of links to a site, search for links to a famous one like Martha Stewart's (http://www.marthastewart.com). These are the results from a search made on October 28, 2000.

---

[2]From http://www.webpromote.com/wpwsrch/detail.asp?aid=2&iid=aug1999vol3 &rw=1&cl=1&sortorder=.

WWW.MARTHASTEWART.COM

AltaVista found **4,406** links to you.

AltaVista found **4,405** links to you *excluding* your own links.

Infoseek found links to you.

Infoseek found **1,131** links to you *excluding* your own links.

Hotbot found **5,000 matches** links to you.

Fast found **10,086** links to you.

Based on this exercise, you can see how logical it is for a search engine to rank a popular site (one with many links pointing to it) ahead of one in the same category with fewer pointing links.

Search engine formulas may consider not only how many links point to your site, but also how important those sites are in terms of size and how many links point to *them*. Another factor is how closely related to the core business of your site are the sites that contain those links to you.

What can you do to benefit from the "popularity factor?" Add your URL to every site you can find in your industry and on large and small directories and lists that permit free and/or purchased text links or ads. If you were to do this, and if a competitor's site was precisely equal to yours in every way *except* in link popularity, then your site, having far more links, would cause most engines to rank your site ahead of your competitor's.

One leader of popularity/relevancy sites is Google (http://www.google.com). Google explains its page-ranking methodology (http://www.google.com/why_use.html) this way:

> PageRank capitalizes on the uniquely democratic characteristic of the Web by using its vast link structure as an organizational tool. In essence, Google interprets a link from page A to page B as a vote, by page A, for page B. Google assesses a page's importance by the votes it receives. But Google looks at more than sheer volume of votes, or links; it also analyzes the page that casts the vote. Votes cast by pages that are themselves "important" weigh more heavily and help to make other pages "important."
>
> These important, high-quality results receive a higher PageRank and will be ordered higher in results. In this way, PageRank is Google's general indicator of importance and does not depend on a specific query. Rather, it is a characteristic of a page itself based on data from the Web that Google analyzes using complex algorithms that assess link structure.

Of course, important pages mean nothing to you if they don't match a user's query. So Google uses text-matching techniques to find pages that are both important and relevant. For instance, when Google analyzes a page, it looks at what other pages linking to that page have to say about it.

To find out how many links point to a site, use the tools on LinksToYou.com (http://www.linkstoyou.com) or on IneedHits.com (http://

www.ineedhits.com/free/popularity). Or visit the AltaVista search engine (http://www.altavista.com) and enter into the search box the following: link:yourdomainname.com. AltaVista will list all the sites it finds that contain links to the domain name you entered. (Note: These results will be only the ones that Alta Vista finds; there may be others that it does not find.) These tools are useful in comparing a site's popularity against that of its competitors.

THE OPEN DIRECTORY PROJECT

Like Yahoo!, the Open Directory Project (ODP) (whose main page is located at http://www.dmoz.org) uses human editors to decide which sites are relevant to a particular topic or category (Fig. 6.5). Because the editors actually look at the sites submitted for inclusion in the search engine's database, the results provided to users are more likely to be pertinent to the search, at least in theory. In other words, human editors improve the potential quality of a search engine or directory.

ODP's editors are volunteers familiar with various specialties and/or geographic areas. As the Internet grows, so does the number of volunteer editors. ODP says this about itself: "As the Internet grows, so do the number of netcitizens. These citizens can each organize a small portion of the Web and present it back to the rest of the population, culling out the bad and useless and keeping only the best content." Volunteer editors present their qualifications to ODP before being approved to edit a given ODP category. Sites submitted for a particular category are evaluated and added (or rejected) by the editor for that category. To ensure quality of site additions and avoid favoritism or other abuse, editors are overseen by other editors. If an editor is found to be selecting only the sites of friends, for example, that editor is replaced.

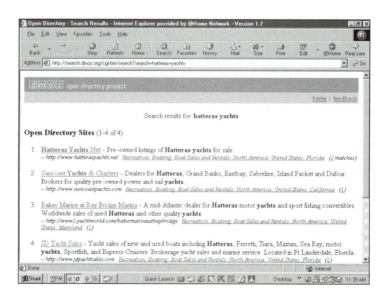

Figure 6.5

ODP search results for the keywords "hattaras yachts," Screen capture from http://search.dmoz. org/cgi-bin/search? search=hatteras+yachts. Open Directory Project, Copyright © 2001 Netscape Communications Corporation.

Besides its potential for creating a high-quality, comprehensive directory, the Open Directory Project is important because many other Internet search engines and directories share its comprehensive database. This means that, if a site is not included in the ODP database, it may well not be included in others, including Lycos, Hotbot, and Netscape. At the opening of year 2001, more than 100 other portals and search engines were using data from ODP directory entries, either exclusively or in addition to their own data. Because the ODP is now the source of information for so many other engines and directories, you cannot afford to miss inclusion in this database. To learn about registering a site or becoming an ODP volunteer editor, visit http://dmoz.org/about.html and http://www.laisha.com/odp.html. Read and follow ODP's site submission directions carefully.

Just as when submitting to Yahoo!, you must first find the category in which you would most like to be listed and submit your URL from there. Unlike Yahoo!, however, you can submit many pages from the same Web site. Pages or sites may be listed in several ODP categories, as long as the pages are relevant and provide, in the editor's opinion, adequate content. For example, a page with nothing but lists of links might be less likely to be added to the ODP than a page with both original content and links.

"PAY-PER-CLICK" OR "KEYWORD BID" SEARCH ENGINES

Unless you have superior Web skills or an exceptional Web master, your firm will probably not be able to rank as high as it would like to on most search engines. But you can buy your way to the top.

"Pay-per-click" or "keyword-bid" search engines, such as the one at http://www.overture.com, auction their top positions for specific keywords. The higher up you want your site to be listed, the more you will have to pay. Each time a user clicks on a "sponsored" link on a keyword-bid search engine, the owner of the site pays the amount bid for that link. So, if you bid ten cents for a keyword phrase (which might or might not be enough money to earn you the *top* spot, depending on other bids) and Overture.com visitors click on your link 100 times in a week, that result costs you $10. When no one has bid on a term, the keyword-bid engine simply ranks and displays sites like any other search engine.

To determine the top keyword bids for your product or service, go to Overture.com (http://www.overture.com) and search for the name of your product or service. Include a city or town name if your business has a local emphasis. The city name plus product name or type of service (refrigeration, maid service, air conditioning, paving, pipe, glass, etc.) is the keyword phrase used most frequently by people searching for businesses in their own city. For example, "oakland traffic signals" or "traffic signals oakland," or even "oakland ca traffic signals" will be used rather than, simply, "traffic signals." A business seeking a dominant position for the entire industry, on the other hand, would leave off the word that defines a geographic area and use only the generic terms.

What's the biggest advantage of ranking high in Overture.com? Sites that rank high in Overture.com also reach about 75 percent of people who use other search engines. Why? Because Overture.com—itself a top-ten search engine—is partnered with a half-dozen other sites, and scores of medium to small ones, that prominently display links to companies in the top Overture.com positions to their visitors.

There are several advantages to keeping your site in the first or second place position on Overture.com. Overture.com claims that the number one position gets three to five times the clicks of secondary ones. Furthermore, Overture.com's top two (sometimes top three) results are displayed, along with other engine results, on America Online (http://search.aol.com), which has 25 million members, Microsoft's Internet Explorer (80.5 percent of Web users use this browser),[3] the Microsoft Internet Explorer default home page (http://www.msn.com), Earthlink (http://www.earthlink.net), CNET (http://www.cnet.com), Netscape Search (http://www.netscape.com), and hundreds more small engines and sites. At least 75 percent of Web users visit some function of these huge sites daily, so a firm's chances of gaining wide positioning on the Web by having high position on Overture.com is multiplied.

Another bid-based site worth investigating is Sprinks.com (http://www.sprinks.com). Sprinks' top ranking sites results are *also displayed* on (your-industry)-related search results at About.com (http://www.about.com), one of the most frequently visited U.S. sites, with 20 million visitors monthly (according to media auditor MediaMetrix, at http://www.mediametrix.com/data/thetop.jsp?language=us).

Other bid-for-position sites include Findwhat.com, 7Search.com, SearchHound.com, Kanoodle.com, OneSearch.com, SimpleSearch.com, and several others listed at http://www.payperclicksearchengines.com.

TRY IT

1. Assume that you work for Andrews Lighting Co. The keywords in the METAtag of the main page of the company Web site are lighting, lights, bright, and special. Use the keyword suggestion tool at http://inventory.overture.com/d/searchinventory/ suggestion/ to see if Andrews is using the same keywords in its METAtag as the ones Web visitors use to search for lighting companies. What would you recommend to the company's Web master?

2. Use the tool at http://linkstoyou.com/CheckLinks.htm to check the popularity of http://www.harvard.edu. Now use the same tool to check the popularity of http://www.yale.edu. Which university's Web site has more links going to it?

3. Now use the same tool to check the popularity of your company's Web site and a competitor's Web site. How many links did you find? Which site is doing a better job of getting links pointing to it?

[3]See http://websnapshot.mycomputer.com/browsers.html for browser information.

Directories

GENERAL INTERNET DIRECTORIES: APPLIANCES TO ZOOS

Portal and vortal sites are often combinations of a search engine and a directory (in addition to advertising). An Internet directory is an index of links that lead users to information. The index is organized into categories, similar to your local Yellow Pages. Users look for the categories most likely to contain the information they seek and then "drill down" through subcategories until they find what they are looking for. Two special types of directories are those specific to an industry and directories in community (city, state, regional) information sites. Most directories depend on human input for the listings and categories. Many sell primary link positions to sponsors or partners.

To have a site listed in a directory, submit a short description for the entire site. Sometimes the directory's editors review sites and write the descriptions themselves. Since the search function of a directory looks only at the descriptions submitted—not of the actual sites—changing a site has no effect on its ranking in the directory. Changing the description, however, might. Changes to Web sites that help improve its ranking with a search engine will do little to improve the position of its listing in a directory. Naturally, an attractive, well-organized, functional site with good content would be more likely to be included with a good review than would a poor site.

You are welcome to advertise in most directories, and some even offer free "plain" links, with additional charges for enhancements. Visit the 4Internet directory at http://www.4internet.com. Once there, drill down to find specific categories and cities. 4Internet's real estate subdirectory is located at http://www.4realestate.com; its New York City subdirectory is located at http://www.4newyork.com; and the real estate subdirectory of the NYC subdirectory is located at http://www.4newyork.com/4newyorkrealestate. shtml. From that sub-section, you can click yourself outside of the site to many others, including the NY Realty Web site (http://www.nyrealty. com), which offers home searching, listings, consumer information, and requests for real estate agent information.

Thousands of other directories are available on the Internet. Many contain separate sections for various industries, often subdivided into state, county, or city sections. Some are called *yellow pages* and show only local telephone company listings. Others, however, let you add your listing at any time. See for example, GTE's Texas State Yellow Pages (http://superpages.com/yellowpages/texas.htm) and note the link at the bottom: Add or Change Your Listing.

Yellow pages and business directories provide minimal data for selecting one company over another. Nonetheless, millions of people use such sites monthly to find businesses and professionals, so you should be in them—at least in the ones that relate to your state, county, and city. Following is a list of large yellow pages or "business directory" sites. Visit the sections of these sites that serve your area and enter your data. It will help position you above all the firms that did not take the time to add themselves to regional listings.

Big Yellow http://www.bigyellow.com/

GTE Super Pages http://superpages.gte.net/

Info USA http://www.abii.com/

Info Space http://www.infospace.com

Internet Oracle http://www.internetoracle.com/findc.htm

Look Smart http://www.looksmart.com/

World Pages http://www.worldpages.com/

Ameritech Pages http://yp.ameritech.net/

Bell Southern US http://yp.bellsouth.com/

Big Book http://www.bigbook.com/

Zip2 http://www.zip2.com/

YAHOO! A SPECIAL ANIMAL

The leading portal began in 1995 as a hobby of two Stanford University graduate students who wants to find sites on the then brand new World Wide Web. Now the firm they started is worth several billion dollars and growing. Their company is Yahoo!, the oldest and most frequently used of the directories. The founders chose the name *Yahoo* because it is easy to remember and it connots excitement; they added the exclamation point to make the name stand out even more.

Technically, Yahoo! is a directory of Web sites, rather than a search engine, but for our purposes that's not important. Let's repeat the important part: Yahoo! is the most frequently used of the directories. The majority of searches begin at Yahoo! This means that your site listing in Yahoo! is very important to your Internet findability.

As mentioned in the Basics section of this chapter, do not attempt to add your site to Yahoo! until you have read everything that Yahoo! says and that other sites say about making such additions. If you make a mistake and Yahoo! indexes you in the wrong area of its directory, correcting the error could take a very long time. The loss to you will be all the people who could have visited your site, but didn't. Yahoo! staffs a giant team for processing the tens of thousands of weekly Web site submissions. To them, "aggregating information" means doing whatever it can, within reason, to keep abreast of "what's happening" (in Yahoo!'s words) on the Web.

As of December 2001, Yahoo! charges a nonrefundable fee of $299 for initial consideration of a site, plus a recurring annual fee of $299 for continued inclusion, which is subject to additional review each year. This fee applies to sites with non-adult content. Sites offering adult content and/or services pay a fee of $600 for initial consideration, plus $600 per year for continued inclusion. For additional information, go to http://docs.yahoo/info/suggest/terms.html.

At Yahoo!, you must decide exactly where you want to be listed before adding your URL. Say your firm is in Davenport, Iowa, and you want to be listed geographically in Yahoo! You would go to Yahoo! and search for "Davenport Iowa (name of your product or service)" (no quotes). Yahoo! will give you two types of matches: *category matches* and *site matches*. When you click on the Site Match link, you will see the list of firms who successfully listed their sites where they ought to be in Yahoo! (See Fig. 6.6.) If you want to be on this page, click on Suggest a Site at the bottom right corner of the page and then follow the directions.

PVC pipe is located in the Yahoo! directory under the headings:

Home > Business and Economy > Business to Business > Industrial Supplies > Fluid and Gas Control

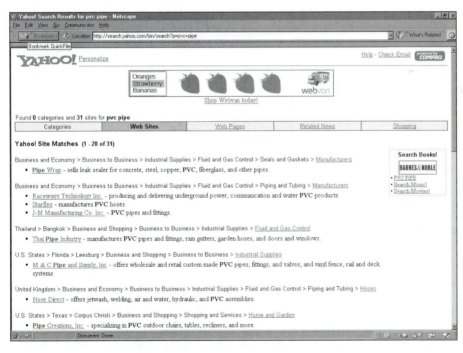

Results of Yahoo! Web pages search for PVC pipe. Screen capture from http://search.yahoo.com/bin/search?p=pvc+pipe.
Reproduced with permission of Yahoo! Inc. © 2000 by Yahoo! Inc. YAHOO! and the YAHOO! logo are trademarks of Yahoo! Inc.

Figure 6.6

And, for "PVC pipe," a search of Yahoo! Web pages results in the display shown in Figure 6.6.

HOW MANY PEOPLE FIND YOUR SITE USING A SEARCH ENGINE OR DIRECTORY?

Various programs or services will track your site's traffic and tell you how many visitors accessed your site, which search engines sent them, how long they stayed, and other data. Ask or pay the company that hosts your site to give you '*log statistics.*' In some cases, they might have to install a traffic reporter on your site (and charge you for it) so you can get the information. You can also buy and install your own program for tracking your site's traffic, but this is not always a simple project.

Visit http://www.webtrends.com/wt_main.htm and read about Web Trends' traffic programs, or visit http://www.hitbox.com and download a free traffic analyzer. One way or another, try to get useful statistics about visits to your site. Why? Because if you know what content captures your visitors' attention, you can emphasize that information or page or approach. If you know which sites' links the visitors use to get to you, then you know what types of sites you want more links on. And if you know general traffic statistics, you can evaluate how well your "getting found" strategies are working.

Summary

The primary tools on portals and vortals are search engines and directories. Hundreds of thousands of Web users rely on these tools to help them find information on the Internet. Although users find Web sites in other ways also—television and radio advertising, newspapers, magazines, direct mail—search engines and directories are responsible for enough directing of Web traffic to warrant attention from site owners.

Web site addresses become part of a search engine's or directory's database when site owners register the site URL with it. Some search engines send out a spider or robot to crawl the Internet finding and cataloging sites, but most cataloging is the result of someone registering a site with a search engine.

Search engines read and catalog various bits of text on the Web sites they visit. They read some or all of: the hidden text of METAtags and mouseovers; the beginning lines of pages; the beginning lines of paragraphs; links; and sometimes whole pages.

Some search engines rank sites according to their popularity, that is, by how many other sites link to the site being ranked. Other search engines sell positioning on their results by allowing site owners to bid on the top positions for particular keywords.

Directories usually look and behave more like the print directories that we're familiar with. They present lists of companies or Web sites according to certain categories.

Review Questions

1. What type of site is used most frequently to find Internet Information?
2. What two sources do people use most frequently to find Web data?
3. List the similarities and differences between a vortal and a portal?
4. A directory is similar to what printed publication found in most homes?
5. Can a portal include one or more search engines? Why is this good?
6. What kind of tool for finding information employs humans to categorize sites?
7. How does a search engine's *spider* or *robot* work?
8. Does the Web currently have millions or trillions of Web pages?
9. Why is it important for a company that markets locally to include its city name in its metatags?
10. Name two directories in which your company should be listed.
11. Why must one be especially careful when entering a URL into Yahoo!?
12. Is Excite.com a search engine, a directory, a portal, or all three?
13. How does having many links pointing to your site give your company more recognition on search engines?
14. What does a meta-search engine do?
15. Why is it important to correct typos when adding your URL to sites?

Internet Advertising of Your Web Site

Links, Banners, Tiles, and More

Many business executives who begin to build an Internet presence for their firm are surprised to learn that the effectiveness of their Internet presence requires that they advertise it. "Advertise my advertising?" Yes, advertise your advertising. Even if your site enjoys superior ranking in search engine results, those results alone are insufficient to help prospective clients find the site and then *select* it to explore. If, of course, yours happens to be the only firm in the country with a Web site in your particular product or service field, you may delay this worry—for a while. The better strategy is to build your dominance while you can. On the other hand, if firms in your industry or regional area are already reaping the benefits of *their* Internet presence, you may find that your site has tough competition. In that case, you'll need to find other ways to win the visibility your site deserves.

As you may already have noticed, the Internet is such an individualized mosaic that defining, describing, or understanding its components is not a simple process. For every generalization we can make, we'll find numerous exceptions. While this fact delights the creative left-brain folks, it makes the job of Internet instructors (and writers) more complex.

THE BASICS

Listings and Enhanced Listings, Banner and Tile Ads

WHAT THEY ARE

Many sites offer a free listing or link "presence," as well as links for purchase. To add a link to your site from sites where they're offered, look for the words "Add URL" or "Link Your Site," or something similar. Usually this link will take you to a form to complete and then submit to the site. When you fill out the form, be sure that every word is spelled correctly and that your URL and e-mail address are correct. Now is not the time for a mistake that would keep people from reaching your site (or a glaring error that would embarrass your company).

Additional enhancements of your marketing presence on a Web site can be in the form of ads—usually banner ads or tile ads. Banner ads tend to be wide but not very high—like a skinny person lying down. Tile ads (also called *block ads* or *button ads*) are usually smaller than banner ads and are square or rectangular. Banner ads are standardized for efficiency and transportability from one Web page to another. Some banner or tile ads are colorful and very animated. But a small square box with plain text is also considered a tile ad.

The primary objective of a banner or tile ad is to motivate the visitor to click on it and visit the advertiser's site. A second important objective is to build brand awareness of a name or product through repetitive impressions made on a Web user. At the end of year 2000, more than 99 percent of the people who saw banners or tile ads ignored them, that is, the *click-through rate* for banners was less than one percent. But some banner ads perform extremely well. Why? Their design and placement are such that they give exactly the right message to the right audience on the right page in the right page position at the right moment.

WHAT THEY COST

The price range for links and banner or tile ads varies widely, beginning with free and increasing to tens of thousands of dollars. A site successfully selling banner ads that produce qualified leads probably charges for the advertising on the basis of the total number of impressions that the ad delivers. *Impression* sounds like something that actually makes an impression on a Web site visitor. In fact, *impression* is a term left over from print advertising. In the context of a Web site, the word *impression* might more accurately be called a *chance* to make an impression. A visitor to a Web site does not have to actually see or read a tile or banner ad for it to be counted by the Web page owner as an impression. The ad simply has to be there on the page where the visitor *could* see it. Does that knowledge make it sound as if you might be buying smoke and mist? Some people think so. Nobody except media firms is completely satisfied with this method of charging for online ads. We expect to hear more discussion during the next couple of years about better ways to display and charge for ads.

WHERE TO PUT THEM

We could simply say "put ads everywhere possible." While this answer has some validity, it isn't very helpful. One approach that might be useful is to prioritize first, second, and third "tiers" of advertising. Identify as the first tier, for example, big sites that have the most unique visitors or offer the most page impressions and that are tied most closely to your product or service. Then look for happy surprises—effective Web sites that don't charge too much for advertising. Some types of sites to consider for the addition of a link or ad are: community information sites, specialty sites, ISPs, media sites, directories, industry association sites, your firm's or home office's site, and leading online magazine Web sites.

COMMUNITY INFORMATION SITES

The primary considerations in placing advertising on the Web are: Where does your target audience spend its Internet time? Where does it look for information? If yours is a firm offering local services, one answer to these questions is community information sites, followed by county (or parish) and state sites. Why? Because nearly half of the small businesses on the Web gain customers within a 50-mile radius. Companies or professionals who capitalize on this fact, and whose competitors do not, will ultimately come out far ahead.

SPECIALTY SITES

A specialty site is one devoted to a particular topic or theme. If your positioning is related to a topic or theme, then search specialty sites for opportunities for linking and/or advertising. For example, real estate chains that specialize in horse properties nationwide might add (or request) a link or ad leading to their site from national horse-properties sites including Equisearch (http://www.equisearch.com), HorseNet (http://www.horsenet.com), and the Equestrian Properties Network (http://www.azl.com/select). After considering these national sites, look for other horse-related sites as potential locations for links or ads: horse breeders, for example, or trainers, veterinarians, supplies/feed/tack, shows, history, breed information, and stables.

ONLINE DIRECTORIES AND YELLOW PAGE-TYPE DIRECTORIES

The Web has a directory for just about anything for any region or country. A firm marketing its products to Spain, for example, might want links in the Spain Industry Directory (http://www.spaindustry.com). A firm that sells a large quantity of valves and piping in the state of Georgia might want an ad in Quicksource.net, an online directory of industrial equipment and supplies for Georgia industry (http://quicksource.net). For a list of directories worldwide, see http://personal.dis.strath.ac.uk/business/directories.html.

Yellow Page-type directories that every substantial business should consider include the GTE SuperPages, Netscape Web Directory, Netscape Yellow Pages, the Thomas Register, YellowPages.com, AtHand.com, and Big Yellow. Why? Because people who have used their telephone company's Yellow Pages for years feel comfortable using online Yellow Pages. Their comfort level with the concept of yellow pages is high, and new Web users especially look there. Firms large and small, local and national, are eager to be listed on these pages with exact wording and other information that builds awareness. Enhancements such as boldface type, active links, or tile ads are sometimes too expensive for small companies, but the basic listing may even be free.

TRADE AND INDUSTRIAL ASSOCIATIONS

Many trade and industry associations—local, state, national, and international—have Web sites with information for members and/or the public. Some association sites offer members a free or low-cost profile page or electronic business card. These opportunities on trade association Web sites are valuable because they give a firm visibility within their industry, and often referrals or cross-selling result.

Trade association sites also sometimes offer enhancements of a firm's name or link in their directory. Don't settle for being just one of the firms listed in a me-too fashion among many others in such sites. Enhanced listings and ads in trade association directories help a firm stand out in its field, and the benefit gained usually exceeds the additional cost. This strategy positions a business compared to similar businesses in the minds of Web site visitors.

PARENT FIRMS

Most large firms now have corporate or company-wide umbrella sites that include pages for divisions and subsidiaries around the world. Is yours a local division of a much larger firm? Be sure your parent firm's Web site has a link to your subsidiary or division's Web site—and vice versa.

Oddly, even major multinational firms may lack comprehensive links to Web sites of their local divisions worldwide. Valuable business may be lost at the regional divisional level as a result of this oversight. As an example, see TRW at http://www.TRW.COM, which operates in 35 countries with 250 locations and is ranked number 103 in the year 2000 Fortune 500. Perhaps this oversight will be remedied by TRW by the time you read this.

INDUSTRY-RELATED DIRECTORIES

Many firms that serve a particular industry improve customer and vendor relations by offering free links to their clients on their city, regional, and even national corporate Web site. This practice can be a valuable source of free links for businesses just venturing onto the Web. Clients should reciprocate; sometimes this offer will encourage a noncooperating site to be more helpful.

SEARCH ENGINES

Search engines (see Chapter 6) offer many opportunities for enhancing a company's Web visibility. Some search engines, such as Overture.com and Sprinks.com, allow users to bid on keywords. The site listing of the high bidders for a keyword or group of keywords will be displayed higher on the list.

Another search engine approach to keyword enhancements is to sell and display a keyword-triggered text-only ad on the results page. This ad appears only when a certain keyword is searched by the user. How often people using a search engine actually see these ads in the far right column of the search results page is unknown. Nonetheless, this context-relevant approach has great appeal: the ad appears only to people who have searched a particular phrase. This "self-selection" approach is far more effective, and possibly more cost effective, than displaying ads at random to any user. See RealNames.com and DirectHit.com for examples.

Reciprocal Links and Banner Exchanges

Reciprocal links and *banner exchanges* are just what the terms imply: Reciprocal linking is, in short, the "I'll-link-to-you-if-you'll-link-to-me" strategy. Banner exchanging is a variation of reciprocal linking: "I'll put your banner on my site if you'll put my banner on your site." Both strategies increase the likelihood that people will find a site. As an added incentive, the number of links on the Internet that take people to a given site can result in higher placement in some search engine results for that site (called *popularity ranking*, see Chapter 6).

With whom should you set up reciprocal links, and where? How should you go about exchanging banners? Are these strategies worth the time and effort required?

RECIPROCAL LINKS WITH OTHER FIRMS

Most companies do business with many firms that do not compete with them. Some are suppliers to the businesses; others are vendors to that company's customers or end users of its products. Some may be wholesalers, dealers, retailers, distributors, or franchisees. Search the Web to find the firms in such categories that have a strong Internet presence. (If you can find them easily, others might also.) Then send them e-mail inviting them to exchange links or banner ads with you. The cost of doing this is your time, and there's win–win potential for both parties.

BANNER EXCHANGE SERVICES

Banner exchange firms can help increase a site's visibility by displaying a banner on a number of Web sites in exchange for displaying a rotating banner of one of their clients. Usually a participating site gets a half a banner exposure in return for a certain number of times that someone clicks on the exchange banner. Some banner exchange firms are more generous, giving two views of your banner for every three views that your site provides theirs. Banners of all participants in a banner exchange are the same size so they can be rotated within the banner frame placed on the sites of the banner exchangers.

The bother, cost, and reduced page loading speed associated with a banner exchange may not be worth the benefit of having more people—who are unlikely to be buying a niche-related product—see the banner. However, a banner exchange for a nationwide retail product that anyone can buy anywhere does have greater potential to increase sales. Note also that having an exchange banner on your site can lead to slower page download speeds and increased design costs. Even worse, different banners showing up on a given page could confuse visitors as to why the banner is there or what site they are really visiting.

Affiliations and Sponsorships

Two other forms of banner or link exchanging are affiliations and sponsorships. An *affiliation* is a link from one site that takes visitors to some other site. If the visitor buys something at the other site, such as a book, CD, or poster, the referring site receives a commission. Note that having an affiliation banner on your site does not bring visitors to *your* site. In fact, it sends your hard-won visitors off to some other location on the Internet. Affiliations are probably not worth your time and energy for the small commissions they may pay. An exception is a bona fide store or a store section whose primary function is to provide a convenient shopping service to visitors and that has links to many affiliated, commission-paying sites.

Sponsorships can be time consuming but effective. Basically, a sponsorship is the recognition on a site or site segment that it is sponsored by a certain person or business. Sometimes the sponsor actually creates the page(s) or provides the information that is hosted on another site. (That's the time-consuming part.) Ideally, the page or information makes the sponsored site more valuable, more useful to visitors. Here's how a sponsorship might come about. Let's say that Darrell Holcomb proposes to the owners or Web masters of a high-traffic community site that his sport shoe outlet create an information section (delivering content or design or both) on regional parks for their site. In return, Darrell requests that the community display a banner at the top of the new parks section crediting his business for sponsoring the section as a community service—with a link to Darrell's site, of course.

Signature Links

Most e-mail programs provide for creating a signature that is added to the end of outgoing messages. The signature may be nothing more than the sender's name, which isn't terribly useful. However, signatures can provide additional contact information, an invitation to participate in a sales promotion, a service tip, or almost anything else that a message can contain—including links to the company's Web site or particular pages in that site. Signatures are usually automated; that is, they attach themselves to outgoing messages with no additional steps. Eudora and some other e-mail programs allow users to create various signatures and then select which one they want to add to a particular message. Depending on how a company uses e-mail, this could be one of the most targeted and effective linking mechanisms available.

BEYOND THE BASICS

Listings and Enhanced Listings

Many community information sites, real estate directories, specialty sites, and other related sites list a Web site address (perhaps linking, perhaps not) for free or for a fee. To add a free link from sites where they're offered, look for the words "Add URL," "Link Your Site," or something similar (as you do for search engines). Usually this takes you to a form to complete and submit to the site. Be sure, when you complete the form, that every word is spelled correctly and the URL and e-mail address are correct. Errors in addresses result in discarded entries, misdirected links, or undeliverable e-mail. Errors in descriptions result in lost opportunities.

If the form asks or allows for a site description using a specified number of words or characters, type a draft of the description into a word processing program first. Use the program's word counter and other features to make sure the description is the best and most accurate possible using the specified number of characters (usually counting a space as a character).

Proofread the description yourself; spell checkers don't catch everything. Then highlight, copy, and paste the description into the form.

Some sites allow you to enter a name for the link in addition to the site address. Some also allow a 15- to 30-word or 90- to 150-character description below the name. Before writing this description, think of the best (truthful) thing to say in this limited space to get people to come to your site. The number of words is limited, so try different combinations to make sure that every word counts. In this situation, a marketing plan and the unique market position or branding statement become important. What position should the business, product, or service occupy in people's perceptions? What are the main emphasis and the primary goal of the site? Who is the target audience? What are they seeking when the message appears? Do you want to attract seniors? cooks? ranchers? golfers? Be certain of all this before you begin (see Chapter 2); then give the link a name and a description that matches what the target audience wants at that moment and still communicates the intended marketing positioning.

Some directories offer a plain listing or listing-plus-link for free and provide listing enhancements for an additional charge. An enhancement might be bold type, different colors, boxes, stars, location above other entries, or more space for additional descriptive text (Fig. 7.1). Businesses with local markets should contact community Web sites in their market area to see if they offer bigger, more visible links for an additional charge.

Buying Search Engine Enhancements

BID-FOR-POSITION SEARCH ENGINES

What? *Pay* a site's way to the top of summary pages on certain search engines? Yes. As mentioned in Chapter 6, some bid-based search engines give the highest ranking to the Web site whose owner pays the most money for each click-through. Site owners (or their Web masters) bid on specific keywords, such as "Staten Island electronic assembly." When a user enters those keywords into the search engine, a link to the site of the highest bidder is displayed at the top of the list, followed by other sites in order of the amount of money paid by the site owners for those keywords. If no one has bid for a particular word or phrase, these search engines display the most relevant sites first. Another variation—and a major advantage—of bid-based search engine results is that bidders can create their own wording for the listing's title and description, which may or may not be the same as the title and description in the site's metatags (see Chapter 6). While bidding for position appeals to some site owners, it creates havoc with the popular notion that search engines

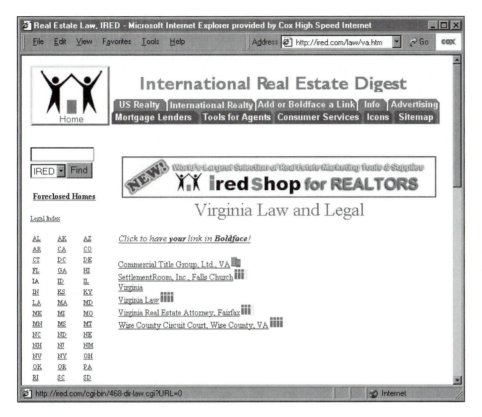

Directory listing. Screen capture from http://www.ired.com.

Figure 7.1

were always meant to stay objective. Conversely, many experts believe that bid sites produce better results, since people willing to pay to have their sites dominate may actually have something more worthwhile to offer.

TIP! **CPC VS. CPM**

Always use caution with "cost-per" terms. *CPC* is significantly different from *CPM*.

CPC refers to cost per click. With sites such as Overture.com, you pay only for "click-throughs"; that is, you pay only when someone not only sees, but also actually clicks on, the link leading to your site.

CPM refers to cost per thousand (impressions). With CPM, you pay each time a user sees the page on which your ad appears, whether or not that user clicks on the link to go to your site.

OVERTURE.COM

This early and acclaimed giant of bid-based search engines, GoTo.com, has changed its name to Overture Services, Inc. and is now located at http://www.overture.com (Fig. 7.2). Overture advertisers pay from five cents to many dollars each time a consumer clicks through a paid-for link to visit their site. If a site wants to be the first link that shows up for keywords that are already bid on by another site, the owner may outbid that site. The previous top bidder's link then moves below the new high bidder's link.

At a cost of $1.00 per click-through, Santa Maria Discount Luggage (http://www.luggageman.com) has positioned itself to appear first (in November, 2001) on Overture.com whenever someone searches for "luggage." Notice that only one cent separates the top three bidders, who can repeatedly leapfrog each other to stay on top, or at least stay in the top two or three positions.

How do you decide which keywords to bid on? Overture.com makes it easy to see how often Web users search for specific words by using their Suggested Search Terms Tool at http://inventory.overture.com/d/searchinventory/suggestion/. The assumption here is that, if people use

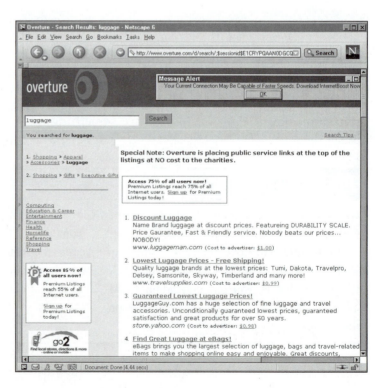

Figure 7.2

Overture.com, a bid-for-position search engine. Screen capture from http://www.overture.com.

Figure 7.3

Keyword search statistics. Screen capture from http://inventory.overture. com/d/searchinventory/ suggestion/;$sessionid$VNE3 WRYADHB5DQFIEFIQSYQ? term=luggage&x=4&y=10.

certain keywords on Overture.com, they use the same keywords on other engines such as Yahoo!, MSN, and Lycos.

Figure 7.3 shows part of the Overture display that resulted when the word *luggage* was entered into the Suggested Search Terms Tool. The word *luggage* was sought more than 23,000 times in October 2001 on Overture.com. Based on the number of monthly visitors to the two sites, the same terms are likely to be searched for on bigger search engines such as Yahoo! 50 to 100 times more often than on Overture.com.

A luggage-related Web site owner might bid on one, several, or all of the above search terms. The higher the bid, the higher the bidder's site will come up on the search results pages of Overture. After the search results are screened for relevance by Overture's editorial team, the company distributes its results to most of the largest search engines on the Web. These sites often display Overture's results higher on a summary page than they do their own search results.

On Overture.com, a deposit of $25 gets you started. Similar, but smaller, bid-based search engines are Sprinks.com (http://www.sprinks.com), 7Search (http://7search.com) and Findwhat.com (http://www.findwhat.com). In April 2001, Findwhat.com began displaying its top results on the major search engines of Excite.com (http://www.excite.com) and Webcrawler.com (http://www.webcrawler.com). A list of keyword-bid search engines is available at http://websearch.about.com/cs/payperclick/. Information is also available at http://www.payperclicksearchengines.com; however, at our last check, the site opened an extra browser window with advertising *in front of* the pay-per-click information, which can be confusing.

Banner and Tile Ads

Some site owners advertise using banner ads or tile ads, with varying degrees of effectiveness. Banner ads tend to be horizontal rectangles. Tile (or *block*) *ads* are usually smaller squares or rectangles. Some small tile ads are called *button ads*. Whereas banners used to be *de rigueur* on the Web and are still used extensively, the use of smaller tile and button ads has grown significantly. Web sites that sell tile ads like them because they are easy to align and fit into almost any format.

The primary goal of banners or tile ads is to have the consumer click on the ad to visit that site. Another objective is to build brand awareness of a name or product through repetitive presentations of the name or logo. Media analysts in the early 2000s generally believe that more than 99 percent of the people who see banner ads ignore them, explaining the average click-through rate for banners and tile ads of less than one percent. According to *The Industry Standard* magazine (December 18, 2000, p. 123), banner click-through rates during year 2000 for at-home surfers approximated 0.05 percent, and for at-work surfers approached 0.25 percent.

Some banners and tiles, however, perform very well. Their design and placement give exactly the right message to the right audience on the right page in the right page position. Remember: Although banners are small, they are actually little billboards, and designing effective billboards is as much an art as a science. The creative people who read the latest reports on effective billboard design and who put considerable effort into designing banner ads reap positive results in the form of higher click-through rates.

CONTEXT-BASED ADVERTISING

Another tactic that Web firms are developing to increase click-through rates for banners is called *contextual* or *context-based advertising*. A media firm such as DoubleClick.com (http://www.DoubleClick.com) might track a particular Web site visitor to discern his or her online habits. If the user visits, say, five pages in a row that deal with a certain type of content (articles, tips, hints, etc.) on outdoor camping, then on the sixth and subsequent pages, many or all of the ads that appear for this visitor will be for camping-related products such as tents, camp stoves, hiking boots, or backpacks. Context-based advertising is based on the theory that a person who exhibits a preference for particular content will be more receptive to ads showing related products.

WATCHING THE COMPETITION

During 2000, a number of firms opened to help businesses keep track of their competitors' activities on the Web. RivalWatch (http://www.rival watch.com) sends crawlers to competitors' Web sites, where they gather information by category, product assortment, price, and type of promotions being offered. RivalWatch customers can then use this data to modify their own offerings.

PriceNgine (http://www.pricengine.com) provides a similar service for tracking product information based on price changes, primarily to keep track of how resellers are offering merchandise. A firm can make adjustments based on PriceNgine information and work to maintain the best sales and pricing positions. As Web competition increases, watch for a growth in services that track online competitors.

ANIMATION

Animation helps catch the Web visitor's eye, and newer banners feature many interactive tricks, including video. Expect to see testing of different sizes and shapes of banner and tile ads during the next few years as advertisers race to break through the less-than-one-percent-click-through-rate barrier.

Better performing ads generally invite the consumer to take some action: "Click here." "Don't click here." "See Something Awesome in Downtown Houston!" Or, they make an arresting offer: "Computers for $99!" "Tune Up Your Web site for FREE!" "Win a New Buick!" A banner or tile ad must be excellent in both design and message to produce results. Those created by firms specializing in small-space Internet ads are often worth the price. Should you use a traditional advertising agency? Only if they have a long record of accomplishment in designing Internet ads; even in that case, have your firm's decision makers interview the agency's clients about the results the ads produced. Some ad agencies that had the tools and experience to prepare them for Web-related advertising have lagged behind in the world of cutting-edge Web site and Web ad design.

SIZES

Some standardization does exist for the size of banners and tile ads. Smaller sites, eager for ads, will still run banners of almost any size. However, most large sites set pricing according to standardized sizes. The Internet Advertising Bureau (IAB) has proposed standard banner sizes, which are shown on their site at http://www.iab.net.

Most sites that host advertising will stipulate a maximum file size for an ad, generally between two and seven kilobytes (KB). Smaller files mean faster loading of a page onto the visitor's screen, which can influence whether a visitor will wait to see the entire page or click impatiently to go elsewhere.

Sites that are more technologically sophisticated offer options of displaying an ad on a given page in a given position 100 percent of the time or of rotating the display of the ad with other ads in that same, or another, position. Buying ads that rotate in a given position decreases the cost, but also reduces the ad's visibility since it does not appear for all visitors. Sites offering rotating banners and tile ads are often the ones that millions of people visit each month. Although a banner rotates with others, the huge volume of visitors assures many views, even in rotation.

Several Internet sites evaluate banners (and other images) and help reduce their file size. These providers are primarily subscription services: for a monthly fee you receive unlimited use of the tools. Optiview.com (http://www.optiview.com, formerly Gif Wizard), for example, "reads" a site and assembles a list of graphics and links. Then it analyzes each of the graphics; ranks them by potential savings in file size; checks for duplicate graphics; and, based on the user's selections, actually reduces the file size of inefficient (bulky, bloated) graphics. These sites have changed names frequently in the past. Some begin as free services and then convert to subscriptions. To find current sites, search for "gif optimizers" on your favorite search engine.

COST

Advertising costs on the Web vary tremendously. Large content sites such as About.com (http://www.about.com) and media firms such as efront.com (http://www.efront.com) charge from under $10 to $35 or more per thousand impressions. Note, however, that some firms are willing to negotiate. Watch for specials and new advertiser programs, and always ask about promotions that might be offered to firms in your budget category.

As the definition of your target audience becomes narrower, the cost of online advertising for that audience increases. The most expensive banner ads appear on pages frequented by a very tightly defined audience. For example, a business with a target audience of people planning to buy a car might request that their banner appear only at specific times. For example, a banner might appear only on the next page a visitor sees after performing a keyword search that includes the phrase "used cars" or, even more specifically, "used cars in Essex County."

Ads can be targeted for even more narrowly defined users. For example, ads can be programmed to appear only to married visitors between 40 and 55 years of age with an income over $100,000 per year who have New Jersey zip codes and who visit art museum Web sites. More parameters selected for a target audience coincide, naturally, with higher charges by the media firm or Web site. Such sophistication usually requires the assistance of professionals, and any number of media firms will help. Firms such as DoubleClick (http://www.DoubleClick.net) help clients define their target audience and plan the placement and frequency of ads on their networks of Web pages to reach that audience. The least expensive banner ads target no specific audience at all. Such ads appear on a "run of schedule" basis, appearing on various Web pages, perhaps in rotation with ads from other firms. In all cases, however, the advertiser is given a guaranteed total number of impressions. When that number is reached, the term of advertising typically ends and the ad no longer appears unless it is renewed.

Also, the more clicks it takes a visitor to reach the page carrying an ad, the lower the cost of that ad. Thus, ads at the top of the home page of a site generally cost the most; ads on pages five clicks away cost considerably less.

WHERE TO PLACE ADS ON THE WEB

According to a survey by the Georgia Institute of Technology, people in the U.S. find out about Web sites in these ways:[1]

Search engines	85%
Links from other sites	89%
Printed media	62%
Friends	66%
Newsgroups	30%

---

[1]Source: GVU's Tenth WWW User Survey, conducted October 1998. See full text at http://www.gvu.gatech.edu/user_surveys. See also http://www.websearchworkshop. co.uk/stats.htm.

E-mail	32%
Television	33%
Directories	58%

These data indicate that links (including banner and tile ad links) from other sites are slightly more valuable than search engines in bringing people to a site.

Should you advertise on the sites that have the most visitors? While well-known general interest sites such as Disney.com, Discovery.com, CNN.com, or ABCnews.com have millions of visitors daily, their visitors probably are not looking for information related to your firm's offerings. Also, the cost of advertising on those sites is well beyond the budgets that most midsize firms allow for Internet advertising. A better approach is to advertise on sites where your target audience spends its time looking for local information or for product- or service-related information.

Where do people look for such information? They spend part of their time at industry-related sites, the sites of firms to which they can sell or from which they can buy. They spend a considerable amount of time searching city, county, and state sites in their geographic area for goods and services they need to keep their business running. If you advertise in these regional sites, they will find you. And, because 48 percent of online small businesses gain customers within a 50-mile radius of operation, it pays to consider advertising in local sites.

Business customers and prospects are also consumers. Consumers routinely visit city, county (or parish), or state sites to learn the schedules, phone numbers, addresses, or Internet addresses of local businesses, clubs, churches, schools, chambers of commerce, city festivals, city offices, stores, utility companies, services, or restaurants. Almost every North American city of any size has one or more city Web sites, and most have business sections that list local businesses in their directories.

Visit some community sites—city, regional, or county—to get an idea of content and advertising. To find city sites in your area, check Official City Sites at http://officialcitysites.org/country.php3, which provides a directory of city sites, organized by state. Knight Ridder, the large newspaper publisher, also operates a national network of regional portals in 58 U.S. markets through its digital division. Those sites are listed at http://www.realcities.com/rc/cityoptions/cities.htm (see Fig. 7.4). A company might consider advertising in one or many of Knight Ridder's Real Cities Web sites.

About its target marketing, Knight Ridder says: "At Real Cities, we offer you a broad range of targeting options—from content- and category-specific offerings (business or lifestyle) to geographic opportunities (local residents of a specific region). You can even pinpoint your targeting to a particular

Figure 7.4

Real Cities from Knight Ridder. Screen capture from http://www.realcities.com/rc/cityoptions/cities.htm. (Shows top portion of screen only.)

time of day, day of the week, or to a consumer's online browser or computer operating system."

Other examples of city sites are:

http://www.coeurdalene.com
http://www.enid.com
http://www.neworleans.com
http://omaha.com
http://www.jacksonhole.com
http://www.orlando.com
http://www.baltimore.com
http://www.darien.lib.ct.us
http://www.newport.com
http://www.marthasvineyard.com
http://www.bennington.com

Some sites operated by city governments do not permit commercial advertising or links. However, chambers of commerce Web sites often *do* offer links, especially to their members. To find out how to advertise in a given community Web site, look for a link on the site called "advertising," "how to be listed in this site," or something similar. That page will give details, an e-mail address, and perhaps a phone number.

Regional cable companies that offer fast Internet connections have created county, regional, and large city Web sites for the areas they serve. They also provide their customers with a custom Web portal site, which might push consumers to places where your link(s) or ads reside. See ocnow.com for an example of a county Web site owned by a cable company (Cox Cable, http://www.cox.com). A portal page within OCNow.com leads visitors to pages or sections for each city in the county. A business that markets countywide in Orange County, California, might have its banner or link appear on this page. If that firm markets only to certain Orange County cities, it would want to place ads only in the cities it serves. Clicking on a category in the center column, such as automotive or banking, takes the user to a related page on which you could *also* buy an ad. Local newspaper sites are also good candidates to consider if they have sections related to your business.

TRY IT

1. Go to http://officialcitysites.org/country. php3 and click into the site to find the links for Golden, Colorado. Visit the city site and the chamber of commerce site. How do the two sites differ with regard to advertising?

2. Find the Web sites for your city and look for a business category. If specific categories are not shown on the first page, check the site's directory, index, or site map. Go to the directory. That's where you want to place your firm's link or ad.

STATE WEB SITES

The business or industry sections of some state Web sites offer links and banner or tile ads. Since many state sites operate as portal or entry points to the entire state, they often charge national advertisers for large ads rather than charging smaller businesses less for small ads. Some state sites maintain business directories. Check your state's pages and look for "Add URL." Then add your firm's site. Some sites add the links free; others charge a fee. See MichiganWeb (http://www.michiganweb.com) for an example.

MAGAZINES, ONLINE AND OFF

Most well established print magazines have Web sites. Advertising in them is easy. Contact the Web advertising representatives from the magazines in which you already advertise by e-mailing them from the magazine's Web site.

Many online magazines and the online versions of print magazines that serve a particular industry are ideal places to advertise a Web site because they shape their content and advertising for a target audience. A company that markets green boards for making circuit boards, for example, may advertise in various publications that are read by buyers of electronic components. Software magazines are the perfect place for a software business to market its wares. Check *Standard Rate and Data* (http://www.srds.com) to see if the magazine profile matches your target audience. As a result of repeated consolidations in the publishing industry, a single publisher today may own many on- and off-line magazines. Check the Web sites of industry journals or other print magazines that serve your market to see if they offer online advertising in their site(s).

VORTALS

We discussed *vortals* (vertical portals) in Chapter 6. Businesses whose positioning is related to a particular topic or theme—a definite 'niche' such as collectibles or gardening—stand to benefit from vortal advertising opportunities. See Chapter 6 for more details.

E-MARKETPLACES

E-marketplaces, including exchange sites, B2B trading hubs, B2B auctions, requests for proposal (RFP) sites, and requests for quote (RFQ) sites (often called simply *B2B exchanges* or *exchange sites*) bring buyers and sellers together to create an efficient online market for trade (Fig. 7.5). A parallel in the physical world might be the New York Stock Exchange. The NYSE is simply a place where investors go to buy and sell securities or stocks. So is NASDAQ. Both are recognized tools for buying and selling ownership in companies. Exchanges should save firms money by streamlining and

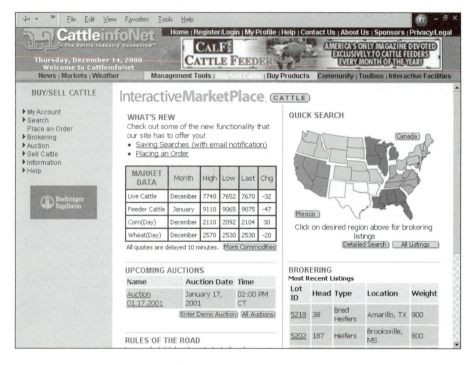

Figure 7.5   Sample exchange site: CattleinfoNet. Screen capture from http://www.cattleinfonet.com.

automating the entire purchasing process. Their exploding growth, however, is being driven by competitive advantages to participants—mostly cost savings—inherent in reengineering supply chains. Some exchange sites also help buyers negotiate national and regional volume-based agreements with suppliers. In this way, they are able to save customers money on commodities, products, and services.

Most business-to-business (B2B) exchange sites deal with the purchase and sale of hard items as opposed to software or services. Some of the biggest exchanges facilitate trading within an entire commodity. Examples include:

aircraft (http://www.myaircraft.com)
aviation parts (http://www.partsbase.com)
bandwidth (http://www.band-x.com)
mortgages (http://www4.imxexchange.com)
insurance (http://www.insureweb.com)

equestrian/horses (http://www.equisourcellc.com)

chemicals (http://www.chematch.com)

steel (http://www.e-steel.com)

industrial metals (http://www.materialnet.com)

coal (http://www.freemarkets.coalhub.com)

oil and gas (http://www.petroleumplace.com)

energy (http://www.altranet.com)

produce (http://www.buyproduce.com)

cattle (http://www.cattleinfonet.com)

poultry (http://www.poultryfirst.com)

seafood (http://www.seafood.com)

used industrial equipment (http://www.assettrade.com)

heavy equipment (http://www.point2.com)

aerospace products and services, and many more.

The largest exchange, Covisint, was formed for the automotive industry. It is a broad industry exchange headed by General Motors, along with its competitors Ford, Daimler Chrysler, Nissan, and Renault. Commerce One, a firm that has built over one hundred public e-marketplaces as well as many private ones, developed the exchange. Having seen the auto industry—a master at buying components and building products efficiently—using an exchange mode, other large manufacturing sectors, led by aerospace, have followed suit.

In early 2001, some large exchanges suffered profitability problems, yet some others performed quite well.[2] Exchanges can be excellent attention-getters for firms through advertising. A large directory of exchanges is Webtomorrow.com, at http://www.webtomorrow.com/ites.htm.

Seafood.com carries ads of firms hoping to improve their position among buyers and sellers, both wholesale and retail (Fig. 7.6). A directory page contains links specifically for consumers to use to contact seafood retailers. Similar sites exist for hundreds of products.

---

[2]Watch for an exchange shakeout. Liquidity and profitability will plague some of the early public exchanges, according to Internetworld.com (Jan. 1, 2001), and perhaps as many as 600 to 1,600 such sites are already in operation. Consolidations and failures are inevitable. Two large exchanges serving the life science and medical industries, ChemDex and Promedix, recently closed their operations; and VerticalNet, which operates exchanges across 58 industries, saw its stock fall from $148 to $8 in 2000. According to a late-2000 study by AMR Research (*Internet World*, Jan. 2001, p. 30) more than 40 percent of respondents plan to join an exchange. *However, more than 30 percent are not even aware that such services exist.*

Figure 7.6 The e-marketplace, Seafood.com. Screen capture from http://www. seafood.com.

INTERNET SERVICE PROVIDER SITES

Some Internet Service Providers (ISPs) offer customers a link in their site, a valuable service because ISPs typically offer a default home page used as a personal home page by thousands of customers of the ISP. Businesses that market in rural areas may be luckier than their urban peers in finding ISPs offering free or nearly free links. A firm may be the only one or one of only a few in a particular industry to be listed in the entire ISP site for a city or region—a definite *positioning* advantage!

Internet service providers in some rural areas often serve several small cities, each with its own city Web site. See, for example, mid-Michigan's Maple Valley Computer Center (http://www.mvcc.com). Check their home page to see all the cities they serve, then visit one, say, Portland, Michigan, at http://www.mvcc.com/comm/portland.asp.

YAHOO! AND OTHER MINI-STORES

Many advertising benefits can be gained by operating a mini-store offered by Yahoo! or an other portal. Yahoo's stores benefit greatly by being, of course, in Yahoo! with its millions of daily visitors. Yahoo! Store (http://

store.yahoo.com) users pay a flat rate depending on the size of the site. There is no per-transaction fee, no startup cost, and no minimum time commitment.

INDUSTRY-RELATED SITES

Industry-related sites, exchange sites (see above) for a given market as well as leading trade associations in a particular field, may be good locations for ads. For example, sporting goods manufacturers such as Rawlings (http://www.rawlings.com), Wilson (http://www.wilsonsports.com), or Spalding (http://www.spalding.com) might consider advertising in the Web sites of two major industry associations: the National Sporting Goods Association (http://www.nsga.org) and the Sporting Goods Manufacturers Association (http://www.sgma.com).

Reciprocal Links and Banner Exchanges

Reciprocal linking and banner exchanges provide ways to increase the likelihood that people will find a particular site. Furthermore, some major search engines place a site higher in their summaries based on how many pages link to it—another reason to get as many links to a site as possible. Visit http://www.linkstoyou.com to get an idea of how many sites already link to yours.

RECIPROCAL LINKS

Search the Web to find industry-related firms that have a strong Internet presence in areas you serve. Then send them an e-mail inviting them to link with you.

Here's a sample message:

Dear (Name of Firm) Web Master:

Because we are not competitors but sell to the same target audience, perhaps we can set up a valuable win–win arrangement.

Would you be willing to put a free link to our firm on your Web site (http://yourfirm.com) if I put a similar free one for you on our site (http://www.myfirm.com)? We could both enjoy increased statewide exposure at no cost.

If you'll send me your text, I'll put it on our company site within four days at no cost to you, ever! Or you can edit the sample that I wrote for you (below), along with a suggested format, and send it back to me.

Cordially,

Name
Title

Enc. Sample ad text, written in our format

(Title That You Want On Your Link)
(25-word description)
(Your Web site URL) (Your e-mail address and phone number)

Moving to Florida?
Get Ready Now, Over the Web.
Before You Move. With a Lender Like Me,
Helping You at Your New Location.
http://www.somemortgagefirm.com
E-mail:
Harry@somemortgagefirm.com
Toll Free #: 888-555-5555

Some commercial sites actively seek reciprocal links and will give you a free link only if you give them one. An example is Seniors Search (http://www.seniorssearch.com). Some sites require that their link be placed on the home (or entry) page to the reciprocating Web site. If this interferes with a home page design or loading speed, the Web masters of the site may negotiate. Sometimes pointing out to them that you have created a special links page that is accessible from a prominent link on your home page will satisfy them. Be sure to follow through with your promises because they will check up on you.

BANNER/LINK EXCHANGE SERVICES

Banner exchange firms help increase a site's exposure by displaying a banner in rotation with others on various Web sites. The banners of all participants in the exchange are the same size. Unfortunately, a banner can appear on any one of thousands of the exchange firm's participating Web sites—most of which are not related to a particular business, target audience, or geographic area. Moreover, exchangers have little to say about what products or services will appear in the banner frame that is fixed (ideally, they request, prominently positioned) on their site, although a site can specify nonporno banners.

To participate, you will need a banner or tile ad of specific dimensions and file size, usually 7 KB or under, which, to be effective, may require the services of a fairly skilled designer. Bottom line: It's probably not worth the bother, cost, and reduced speed in page loading simply to have more people who are unlikely to be interested in those products or services see your banner.

The exception? For some firms, banner exchanges are a smart tactic. For example, if a small entrepreneur is selling a book nationwide titled *The Best Way To Buy or Sell Anything*, then the book could apply to anyone, anywhere, and a shotgun marketing tactic such as a banner exchange might be valuable. Remember, however, that the number of times a banner is displayed depends entirely on the number of times that the exchange banner is displayed on the reciprocating site. If a site lacks heavy traffic, not much will be gained from a banner exchange program.

For full information on how Microsoft's bCentral establishes and manages banner exchanges through its free Banner Network, see http://www.bcentral.com/services/bn/default.asp.

Affiliations and Sponsorships

Some companies, especially booksellers and software companies, pay a commission for sales they make that originated at another site, referred to as an *affiliate* or *dealer*. Here's how it works. You put their icon on your site, and for each person who clicks on the icon, goes to their site and then places an order, you get a commission, usually 5 percent or more of the sale amount.

The selling site's computers record which site the buyers came from, and if they came from your site—one of their dealers—you get the commission. Is this worthwhile? Some shopping mall sites estimate that one of every 200 visitors places an order—and those are visitors who have chosen to be in an online shopping mall, supposedly already there and in a shopping mood. Why are people visiting your site? Probably to look for help with a product or service that you sell. It's fairly unlikely that they will click on an unrelated icon and dash off to buy a book or product.

What are the costs to you? Every image or word added to a site increases its loading time for visitors—and Web visitors are not patient. Adding new icons to a Web page inevitably requires some level of redesign or reorganization of the page. Worse, if visitors click on an icon to buy something, you have just lost them from your site. So, is it worth adding affiliate icons? Probably not, unless your site is logging hundreds of visitors each day who aren't interested in your main product or service anyway.

On the other side of the transaction, however, if you are a nationwide marketer of consumer products, it may be worth your while to set up your own network of affiliates. Your icon on hundreds of other sites can help build brand awareness. The sales monitoring technology and bookkeeping, however, are somewhat intimidating for most businesses.

Some of the best-known affiliate relationships are Amazon.com (http://www.amazon.com), 1-800-Flowers.com (http://www.1800Flowers.com), and Omaha Steaks (http://www.omahasteaks.com). The affiliates information shown in Figure 7.7 for 1-800-Flowers.com shows how a typical affiliate program works.

Sponsoring a section of a site usually refers to providing the content and maintaining a section of a high-traffic site in return for the display of logos or links in that section, sometimes to the exclusion of competitors. Sometimes sponsorship refers to the payment of a fee to have company information displayed and the company cited as the sponsor somewhere on the page(s). For example, a local nursery might sponsor a gardening section of a city or community Web site. Why would a nursery with its own Web site do this? Primarily for the traffic that the city or community Web site enjoys. Although sponsorships on sites with the traffic and market power of high-traffic sites may be too expensive for small firms, sponsorship of a section of a community site may be worth investigating. Chambers of commerce and city, state, or county Web sites or portals are likely candidates. Other community sites that might entertain such an offer include a local historical society, city recreation program, city government, local Internet Service Providers (ISPs), local clubs and organizations, a visi-

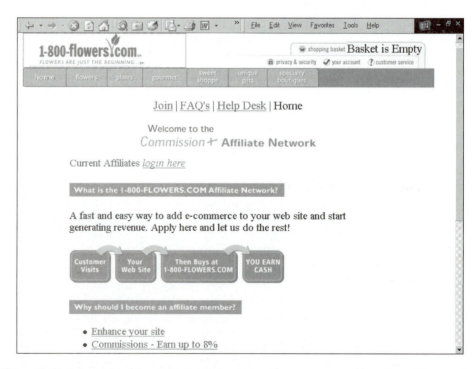

Figure 7.7   Affiliate program from 1-800-Flowers.com. Screen capture from http://www.1800Flowers.com, Affiliate Program tab.

tors' center, local moving and storage firms, and other sites tied to a local or regional market.

How does a company ask about being a sponsor? One way is to call or e-mail the organization to identify the decision makers. Then contact them and offer to provide all the content for a special section about your industry or product category on their site in exchange for being listed as the sponsor. You may have to sell them on the idea of even creating a special section; they need to understand how it can produce revenue or traffic for them.

ASKING TO BE A SPONSOR

The head of a regional office of a realty firm might write something like this to the owner of a state- or county-wide site:

Dear (name):

People from all over the nation visit your excellent site to learn about our part of the country. Would it benefit these people even more to include a comprehensive section on the local housing market, loan and credit information, new home developments, mortgage payment calculators, and even a home-search function?

I'll create a Web site with all this information, keep it updated, and make it available to you if you will put my clickable banner and link at the top of the section with a statement such as, "Sponsored by (firm name) as a Consumer Service."

Once the section is up, other real estate-related firms may pay you to have their names and links there also. It's a win–win situation. You get a valuable new section and service for your site; we get prominence on it forever. And the new section produces revenue for you for years! If this idea appeals to you, when would you like to start?

Tracking Ad Performance

The effectiveness of an ad should be measured. Statistics on link performance such as impressions and click-throughs will tell you the degree to which an ad or combination of ads is driving visitors to your site. Increases in visitor communications, downloads, purchases, or other actions following ad placements will indicate the degree to which an ad (or combination of ads) is working in conjunction with your site content and functions to help you reach site goals.

One helpful approach is to conduct a 30-day test before committing to a long-term ad purchase. This test allows you to track performance and adjust an ad or link before you commit large amounts of money. You can track many types of visitor and site behaviors, but only a few concern you as a banner advertiser, including:

- Impressions or page views. The display of a page containing your banner ad on a visitor's monitor. You must rely on the page owner's statistics for data on impressions.

- Click-through rate (CTR). The percentage of users who clicked on an ad. Calculate the CTR of an ad by dividing the number of clicks on the ad by the number of impressions.

- Referral. The page last visited by a user before entering your site. By capturing referral data, you discover which sites—and which marketing tactics, such as banner or tile ads, text links in directories, or links in the text of a paragraph—are sending you visitors. Various programs can capture this information for you, such as those offered by HitBox (http://www.hitbox.com/).

Summary

Creating and launching a Web site is only the beginning of Internet marketing. The next critical activity is getting people to visit the site and use the information and tools there, including interactive communications and purchasing.

Online advertising encompasses a range of tools, including listings and enhanced listings, banner and tile ads, affiliations and sponsorships. Depending on their placement, some of these tools can be created at no cost; others can be extremely expensive and are feasible only for large firms.

Where are links and ads most profitably placed? On sites frequented by the target audience. These sites may include portals and vortals, area (city, county, state, region) community information sites, online magazines, online stores, or exchange and auction sites.

Online advertising should be evaluated. The most common measures of effectiveness are impressions and click-through rates. Other measures include comparisons of visitor communications, downloads, purchases, or other actions taken before and after placement of a link or ad or combination of ads.

Review Questions

1. Why do site owners need to advertise their advertising?
2. What percentage of online small businesses gain sales from their local area?
3. Describe the difference between a *listing* and an *enhanced listing*.

4. Name two objectives of banner ads.

5. What percentage of people who see banners actually click on them?

6. Give two examples of *specialty sites.*

7. Name one disadvantage of exchanging banners with other sites.

8. What kind of search engine is Overture.com?

9. What is the difference between CPC and CPM?

10. Explain how context-based presentation of banners or tile ads works.

11. How do standard banner sizes make planning of online advertising easier?

12. Is the price of advertising that reaches a carefully defined target audience higher or lower than advertising to a larger but more general audience?

13. Why does an ad on a page that is five clicks away from a home page cost less?

14. Why is it worthwhile to advertise on Web sites of internet service providers?

15. Do people use search engines or links more often to find pages on the Web?

16. Why is it usually not worth creating an affiliation to sell products of another firm on a business site?

Promotion On and Off the Net and Print Advertising

You mean there's more *besides* advertising? If you're serious about Internet marketing, then, yes, there's definitely more.

Some of these tactics are obvious, inexpensive, and easily accomplished—and you would probably think of them and do them anyway. Tasks such as adding your Web site address and e-mail address to your business cards, letterhead and envelopes, flyers, post cards, invoices, and print ads seem obvious, but can be easily overlooked.

Other tactics discussed in this chapter are also matters of common sense and are inexpensive, but are not so easily accomplished. Newsletter articles, press releases, and other public relations efforts require time and effort, both in their preparation and in their placement. This chapter provides step-by-step guidance for attaining effective target market visibility.

THE BASICS

Public Relations

Professionals define *public relations* as "good performance, publicly appreciated." *What* about your performance is *good? How* can you obtain public appreciation for it? One method is to use *publicity*, a major tool of the public relations profession. Here's one approach to getting publicity.

The first step involves identifying the good performance that a business wants to highlight. Good performance should spring from strong points—from *positioning*, from *branding*. What has the company or the business owner, entrepreneur, or employee done that educates people about using or choosing its products or services? Or that helps them solve a problem or answer typical or unusual industry questions?

Imagine that you are the oil field drilling products expert and you provide information about buying or selling new or used oil patch equipment. News? If you are making this information available for free on the Internet, maybe so. Or perhaps you're the golf club manufacturer who has added 360-degree virtual tours of major national golf courses to your site for all to see. Or perhaps you're the Coastal Homes realty chain that has set up a volunteer group to keep the Southern California or Myrtle Beach shorelines clean. Keep thinking; you'll find it—the *hook.*

The next step begins the process of obtaining public appreciation. Write a one-page summary of how a genealogy software company is using the Internet to provide valuable and much-needed services online. Or write a one-page summary of how a local business helped the firm from Zaire find, preview, purchase, and inhabit the perfect U.S. branch office without the expense and hassle of travel, hotels, temporary rentals, and storage. Or write a release on some other topic that builds on a unique market position and related activity.

The key is to get the critical information down on paper (or into a word-processing program or e-mail) in a short form. This will probably not be the final article; it is the information that will interest a newsletter, magazine, or Web site editor in your story. Such publicity efforts may, of course, be the full-time job of a staff person in a larger company; or they could be hired out to an advertising agency or promotions firm. But for smaller to midsize businesses, the job usually falls to a sales manager or the owner or a vice-president.

The third step is to distribute the summary to the editor of the local paper; the local, state, or national trade or industry magazine; business journals in your area; magazines and newsletters of all the groups related to the industry—even the magazine or newsletter published by the firm itself. Besides getting public recognition in print media, target Internet sites that will give you the recognition you're looking for and link to your company's site. News services, e-newsletters, and e-zines (Web magazines) are often hungry for content.

More Visibility

Don't overlook the following locations for publicizing your Web site: Internet bulletin boards, news groups, chat rooms and usenet; business cards, flyers, seminars; conferences, talks at community functions; vehicle door signs, grocery-cart panels, shopping mall kiosks, and bus stop benches and shelters; waiting rooms, lobbies, cash-register counters, and front windows of your own nationwide dealers, representatives, distributors, franchisees and other businesses listed on your site. Use your imagination and your knowledge of your business, your strengths, your position, your community, and your target audience to think of many more possibilities.

BEYOND THE BASICS

Many marketing professionals believe that editorial matter is seven times better read and remembered than ads. In the ad industry, writing and placing articles and news releases or press releases to gain free publicity typically costs about one-tenth as much as buying display ads. Most small to midsize businesses need to allocate considerable time and resources to articles and press releases to promote their site and services. In many cases, editorial content is the very reason people subscribe to magazines, newspapers, and online newsletters.

Public Relations

If, as advertiser lore would have it, public relations is "good performance, publicly appreciated," a business or person actually has to do or say something newsworthy (even meritorious) in order to get public appreciation. Being newsworthy is not as momentous as you may think. You need not rob a bank or donate a new wing to the hospital. *Newsworthy* refers to facts that are timely, interesting, or educational to the audience that receives them.

The most common news releases issued by manufacturers and industrial companies for customers and potential customers announce new products or services. Releases for the industry and investors often announce new company leadership, resources, attainment of sales goals, or acquisitions or mergers. Less common but powerful are releases that report how a firm or a representative of the firm used its product or service to solve a problem for a customer. Such case histories can help position a firm as an industry leader, an authority on solving customer problems, a company that understands its customers' needs.

ARTICLES GIVE YOU CREDIBILITY

To get news articles about a business, service, or product published, you will need to capture the interest of a reporter, editor, or Web master. Ask yourself, What does this firm do that is interesting or useful for its target audiences to know? What has it (or its staff or workers or management or vendors or products) done lately that those audiences could benefit from knowing? Or, How can we educate people about (something) in a way that helps them?

Then ask those questions in the context of positioning or branding (see Chapter 2.) What has this business (or product or service or professional) done that is interesting and related to the firm's market positioning as, for example, the "quality door hardware manufacturer," or the "nation's number one inflatable mattress chain," or the "freshest flower delivery firm"? Sometimes simply writing the headline will help write the story. For example:

- Door Knob Maker Offers Free Home Safety Brochure

- Inflatable Mattress Leader Launches Consumer Safety Web Site

- Homes Realty Chain Helps with Lake Cleanup

- Apple Orchard Announces Free Samples Tuesday

- Attorney Provides Free Information for Beneficiaries

- Local Golf Pro Addresses Area Youth at Career Day Event.

Try It   Write a one-page summary of an event, activity, or accomplishment. In essence, this summary consists of the reasons why the publication's audience (not necessarily the firm's immediate audience) should be interested in your feature article. What you are seeking here is an *angle*—a point of view that should be inherently appealing to the publication's audience. Without an angle—a reason why the story should be published—you will not impress editors.

Businesses that market locally should send this summary—by e-mail, snail mail, or personal delivery—to a local newspaper (to the attention of the section editor most likely to be interested in the subject or, lacking such a section, to the editor of features or the general interest section.

Businesses that market nationally should send this summary to editors of print and online publications for the industry; area business journals, newsletters, or magazines of related professional organizations; organizations that it supports; and area commerce magazines, plus industry columnists. The latter group, columnists, is often ignored; but just a mention by one of them in a well-read column or one that is syndicated nationally can draw valuable attention to your firm.

A firm that is a division or wholly owned subsidiary of a larger firm should contact all the publications in which the parent office or corporation places advertising.

Note that your summary need not be great literature. Recipients use the summary to evaluate the merits of doing a story on the solution, event, or other information included. If they like the summary, they'll call for an interview or some additional information, and then they'll write the final story themselves.

LOCAL MEDIA PRESS RELEASES TO THESE MEDIA'S OR OUTLET'S

Local newspapers are often quite generous with their publicity in specialty sections, especially for their advertisers. If you are assigned the task of getting an article in the local media, you should talk to the advertising reps from local newspapers and business journals in which the company advertises. Advertising representatives of smaller papers have considerably more impact on what editors run than do those of larger papers.

Sending your publicity items out in the proper format makes editors more receptive to your submissions. The format shown in Figure 8.1 is the standard used in the public relations field. Note how an editor can scan the top fifth of the press release in seconds to know exactly what the subject of the story is. Writing your headlines for the editor's eye is most important at this stage. In most cases the editor will rewrite the headline to his or her own taste. However, your *first paragraph* must appeal to the readership of the publication to which you send the release.

It is relatively easy to get publicity into occasional or periodic special sections, which are often primarily vehicles for the newspaper to sell more advertising. The representatives for these sections have considerable influence regarding what goes into such sections, and sometimes the newspaper employs special editorial staffs just to compose these *advertorial* sections. While the articles in these sections sometimes seem "puffy" and may tend to oversell the subject, they draw attention to a firm's announcements. Frequently, simply summarizing a company's glowing sales figures to date or writing about a professional's work as "The [insert brand or position] Specialist" is sufficient to move a story into print.

Ask the sales or marketing director of your company what criteria the firm uses to publish articles on individual employees. Or discuss company successes in its widely distributed corporate or local newsletter. In many firms, an attorney must approve all publicity items before distribution.

Bacon's Publicity Checker (Newspapers or Magazine version, http://www.bacons.com) and Gebbie's, Inc. (http:/www.gebbieinc.com) provide

(Company Letterhead)

For more information, contact:
Jake Lamotta, PR Director
(800) 555-5555   **News Release**
Jake@SavingOnBlinds.com   **For Immediate Release**

John Campbell Joins SavingOnBlinds, Inc.
as Vice President–manufacturing,
to Spearhead Introduction of New Products, Services

Orange, California - June 23, 2001 - John H. Campbell, with more than
18 years experience in window treatment manufacturing and sales, has
joined national franchiser SavingOnBlinds, Inc., as Vice President-
Manufacturing.

Campbell is spearheading a new and significantly expanded line of products to be announced by SavingOnBlinds during 2001. SavingOnBlinds
(http://www.SavingOnBlinds.com) is the country's leading in-home window
treatment firm, with more than 200 franchisees.

Previously, Campbell was National Sales Director of M & B Window Fash-
ions, Los Angeles, a division of Hunter-Douglas, the leading brand and
volume leader in its field. Before that, he was Western Regional Manager of Louver Drape, Greensboro, NC, a division of Levolor® Home Fash-
ions, and National Sales Manager of Blind Design, Inc., San Diego, CA.

Campbell also owned his own storefront retail window covering business
for four years and, before that, was with James Madden Company, specializing in Levolor products, drapery hardware, service, and supplies.

Chad Hallock, President of SavingOnBlinds, Inc. says, "We are most
gratified to have found a seasoned industry veteran such as John Campbell. Because his career spans virtually every aspect of the window
coverings business, from retail to hardware supplies to manufacturing
know-how, he becomes a valuable addition to our team as we prepare to
launch many new lines and services during 2001."

SavingOnBlinds Inc. headquartered in Orange, CA, is a nationwide franchiser with more than 200 independent franchisees in 35 states, offering brand-name window treatments and products at discounted prices. The
firm's shop-at-home-convenience concept is most appealing to today's
busy consumers and to those engaged in buying or selling a home that
needs remodeling. The national Web site is
http://www.SavingOnBlinds.com.

SavingOnBlinds, Inc. is located at 4050 W. Bates Ave., Orange CA 92865-
4429 - Telephone: (800) 555-5555

#

Figure 8.1   Standard format for publicity release.

lists of publication editors and contact information. Read more about
publicity at http://www.free-publicity.com/faq.htm. See the many resources at The Public Relations Society of America (http://www.prsa.org)
and their links to other resources (http://www.prsa.org/ppc/prlink2.html).
Also, check the Writer's Resource, InkSpot.com (http://www.inkspot.com).

Check published media articles on your subject to verify facts at http://www.findarticles.com.

WHAT WORKS?

One way to know what editors like to see or announce about an industry, business, product, or service is to ask them. Because editors are busy trying to meet the next day's (or week's) deadlines, if you do call them, have your "pitch" down to 15 seconds or less. "Fred, tomorrow morning, 100 of our 102 employees are going to show up at work wearing chicken suits to promote our new line of frozen Blazin' Chicken dinners." Or, "Fred, consumers can now get from BiggieBytes.com 1,000 free megabytes of Web-based storage space for their computer files. This beats any other offer by 700 megabytes. Let me send you the story right now."

Another, possibly more effective, tactic is to pay close attention to the relevant sections of the publication for several weeks (or months) until you develop a sense of what topics and "hooks" have been successful in getting into print.

CONTACTING EDITORS, LOCAL AND NATIONAL

Emphasize a story's angle when you talk with or e-mail an editor. The first thing an editor looks for is the hook. Call editors only about articles, not about news releases. Figure 8.2 provides some acceptable scenarios of query calls or e-mails to an editor.

LOCAL PROMOTION TO SMALLER PUBLICATIONS

If your business markets locally, and if part of its audience is middle-income families, an article in miscellaneous local tabloid "throwaways" and "driveway publications" can be easy to place and worth the time invested. Because the editorial staffs of such publications are usually very small, they may view an offer of free written material as a cost-effective blessing. Always include your firm's Web site address. Even more effective, post a longer, more detailed version of the same article on your Web site and ask the editor to include a link to it in the story. Archive the article in your site for all future visitors to read.

INDUSTRY-RELATED NEWSLETTERS, ONLINE AND OFF

Scores of editors of e-mail, Internet, and print newsletters struggle to find enough valid content to meet their deadlines. Some entrepreneurs help them by writing a guest column; your firm could provide such a guest columnist. A simple case history, for example, about how a customer solved a problem using a product can add significant material to online and offline newsletters.

Dear Bob:

Rare Flu Shots Being Given
Tuesday at Local Radio Hut
(Headline for print communications only.)

I'm Fred BrickandClick from the local Radio Hut electronics store. On Tuesday, the 21st—ten days from now—we will have nurses on hand to administer flu and pneumonia shots. Most hospitals and doctors in this area will not receive flu shot serum for another month. But we will offer flu shots for only $15 per shot. We were hoping, as a community service, that you might help us spread the word about this valuable program. What would you like to receive? A news release? An interview with one of our people at your office? We think this is an important community service and want it to go well. Full details are available on our Web site (give URL here).

Dear Bob:

Citywide Flying Disk Tournament Benefits Boys and Girls Center
(Headline for print communications only.)

I'm Fred LocalBigEmployer from Flying Disk, Inc. As you know, last year we worked with the city recreation department to fund and build three new Frisbee-type disk-golf courses for public use. Next Saturday we will be hosting the first annual citywide disk-golf tournament to benefit the Boys and Girls Center. In what format would you like to have us provide the details of our event? Your coverage will have a lot to do with how much money we raise for the Boys and Girls Center. Full details are available on our Web site (give URL here).

Dear Bob:

Battered Wives Organization
Astonished by $175,000 Donation
from Wingnut, Inc., Employees
(Headline for print communications only.)

Your county business journal readers might be interested to know that our 1,010 employees at Wingnut, Inc. have collected and will contribute more than $176,000 this year to our local battered wives organization, Paula's House. Paula's House executive director Susan Smith is astonished: her entire annual budget has never exceeded $80,000. We think this donation can serve as a good model for your many business readers. Presentation ceremonies will be held next Tuesday, October 14, at Paula's House. What information can we provide to you for your readers? Full details are on our Web site (give URL here).

Dear Jim: [editor of large national franchising magazine and Web site]
Ken Dilley, our Vice President Communications of national franchiser SavingOnBlinds, Inc., has written an article called "How Home-Services Franchisees Can Get Leads Easily by Finding Homes for Sale on Realty MLS Web Sites.

The 1,200 word story gives step-by-step directions on how franchisees can locate in minutes the addresses of all homes for sale in a given city or ZIP code using the Internet. Because homebuyers and sellers make a huge portion of home service-related purchases, this article may be most educational and valuable to your readers. Ken has included excellent screen shots to illustrate the article. Would you like to see the article?

Figure 8.2   Examples of query calls and e-mails to editors.

FRONT PAGE NEWS?

Columnist Bill Koelzer followed the suggestions described above in consulting work he did for Pallotta Team Works, a Fund Raising firm that was announcing a series of AIDS Vaccine Bicycle Rides. Among many other places, the story appeared in a health-related Web site (Fig. 8.3), complete with photo.

Koelzer also followed the steps outlined above in placing a story about how the Internet is changing the way people search for homes and how Debbie Ferrari embraced online technology to help remote buyers moving to her area. The local newspaper ran a front-page story with a photo. Then Debbie placed a scan of the article on her Web site to reinforce her positioning as Internet Realtor® (Fig. 8.4).

BECOMING A COLUMNIST FOR A TRADE MAGAZINE,
BUSINESS JOURNAL, NEWSLETTER, OR ONLINE E-ZINE

A business or professional in a field or specialization qualifies as an authority in the eyes of a trade magazine, business journal, newsletter, or online e-zine. (Generally public relations staff write the bylined articles and columns for executives of large companies.) Following are some tips for writing a guest column or article.

1. When the editors agree to accept an article from you or your company, send them an outline, not the final article. They can approve the outline before you spend time writing the final text.

2. Always ask how many words the article should contain.

Public Relations Results. Screen capture from http://www.statehealthclips. com/stories/20001110_ aids_bicycle.htm.

Figure 8.4

More results. Screen capture from http://www.debbieferrari. com/sunpost.html.

3. Polish the article before sending it to the editor. Have colleagues read it and critique it before you submit that final version. (You may need to prepare yourself for colleagues' negative feedback. Keep that in mind when you select your helpers.) Be sure to include your Web site's URL in the text of the article to drive visitors to your site whether your article appears in a print or an online publication.

Some business writers have become the regular columnist for trade news in their industry, especially for smaller trade magazines. Even so, there's no harm in approaching larger trade and online sites with a proposal. Bill Gates of Microsoft has no trouble getting columns placed—but neither should CEOs of businesses in other niche markets.

TIP!

Some firms require that their legal department review any material sent out for publication, particularly comments made by CEOs and other top management.

Guest columns lead to added visibility for the business's Web site, since each column includes a Web address, plus photo(s) and contact information. An executive's presence as an authority enhances the firm's market position and industry reputation. And each time an article or column is accepted, the writer and the company gain credibility with editors. Over time, case history articles can be assembled and displayed at trade shows, brochures, handouts, and on Web pages. Such publicity increases credibility for the company and, even more important, helps the firm position itself in customers' minds as a leader in its field.

Figure 8.5 shows a screen capture from *Western Roofing* Magazine's Web site. Their articles appear both in print and on the Web site. Note that the writer, Heidi Ellsworth, is prominently named and credited for the article, giving her and her company more visibility and credibility.

TIP!

To speed up approval as a specialty columnist for a publication, write four or five columns and deliver them to the editor all at the same time. This tactic shows that you know your topic and gives the editor several weeks worth of columns before having to worry about your integrity in meeting deadlines. Remember that positioning works best when you get there first. If you don't submit a column, sooner or later a competitor will.

Will a publication's editors let small business owners or managers of midsize businesses write a regular column? Some local papers charge a

Figure 8.5

Western Roofing Magazine. Screen capture from http://www .westernroofing. net/html/wr_current_issue. html.

modest fee for publishing each column—usually to avoid problems in their relationships with other prospective columnists, especially those who are advertisers. On the other hand, many e-zines are thrilled to have a leading firm in their industry provide expert content; that content is displayed in a prominent location temporarily, and then is archived on the site, and is thus available for years.

If the publication or online magazine or newsletter agrees to such a columnist arrangement, the writer should focus the columns on tips, how-to, and educational topics that are valuable to the audience. Columns are usually short (ask for an exact length—usually 1,000 to 2,000 words).

Try It　　Olden Days Book Publishing in Smallville, YourState, publishes and distributes books on the history of YourState. The company publishes books on state and town history, as well as architectural, economic, social, political, family, and religious histories. Olden Days will soon release a new book entitled *Nineteenth Century Wagon Manufacturing in Smallville*.

1. Write a press release for this new book.
2. Make a list of the newspapers and magazines to which you would send the announcement.

Publicity on the Internet

Online business newsletters and Web sites routinely publish articles on ways to provide better service. In the real estate field, for example, nationwide realty and home search sites such as Realtor.com, ired.com, Agentnews.com, RealtyTimes.com, realestateabc.com, RELibrary.com, magazines and Web sites of state associations, and others generally welcome industry insider articles to appear in special sections or promotions. Determine what large organizations, Web sites, and associations are leaders in your industry. For lists of associations, visit the American Society of Association Executives (http://www.asaenet.org).

TIP!　**SUBSCRIBE TO BUSINESS NEWSLETTERS**

Wise managers ask their key marketing people to subscribe to several marketing or general business educational newsletters designed to keep readers attuned to changing market and marketing trends. The top 100 business newsletters are listed at http://www.100hotnewsletters.com/business.html.

Every industry has its own online newsletters, many of which are extensions or versions of trade magazines that operated long before the Web began. To find newsletters in your field, search for "business newsletter

Figure 8.6

Web marketing information site. Screen capture from http://www.wilsonweb.com.

lists" or "(your industry's name) newsletter lists." Dr. Ralph F. Wilson's site (http://www.wilsonweb.com, Fig. 8.6) provides useful information about Web commerce and e-marketing in general, mailing lists, and more.

LOCAL WEB SITES

City, county, and state Web sites are often in need of helpful hints for their site's visitors. E-mail the designated editorial or advertising person listed for the target city, or the Web master, and attach the summary of your article idea. Explain why their visitors would be interested. Or offer to perform some service for the site in return for a mention and a link to your firm's site. Following is a sample request.

Dear Fred:

The section of your Web site on "Our City's Scenic Spots" is terrific. Those photos are magnificent. Did your photographer daughter take them? Some people might like to know more about each photo than is provided by the brief captions. I'd like to offer to write a paragraph or two about each picture, in return for a credit.

After I have written the 20 descriptions for the images, I'd appreciate your showing the following paragraph in return near the middle of the page of photos:

Photo descriptions by Lamont Cranston, CEO, Shadow SandalWear. Shadow SandalWear has manufactured tough, high-fashion sandals in Florida for 37 years. For a special discount coupon and more info, click here.

I can have the captions to you within a week. Please reply by e-mail or call me at 800-555-5555.

Sincerely,
Lamont Cranston
ShadowKnows@Sandalware.com

USEGROUPS

Usenet and its many newsgroups (*usegroups*) and online forums enable people in a given industry or profession—or people who share some other interest—to discuss topics of mutual interest, ask and answer questions, and, in general, learn from one another. Participation in these groups may provide you with a forum for drawing attention to your personal expertise or to your firm. Exercise considerable restraint if you choose to use this forum: observe the "netiquette" that applies among newsgroup participants. Blatant advertising of your services will be sure to draw fire.

Note that usegroups can be very time consuming, and the benefits may be negligible. Consequently, usegroup participation rightfully earns very low priority in the repertoire of Internet marketing tools. The Internet FAQ Consortium (http://www.faqs.org/faqs/usenet/what-is/part1/ and http://www.faqs.org/faqs/usenet/what-is/part2/) describes Usenet as "a worldwide distributed discussion system." The Consortium document continues:

> It [Usenet] consists of a set of "newsgroups" with names that are classified hierarchically by subject. "Articles" or "messages" are "posted" to these newsgroups by people on computers with the appropriate software—these articles are then broadcast to other interconnected computer systems via a wide variety of networks. Some newsgroups are "moderated"; in these, the articles are first sent to a moderator for approval before appearing in the newsgroup.
>
> Usenet is available on a wide variety of computer systems and networks, but the bulk of modern Usenet traffic is transported over either the Internet or UUCP [don't ask].

A typical Usenet scenario consists of one person making a statement and others commenting on it. Newsgroups are generally topical, and they deal with every imaginable subject. Most subjects of usegroups, also known as *newsgroups*, are searchable by topic, usually by entering "usegroups" into a search engine, adding a topic name, and hitting Enter or by entering "alt. (nameoftopic)" [no parentheses, and insert a space between the dot and the name of the topic] into the location box of your browser. Using your browser's location box, you can also take yourself into a chosen newsgroup by using this format: "news:alt.(yoursubject)." Enter, for example, "news:alt.autos or news:alt.marketing". Then hit the Enter key.

TIP!	E-MAIL ADDRESS FOR USENET MAIL

Before you join a usenet, you will be asked to create a screen name that newsgroup people will see and to provide an e-mail address for receiving the responses to your postings. Usenets can deliver hundreds of e-mails a day, so having a special e-mail address/inbox to collect them—one that is separate from your normal e-mail address—is a very good idea to avoid being overwhelmed. One of the free Web-based e-mail addresses is a good choice for this purpose. These addresses are offered by Yahoo! and others. Simply search for "free e-mail."

The browser will return a list of related newsgroups that you may want to explore, such as:

    news:alt.business
    news:alt.Web
    news:alt.marketing.issues
    news:alt.education.e-mail-project

To find extensive information on newsgroups, go to Deja.com (http://www.deja.com/usenet), where you can learn the basics at http://www.deja.com/info/usenet_faq.shtml. Save time. Deja.com's Usenet Discussion Service is the largest such archive on the Net, including Usenet newsgroups and other popular forums.

BULLETIN/MESSAGE BOARDS, GUEST BOOKS

Thousands of local ISPs; business groups; state and national business associations; and community, county, and state Web sites have bulletin boards on which people can leave messages. Users go to the bulletin board Web page, enter their identification information, and then type in a message for all users to see or for only persons sharing a particular password. Such postings tend to be of marginal value unless a particular target audience routinely accesses the bulletin board. Bulletin boards for users local to a company store or office, or those for an industry association or trade group Web site (e.g., National Association of Whatevers) offer more potential benefit.

Most guest books allow a visitor to add a comment to the entries from other visitors. They also allow visitors to view previous entries. Few visitors, however, take time to leave a note in a guest book. Of those who do, most leave favorable messages, which add credibility to the claims made in the site and improve market positioning.

WEB SITE ADMINISTRATORS

Making the acquaintance of the owners and/or managers of key local and national Web sites can lead to significant benefits for small or medium businesses. At the very least, establish an e-mail relationship with them. If you like their site, tell them so. Tell the owner of the site that you would like to be the first to know of any new promotions or link enhancements offered. Invite the owner to ask you about your industry, no strings attached. Write an article about the current or future state of your marketplace, or write a series of helpful tips for those who buy products in your industry and give the article to the site owners to post, free, on their site.

Why be so generous with your time and knowledge? Because your competitors will probably not think of doing this, especially for local and smaller regional Web sites. If yours is the only firm helping them improve service to their audience, the site owners may well turn to you for advice, notify you when they have new advertising opportunities, or even refer people to you as a resource or vendor. The result will be an improvement in your marketing position.

OWNERS OF LARGE INDUSTRY-BASED SITES

Get to know the owners/managers of key national Web sites in your field. Send them an e-mail thanking them for building such a terrific resource for your industry. Rarely do builders of huge and valuable business-oriented Web sites receive such e-mails from corporate executives or managers. They will remember you.

Go one step further. Try to become acquainted with the owners and editors of the major Web sites and newsletters that reach your key audiences. If you are the owner of a small business or the manager in a midsize business, make a point of contacting Web site executives well ahead of the next industry trade show or convention; ask if they'll have time to see you or one of your team members. If the site owners will be in your town for a convention, seminar, or trade show, offer them a company tour. Stand out from your peers—that's a big part of positioning yourself and your firm in an industry. You are creating a personality for your business, product, or service, and that personality is part of positioning. You will build a win-win relationship that benefits everyone. In addition, key Web site staffers may have the power to give your firm special placement or promotion on their site.

YET MORE WAYS . . .

Your Internet marketing information should be clearly visible on everything you include in your store of printed materials. On brochures, flyers, and other materials that provide sufficient space, add a box with text directing readers to your site. Create an entire print brochure or flyer as an announcement of helpful resources available on your Web site. Offer your audience strong and specific reasons to visit; tell them that your site offers . . .

- solutions to the ten most common objections of their buyers

- direct streams to daily industry headlines for info they can use to sell

- sure-fire tips that help them sell your products

- ways to avoid callbacks and reduce maintenance on your products

- helpful illustrations and instructions for installation/use of your products

- troubleshooter's hotline, both in whiteboard chat and by phone

- seasonal discounts on certain models of products

- certain free accessories with the purchase of a major product that uses them

- certain free product upgrades for a limited time only

- free software when X and Y product are purchased together

- a list of all industry trade shows that relate to your audience

Include some humor. Many corporate Web sites are incredibly boring (surely you must have noticed). The main reason for promoting a business or service or product on the Web is to get more visitors to come to your site. Visitors won't return to a ho-hum site.

ROLLING BILLBOARDS: SIGNS ON VEHICLE DOORS

Companies with their own delivery trucks have a mobile advertising advantage. All those trucks should carry both the URL of the company Web site and the e-mail address. Along with the URL, include a positioning statement or a reason for people to visit the Web site. How about this?

Get FREE Decorating Advice at
www.OakFurnitureHeaven.com

The same tactic applies to vans that your dealers, branch offices, or franchisees drive around the local community. In smaller towns, another option to gain community favor might be:

Use The (Town) Community Calendar at:
www.OakFurnitureHeaven.com

Compare the benefits offered by these presentations of a firm's URL with this one:

www.OakFurnitureHeaven.com

A Rule
Here's a simple guideline: *If your phone number appears, add your e-mail and Web site address as well.*

Offer something valuable to the audience at hand. Ann Arbor, Michigan, Transportation Authority (http://theride.org) city buses display their Web site address prominently (Fig. 8.7). This drives more citizens to the site to learn about schedules, routes, and fares.

OTHER WAYS TO ENCOURAGE YOUR TARGET AUDIENCE(S) TO VISIT YOUR SITE

Use your creativity to identify ways to increase the visibility of your site. Here are a few more ideas:

- Display the unique market positioning statement or brand prominently on your business cards, letterhead, ads, flyers, brochures, product wrappers or boxes, along with the e-mail and Web site addresses.

- Advertise *your site* in publications that your target audience reads. Announce features that are unique in the industry and/or offer tools, hints, tactics, shortcuts, or resources of value to your audiences.

- Hold free seminars for target audiences—perhaps "How to Use the Internet and E-Mail to Get More Sales"—at your next trade show. Provide handouts, business cards, and other materials that display your Web site, tell what information it has for visitors, and list your e-mail address.

- Exchange or share visibility with firms or merchants favored by your target audiences. For example, you put merchants' coupons or announcements on your Web site, and the merchants put a display promoting your business on their site or in their stores.

Figure 8.7

Ann Arbor Transportation Authority bus. Screen capture from http://theride.org.

Some strategies that have potential for increasing visibility are not widely used or are only used regionally. Among these are advertising on screen-clips that run before and between movies, taking advantage of a captive audience) at local theaters; bus stop advertising on the shelter posters and benches; car door signs; and (a Koelzer favorite) grocery cart ads. Local grocery-shopping-cart advertising is often overlooked as a way to build visibility for Web sites. The cart ad shown in Figure 8.8 could just as easily say "Kitchen floor ideas at www.kitchenfloors.com" or "Order your next pound of fudge online at www.chocolatecaramelfudge.com."

For most grocery cart ads, a firm that has rights to such advertising in various grocery stores in your area, puts your ad on the carts for a fee. Often the ad is placed next to a store map or aisle directory on the cart—where shoppers look for item locations.

Stores in suburban areas average from 100 to 250 shopping carts; megagroceries may maintain 500 or more. Costs vary widely, according to number of carts, regional pricing, and size of the ad. Get statistics from the company that sells the ad space in your market area(s). Compare the cost to that of your general newspaper ads for a given area for six months to help you decide if such an investment is worthwhile. Make similar comparisons for other types of public advertising.

A FINAL WORD ON "GETTING FOUND": KNOW HOW MANY PEOPLE FIND YOUR SITE AND HOW THEY GOT THERE

Web masters or managers can obtain site traffic statistics in various ways. For a fee, the company hosting the site will usually provide *log statistics* gathered by a tracking program or traffic analyzer. Businesses maintaining their own sites can purchase and install their own program to track their site's traffic. Such programs indicate not only how many visitors accessed the site, but what site or search engine sent them there; what browser they

Figure 8.8

Realtor Debbie Ferrari with shopping cart ad directing shoppers to her Web site.

were using; their location; which pages they visited first, second, third, etc.; how long they lingered on each page; and more.

Why is this information valuable? Because if you know what types of sites users were visiting before they came to your site, then you'll know what types of sites to advertise in and target to get more visibility for your site. You'll *know* what types of sites to spend your time and money on. Furthermore, you'll be able to evaluate how well your "getting found" strategies are working. Are you reaching your traffic goals? Which strategies, links, ads, and so forth are working to bring visitors to your site? Which are not? For example, say a Web master changes certain key words in the metatags on the company site. Traffic data could indicate whether this has affected the number of visitors. (Conversely, if you can't determine the effect on traffic, how do you know that you're adding the correct words and tags?)

Yes, you can deduce increases or decreases in traffic to some degree based solely on the fluctuating number of e-mail inquiries that you receive. But hundreds of visitors could be visiting your site but not sending inquires. And here's the rub: they might send you an e-mail inquiry if only your site were designed or worded a bit differently.

You may have no idea which page your visitors go to after seeing your home page, or how much time they spend on each of the succeeding pages. If you knew, you would be able to modify the prominence of your pages to your advantage.

TRAFFIC ANALYZERS

Statistics gathered by one version of the Web Trends (www.webtrends.com) traffic analyzer include:

Most Requested Pages	Least Requested Pages	Top Entry Pages
Top Exit Pages	Single Access Pages	Top Paths Through Site
Most Submitted Forms	Most Active Organizations	Top Authenticated Users
Most Active Countries	Summary of Activity by Day	Activity Level by Day of Week
Activity Level by Hour	Technical Statistics	Forms Submitted by Users
Client Errors	Server Errors	Most Downloaded File Types
Organization Breakdown	North American States	Most Active Cities
Bandwidth	Most Accessed Directories	Top Referring Sites
Top Referring URLs	Top Search Engines	Top Search Keywords
Most Used Browsers	Netscape Browsers	Microsoft Explorer Browsers
Visiting Spiders	Most Used Platforms	Glossary

Another source of useful information about site traffic analysis is Hit-Box (http://www.hitbox.com). Smaller firms with limited budgets will be glad to know that one version of the HitBox traffic analyzer is free.

For each of the Web site addresses listed below, write a *hook* to motivate that site's target audience to visit the site. Example: For http://www.beadsbybetty.com you might write: "Free design ideas at http://www.beadsbybetty.com."

1. www.lampsforenlightenedliving.com
2. www.topnotchroofrepair.com
3. www.foodforthenest.com
4. www.eliteofficefurnishings.com
5. www.apexofficesupplies.com
6. www.yardart.com

Summary

Promotion on the Web is similar to promotion anywhere in many ways. You need to emphasize positioning or branding, along with what valuable products or services you can offer the customer or client.

Put your firm's phone number on everything that you print or publish; do the same for your Web site and e-mail addresses.

Professionals define *public relations* as "good performance, publicly appreciated." Much of getting your firm promoted is common sense. It makes sense to send editors news releases and articles about your firm, especially since this space usually costs so much less than ads purchased in the same media.

Be creative about identifying alternative places to promote your site. Grocery carts, theater screens, tailgates of city vehicles, buses, towed airplane banners, hot air balloons, barges in the river or on the lake, banners with smileys cut in them and hung across main street, trucks with billboards parked on the street near the entrance to your industry's biggest trade show. . . . How many more can you add to this list?

Remember that engaging in effective promotional tactics requires creativity and careful planning.

Review Questions

1. What is "good performance publicly appreciated"?
2. What does *newsworthy* mean in the context of public relations?
3. Why would a golf equipment manufacturer want to show 360-degree views of golf courses on its Web site?
4. Which is better remembered, an ad or an editorial item?
5. What is the most common type of business press release?

6. Why is a case history describing a problem solved by the use of your products or services a powerful marketing tool?

7. Why does an audience give you more credibility when they read a favorable article about your firm or its products?

8. Why is it easier to get publicity into local media than into national media?

9. What is meant by a story's "angle" or "hook"?

10. Are newsgroups time consuming, or do they save you time?

11. Is advertising encouraged in usegroup postings?

12. How does a Web site's guest book work? What benefits can it offer a company?

13. Name two services that Web site owners can provide to your firm?

14. What should appear on your business cards, fliers, brochures, e-mails, newsletters—basically on everything that your company publishes about itself?

15. Why should you offer specific reasons for your audiences to visit your site?

16. How can adding humorous or lighthearted content improve your Web site?

17. What is the value of displaying your URL and a tagline on your firm's vehicles?

18. What is meant by offering something valuable *to the audience at hand?*

19. Why would you announce a special new edition of Web site content to your audiences?

20. Name two things that you can learn about your Web site visitors from the site's traffic statistics.

Part Four
Effective E-Mail

Effective marketing of your business, products, or services in today's world means that you must communicate by e-mail. You must. Even if you have no Internet presence—no Web site, no listings on Web directories, no pages in a mall—you must be able to communicate by e-mail.

1. Your clients—current or future or both—want to communicate with you by e-mail.

2. E-mail is fast. You can ask and answer questions, send marketing information, and keep your clients updated continuously. This means that you can build rapport with prospects that you could not build using regular mail through a series of messages.

3. E-mail offers many features that make your communications more effective, including forwarding messages; sending messages to custom lists of clients and/or prospective clients; sending Web pages, links to Web pages, photos, attachments with reports and proposals, and much more.

E-mail is much more conversational than other written communications. Why? Because e-mail users are accustomed to fast responses. When e-mail assumes a conversational style, your readers can ask questions about your message immediately. And they expect immediate answers.

A conversational style can lead to some sloppiness, which can result in missed opportunities and a poor impression. Opportunities are lost when a writer simply doesn't take time to ask one more question, or add one more point, or clean out extraneous and distracting comments that make the message less understandable or less useful to the reader, or provide requested information. If you don't provide good responses, the business next door—the one using e-mail—will.

The chapters in Part Four are:

1. E-Mail Marketing

2. E-Mail Mechanics

3. Composing E-Mail

LEARNING THE LANGUAGE

The following terms are used in Part Four. Familiarize yourself with them by reading the plain language definitions provided.

@   Symbol most often seen in e-mail addresses, as in "johnandjane@earthnet.com"; in general, the Internet symbol @ means "located at."

attachment   A file attached to an e-mail message. The file may be a photo, text, a Web page, or any other type of file. Do not send files unless you are certain the recipient can find them, view them, and open them. If your e-mail recipients can browse the Internet, then .jpg and .gif graphics files, html files, and simple text files will work fine.

Adobe Acrobat An excellent tool for exchanging documents over the Internet if you and your recipient do not have the same software. Acrobat will create a .pdf file (portable document file) which can be viewed using the Acrobat Reader, a program downloadable for free. Such .pdf files can be read even across platforms (that is, whether you are using a PC, Macintosh, UNIX, or other type of computer system).

bcc   Abbreviation for *blind carbon copy* or *blind copy*; indicates a copy of an e-mail message sent to recipients whose addresses do not show on the message. Think of a blind copy as a "secret" copy. For example, if Mr. Agent sends a message to Mr. Buyer with a copy (cc) to Ms. Broker and a blind copy (bcc) to Mrs. Attorney, only Mr. Agent and Mrs. Attorney know he sent her a copy; Mr. Buyer and Ms. Broker do not see Mrs. Attorney's name or e-mail address on the message.

emoticon   Term coined for *emotion icon*; a small icon composed of punctuation and other characters, such as colons and parentheses. For example, :-) is the symbol for a smiley face (look at it sideways). If the colon is changed to a semicolon, ;-), the emoticon is winking, indicating jest or humor.

folder   An object in a graphical interface, such as Windows, that can contain multiple documents or other types of files. Folders are useful for organizing or holding e-mail messages, graphics, scanned photographs, and documents created with a word processing or other application.

forward   To send an incoming e-mail message to another recipient or recipients.

listen back   To reply to an e-mail message only after verifying that you have understood and noted ("listened to") every point that the sender made, and have responded completely, point by point.

MAPI   Acronym for messaging application programming interface, a built-in Microsoft Windows system that enables various e-mail applications (MAPI-enabled ones) to send and receive messages.

Reply, Reply All   To answer an incoming e-mail message. Reply sends the response only to the address of the originating message; Reply All sends the response to the original writer and to everyone who received a copy (cc) of the original message.

signature   Generally, a statement and a selection of links and/or images that are automatically attached at the end of outgoing e-mail messages.

spam   Electronic junk mail or junk newsgroup postings. Unsolicited, advertising-oriented e-mail comprises most *e-junk*.

E-Mail Marketing

The subject of this chapter is e-mail-based marketing to groups. The recipients may be past customers, frequent customers, prospects, or some other identifiable e-mail group. Less effective is sending a promotion to e-mail addresses obtained by renting or purchasing a list, even though some mailing list suppliers claim to have millions of e-mail addresses.

Sophisticated merging programs allow *individualized* messages to be sent to thousands of recipients with the same information, promotion, or other material. Many large companies have their own proprietary e-mail-merge programs, and various commercial merging products are reasonably priced.

The goals for e-mail marketing are basically the same as for other marketing communications, particularly direct mail. The e-mail marketing should be an integral part of a business's overall marketing efforts. Marketing by e-mail provides opportunities to place an array of graphics and links before a target audience fairly inexpensively.

THE BASICS

E-Mail Marketing Goals

The primary goals of e-mail marketing are acquiring new customers and retaining existing ones. Building brand awareness and reinforcing positioning both contribute to acquiring new customers. Increasing sales to existing customers and improving customer satisfaction contribute to retaining existing customers. Surveys and other market research data contribute to the attainment of both goals. Whatever the goal, it needs to fit into the overall marketing goals for the company, product, or service.

E-Mail Marketing Lists

Recipients of e-mail marketing should be identified and grouped, or *segmented*, just as they are for other types of marketing. The most successful e-mail campaigns are those directed to and designed for specific segments of customers or clients or potential customers or clients. For this reason, most purchased or rented lists of e-mail addresses are not satisfactory: they are usually not sufficiently focused. Also, users change their e-mail addresses frequently, so the recency (how recently the list has been updated or corrected) of purchased lists is an important criterion. That is, older lists contain more addresses that are no longer valid or that users do not access. Still, some e-mail lists obtained from subscriptions to magazines, e-zines, newsletters, and other sources within a company's area of business may well merit investigation.

Far preferable to rented or purchased lists are lists accumulated from correspondence with customers, product registration cards, order forms (online and off), and e-mail inquiries. A company whose Web site and other communications offer an online subscription to an informative, valuable newsletter or product updates by e-mail offers one of the best opportunities for successful, targeted e-mail marketing. This strategy targets not only certain groups that self-select themselves to receive the e-mails, but also gains the *permission* of the recipients for the e-mailings. Furthermore, this "opt-in" strategy helps firms avoid sending unwanted spam (junk e-mail) to thousands of Internet users who are not interested in what the business has to offer.

E-Mail Marketing Content

What should businesses send via e-mail? They should send materials that will help them achieve their overall sales and marketing goals. This material differs from industry to industry, company to company. Some common materials, however, include the following:

Product/service/company announcements; press releases
Newsletters; infobytes
Surveys
Sales/specials
Web site updates

BEYOND THE BASICS

Goals

Most e-mail marketing goals are related either to acquiring new customers or retaining existing customers. Several studies by large research firms have reported that companies spend as much on e-mail marketing for purposes of retention as on acquisition of new customers. In April, 2001, eMarketer reported that spending for retention comprised 50 to 65.9 percent of all e-mail marketing spending (Fig. 9.1.) The goals of e-mail marketing coincide with those for various other marketing communications, particularly direct mail. But the interactive nature of e-mail communications, along with their harnessing of Web pages and functions, make them different from direct mail and all other media.

E-mail marketing goals and efforts must be part of a business's overall marketing goals and must be integrated with the company's other marketing efforts. The critical goals include:

Build brand awareness/recognition

Reinforce positioning

Retain and increase depth in existing customer base (increased sales/customer)

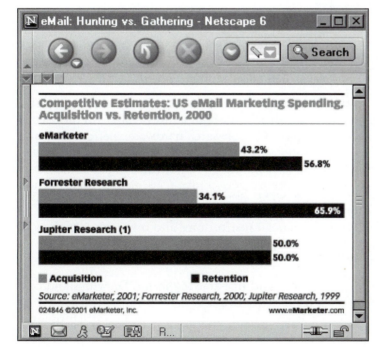

Figure 9.1

Comparison of e-mail marketing spending. EMarketer, Inc. 2001. Screen capture from http://www.emarketer.com/analysis/images/024846.gif.

Maintain or build satisfaction and positive interactive relationships with customers

Gather data (market research)

Refine segmentation

Identify prospects (leads)

Increase sales depth in target segment (get new customers)

Specific objectives for an e-mail campaign might include the following:

Promote new merchandise and send recipients to a Web page describing that merchandise

Promote items on sale and send people to a Web page describing those items

Promote items in a print catalog sent to recipients by U.S. Mail; direct them to a Web page order form with their name and address already filled in

Audience

In Chapter 2, you identified your target audience or audiences. Of course, these audiences may vary even within a business according to products or services. For e-mail marketing, the audiences can and often should be even more narrowly defined—this time according to the objective of a given promotion or announcement.

E-Mail Address Lists

Once you identify your audience, how do you obtain their e-mail addresses? The *most* effective list—the one that will reap the most results—is one that a business assembles for itself from various interactions. For example, provide a space for the e-mail address on the following *print* materials:

- Product registration cards. Many product registration cards request a customer's e-mail address, although e-mail addresses are still more commonly requested on cards for software, hardware, peripherals, and other computer-related items. No matter what product you sell, if you ask customers to register that product, request their e-mail address.

- Open-house guest books. Open houses are usually intended to attract potential customers or clients. They are typical for residential real estate, banks and other financial institutions, and other organizations or businesses that the general public does not enter as casually as they do shopping malls.

- Grand-opening guest books and free-drawing forms. Drawings and contests have been used for decades to get contact information. Now that many business cards carry e-mail addresses, drawings that use the drop-your-business-card-here approach can benefit B2B marketers. Businesses that wish to attract consumers, however, need to use forms that ask specifically for e-mail addresses.

- Reception sign-in books. Usually a reception sign-in page asks for name, company, and the person or department being visited. Add a space for an e-mail address. Then distribute the information to each department. Physicians, dentists, veterinarians, and other medical offices or labs usually have a sign-in sheet, but few of those sheets have a space for a client's e-mail address.

- Gift or donation cards/envelopes for your nonprofit organization. These envelopes are frequently blown into an organization's magazine or newsletter or included in direct mail (print). They may be available in the lobby of a nonprofit business; in book holders on the back of pews; or next to checkout desks of libraries, thrift shops, and other nonprofit organizations.

- Update cards or forms printed on physical newsletters—at least twice a year.

- Cards used to request catalogs.

- Catalog order forms—and every other order form printed for consumer use.

- Customer satisfaction cards for restaurants, hotels/motels, tours, airlines, car rentals, and all travel-related businesses; tax preparers, cleaners, doctors/dentists, veterinarians, auto repair shops, computer repair shops, plumbing and electrical services, insurance claim processing, gardening/landscape services, show repair—you name it. If you provide a service, you have a terrific opportunity to gather e-mail addresses of current customers using a short, easy-to-complete satisfaction card.

- Customer satisfaction cards for stores of all kinds—bookstores, hardware stores, home furnishings stores—*any* store. Simply place a card by the cash register or by the exit and ask shoppers to rate your store on service, selection, cleanliness, or any other pertinent categories.

- Charge slips. If your business allows clients to use VISA, MasterCard, or other charge cards, ask for the client's e-mail address—especially if you use the cash register type charge procedures.

- Applications of all sorts: applications for a store account, employment, a fishing license, a dog license, a video rental account, etc.

- Anything consumers sign and return to you: rain checks, special orders, catering orders, cake decoration orders, equipment rental receipts, and so forth.

Create opportunities for visitors to your Web site(s) to give you their e-mail address:

- Sign-up forms for anything you offer as a free download, product sample, or access to a database

- All online order forms

- Surveys, polls, daily quizzes, etc.

- Memberships to user groups or Web site functions

- Sign-up forms for (daily, weekly, monthly, occasional) tips, newsletters, cartoons, quotations, etc.

- Web site guestbook

- Bulletin board

And be sure to *store* every e-mail address you collect.

Collection of e-mail addresses will be more effective—more addresses and a higher proportion of *correct, current* addresses—if you offer some incentive, such as: "To receive occasional discount (new product, upgrade, etc.) announcements by e-mail, please give us your current e-mail address."

Try to make the e-mail addresses you gather fit clear "opt-in" criteria. Give users the *choice* of receiving information from you or allow them to choose which types of information they are willing to receive by e-mail (product updates, new product announcements, industry updates, user newsletters, etc.). Abiding by the users' choices gives you *their permission* to market to them.

Permission Marketing

Mass e-mail campaigns sent to thousands of addresses—*spam* or *junk e-mail* or (our own term) *e-junk*—inevitably provoke hostility. Spam is considered by the vast majority of e-mail users to be an invasion of privacy—worse even than the junk mail that arrives in the physical mailbox because it is so ubiquitous and because it lands in the users' computers in their offices, dens, or family rooms. E-mail marketing should be done by the recipients' permission only.

Does this mean that all e-mail addresses must be obtained through direct contact with the customer, client, or prospect as described above? No. But if you rent or purchase a list, do your very best to assure that it is a highly targeted list and, preferably, that the addresses were obtained with permission for mailings.

If you use a rented or purchased list, give recipients various clear ways to remove themselves from your list (*opt-out*), either by replying to the e-mail with the word *remove* or by providing a link to a page where the user may click on an option to be removed. In some ways, the latter strategy is preferable. One reason is that many e-mail marketers use the reply-to-remove strategy simply to confirm that an e-mail has reached a live person and is active. Rather than removing the person, they send even more e-junk. E-mail users have begun to understand this concept and tend to delete the message rather than reply. Not only will sending unwanted e-mail limit your ability to maintain a solid opt-in list, recipients' irritation with you will continue to grow. Second, by asking recipients to go to a Web page, you can give them other choices. Perhaps they don't want information on new gardening equipment, but do want a checklist of garden tasks they should attend to weekly. Giving choices not only improves your list; it also enables you to begin to create qualified or segmented lists for specific purposes.

PUBLISH YOUR INFORMATION POLICY

Concerning information policies, Regina Brady, Vice President of Strategy and Partnerships, FloNetwork Inc., says:

One of the most important steps that a marketer can take to ensure that its e-mail campaigns are implemented responsibly—and thus respect the privacy of Internet users—is to publish an online notice of information practices that is easy to find, read, and understand.

This notice should cover

1. The nature of the personal information that is collected with respect to individual consumers;
2. The manner in which such information is collected;
3. The nature and purposes of disclosures and the types of persons to whom disclosures may be made; and
4. The mechanism by which the individual may limit the disclosure of such information, should they desire to do so.

This careful attention to online etiquette magnifies the power of the medium. Similarly, tapping all of its potential—from its capacity for dynamic, personalized creative [potential] to its ability to support instantaneous, detailed response analysis—unleashes that power and focuses it on the market. Indeed, when designed and executed as a comprehensive, integrated strategy, e-mail delivers unprecedented advantages to the marketer. As a consequence, it is now the most exciting and powerful new capability in the direct marketing field.

Source: http://www.thinkdirectmarketing.com/dmlibrary/tutorials/email_market2.html.

Double Opt-In Permission

In most cases, people opt in for e-mail by registering themselves for some offer (membership, newsletter, certain types of e-mails, reports) by clicking or unclicking a box on a Web site or checking a box on a printed form. When opt-in clients or prospects confirm by e-mail or Web page that they did, indeed, opt in, they become *double opt-in* recipients. You know these people want your messages.

Why bother with *double* opt-in? Many serious marketers are shifting to double opt-in as their standard. They make sure they can prove that they have users' permission and are complying with their wishes.

THE PERMISSION RULE

Never send unsolicited e-mail messages. Always get the permission of a recipient before e-mailing anything. There is nothing more to know about this rule.

Double opt-in provides better protection for your reputation by helping you avoid being identified as a spammer. Furthermore, double opt-in can protect you if, under new consumer protection laws regarding spam, recipients claim you sent e-mail to them without their permission. Legal issues remain to be untangled in the courts. But if you want to be safe, choose the double opt-in.

Refining the Lists: Track E-Mail Visitors

Using database technology, you can gather and archive key marketing and behavioral information about every opted-in message recipient. You can determine which customers purchased, which wanted more information about your new merchandise, which wanted to order more traditionally from a catalog, and which did not respond at all. With this information, future e-mailings can be tailored for each customer, carrying exactly the kind of message they've historically acted favorably upon, in the format they prefer. This process lets you know who your best customers are and lets you send them hand-tailored offers.

Try It

1. List eight non-online potential sources that your business could use to gather e-mail addresses for its mailing list.
2. List three ways your business could use its Web site to gather e-mail addresses for its mailing list.

What to Send

E-mail marketing campaigns must contain material that interests the target audience, has value for the recipient, and builds on the positioning of the company, product, or service. Campaigns should be planned to help achieve the overall sales and marketing goals. Random messages sent 'shotgun' to a general audience seldom bring the intended results. Individual messages vary significantly from one product or service to another. Nonetheless, the most common types of messages include product, service, or company announcements; press releases, newsletters; short tips or daily (or other periodic) messages; surveys; sales and special offers; and Web site updates.

PRODUCT/SERVICE/COMPANY ANNOUNCEMENTS; PRESS RELEASES

Announcements of new products or services are good candidates for e-mail to your customer list or to a 'prospect' list. Product updates, especially the type that can be downloaded from your Web site or that of a distributor, may have special appeal for current customers. New manuals for assembly, installation, or maintenance, especially downloadable ones, could be greatly appreciated by the owners of the corresponding products. High-light the features and benefits of whatever you announce that will be most important to your audience. The opening of a new office or store also merits its own message, especially if you can target the list to the geographic area of the store.

Press releases concerning company sales, new leadership, or recent awards may be of interest to some audiences, especially investors and employees. See Chapter 8 for more on this topic.

SHORT TIPS OR DAILY MESSAGES

What would your customers or clients find interesting? Something related to your business. Retailers of camera equipment may send tips for photography. Retailers of toys and games for children may send parenting tips. Retailers of office supplies might send an office cartoon of the day. Tips or other items not *directly* and clearly related to your own products or services can build brand awareness by using a brought-to-you-by line or banner with active links to your Web site.

NEWSLETTERS

In general, topics discussed in your newsletters have more impact than ads. As you know from Part Three, banner ads have low click-through rates; but the same banner ad in a newsletter can generate many times the activity. Why? Because the recipients chose to receive the newsletter. Self-selected recipients' interest level and responsiveness will be much greater than that of the general Web-surfing public.

Newsletters with more copy about the company or product and less about the customers or clients and their needs and priorities are often ineffective. One key to a successful newsletter is frequent use of the word *you*. Relate as much newsletter content as possible to the reader. Rather than discussing how your brilliant engineering department created a terrific widget ("We spent six years testing our new weed-pulling SuperTool"), discuss how it makes work or play easier or better for the intended users ("You can cut weed-pulling time in half when you use our 'Roots 'n' All' SuperTool").

Besides product and service and company "news," include letters from customers, suggestions from employees, reviews of and links to articles of interest to your readers, calendar notes, how-to hints, a contest or challenge or puzzle. Pack it all with links to pertinent pages on your Web site.

Newsletters are often more effective when they come from an individual rather than a company. Consider having each newsletter be from your CEO or president, or a customer service or sales manager. Send newsletters to dealers, distributors, or manufacturer's representatives from the national sales manager and show his or her photo at the beginning and signature at the end. And keep e-mail newsletters short. Put the details on the Web site. Users who see a long, involved message in their inbox may be tempted to hit the Delete button.

SURVEYS AND POLLS

Many people *like* to respond to surveys or polls (see Chapter 4). Surveys by e-mail can also engage your target audience. The message could contain the questions and ask the recipient to reply by e-mail, a tactic that works best with only one question. Respondents can give as much or as little information as they wish, so give them some guidance. Tell them to rate something on a scale of 1 to 5, or to select their favorite item from a list, or to answer a more complex question in their own words. Alternatively, the message could contain a direct link to a survey located on your Web site. Users can click in circles or boxes, answer multiple-choice questions, or write some statements of opinion. With either approach, you stand to gain valuable information about your target audience's opinions, needs, and even demographic characteristics. What do they gain? Usually two things: (1) the satisfaction of making their opinion known or helping you understand their needs, and (2) statistical information about the other respondents' replies.

SALES/SPECIALS

E-mail specials or Web promotions can be started and stopped within days—virtually no printing is required. Alert your customers and distributors of any special or seasonal sales or discounts or other promotions. Free shipping, 20 percent off, gift with purchase, and other promotional schemes work just as well or better in cyberspace than in the brick and mortar market. Inform the target audience about regional, or even local, store promotions. Include a coupon they can print out and take to the local retailer or office. Encourage forwarding of the valuable coupon to friends and family, a technique called *viral marketing.*

WEB SITE UPDATES

Some Internet users want to know when a particular Web site is changed or updated. They may use an automated service that provides this information. More effective for the owner of the Web site, however, is to offer to let visitors know when your site changes. You add a user to your maillist and you have an opportunity to build the relationship with that user each time the Web site is updated. What types of updates are appropriate? Announce the addition of a new Web function, such as a calculator (gallons of water needed for 20 koi; calories burned today; energy saved by replacing conventional lightbulbs with new, energy-saver bulbs, etc.), puzzle, or search function. Send information about the addition of a major information section, a new catalog (especially if you sell unique or semi-unique items such as houses, antiques, art, etc.), or a new activity report for the month, related to your business or to the specific interests of your target audience.

AUTORESPONDERS

Autoresponders, as discussed in Chapter 4, send prepared e-mail messages in response to (a) a user's request from a Web site; or (b) an e-mail to a particular address. One use of autoresponders that has been considerably successful tells e-mail writers that you have received their inquiry (help request, complaint, etc.) and will reply within a short period of time, say, 24 hours. Of course, you need to be sure that you *do* get back to the sender within the promised time. Many offices use autoresponders to let people know that they are out of town and ask you to contact a particular colleague if you need assistance before they return.

Another use of autoresponders is to send reports or data that have been requested from a Web site. Why not simply post the reports on the Web site itself? One reason is that using autoresponder puts your name and e-mail address in the e-mail box of the requester. Even after they have left your site to pursue other interests, your e-mail address and links to your site will be easily available to them. Another reason is that you will collect an accurate, active e-mail address, which you can use to invite the requester to join your opt-in maillist for updates and other material.

Make Each E-Mail Count

Several proven tactics to use e-mail more effectively are cited by Regina Brady, a leading authority on Internet direct marketing and vice president of Strategy and Partnerships, FloNetwork Inc. (http://www.floNetwork. com), which manages permission-based direct marketing.[1] These suggestions appear in her article "E-Mail: The Future is Here for Interactive Marketing."[2]

> Link e-mail with other Web content. Embed hot links in the message, which will make it easy for the reader to visit its Web site or, even better, the area of the Web site, which provides additional information about the specific offer to which the reader responded.
>
> Keep its initial mailings short (1 to 2 screens) because people are reading these messages on a computer screen, and the dynamics are different from those of a traditional direct mail letter.
>
> Employ the one-to-one marketing functionality of the medium to establish real two-way communication with customers.
>
> Measure the performance of each call to action or link in its mailing so that it knows what works and what doesn't and archives that knowledge in its database for future use.

And . . .

> Embed multiple calls to action in the e-mail message, offering each recipient several choices or hotlinks based on their specific need or interest. E-mail is not a passive medium; by including a number of exciting offers and live samples, the marketer will encourage the customer to interact with the message, and that involvement, in turn, both increases the probability of a sale and generates valuable new information which can then be appended back to the marketer's database for future use.

Try It   Describe an e-mail campaign that would be appropriate for your customers or clients that uses daily tips, cartoons, or other items. What items would you send, and why?

---

[1]Brady serves on the Board of Directors for the Internet Alliance and the Ethics Policy Committee for the Direct Marketing Association. See http://www.ftc.gov/acoas/nominations/bradybio.htm.

[2]http://www.thinkdirectmarketing.com/dmlibrary/tutorials/email_market2.html.

The Sending Process: E-Mail Merge Programs

As is the case with most Internet developments, e-mail merge programs are far more sophisticated than they were even a few years ago. Today you can use standalone programs, enhancements to word processing or database products, Web-based e-mail marketing tools, or full-service companies to handle it all for you.

Among the current products that support e-mail marketing is E-mail Merge for the Macintosh, a program for merging database information into messages to create individualized messages (http://www.sigsoftware.com/ emailmerge). Word Merge Pro, also for the Mac, allows you to perform merges that are similar to the built-in mail merge feature of Microsoft Word without an intermediate export/import stage (http://www.word-mergepro.com). For the PDA/Newton, there's Merge, a mail merge tool for the Works application (http://www.standalone.com). Search http://www. zdnet.com or http://www.tucows.com or other software-review Web sites for more.

Advanced Access uses a Web-based e-mail merge program that allows for embedded images, time-specific repeated e-mailings, and other features (Fig. 9.2). The program automatically sends out your preselected cam-

Intellic@rds. Screen capture from http://www.democards.com/ default.html.   **Figure 9.2**

paigns—campaigns that you design and write using Intellic@rd tools or campaigns created by Advanced Access. The program includes online management of lists, making possible campaigns to specific groups of clients or customers. Advanced Access provides predesigned campaigns for use by real estate professionals. (We encourage them to develop campaigns for other industries.)

Some of the functions offered by Jumpstart by Responsys (http://www.jumpstart.responsys.com) include:

- Customers and prospects can register directly on your Web site.

- Automatically sends great looking, personalized announcements, promotional offers, and interest-based newsletters.

- Manages customer and prospect lists.

- Grows customer relationships with every interaction.

- Manages customers' permission preferences, protecting you from sending spam.

- Tracks e-mail marketing success with real-time results reports.

Jumpstart will automatically send a follow-up confirmation e-mail to those who fill out your Web site sign-up form. Once the recipient clicks on the confirm link, their opt-in status in your contact list changes to "in" and they can be included in other outbound campaigns. Note that larger firms with huge e-mail volume may exceed the capabilities of Jumpstart.

Try It   What would you want an e-mail marketing program to do for your business? What tasks should it perform?

Setting a Good Example

Turner Sculpture of Onley, Virginia, uses effective e-mail marketing to reach its customers and others interested in the Turners' works. Turner's collects e-mail addresses online through its active e-mail links, the order form, and its newsletter request page (see Figure 9.3). Visitors to the (physical) studio and foundry enter their e-mail address when they sign the guest book. Web visitors who request the newsletter *Tracks* are also asked if they would like to receive occasional announcements by e-mail.

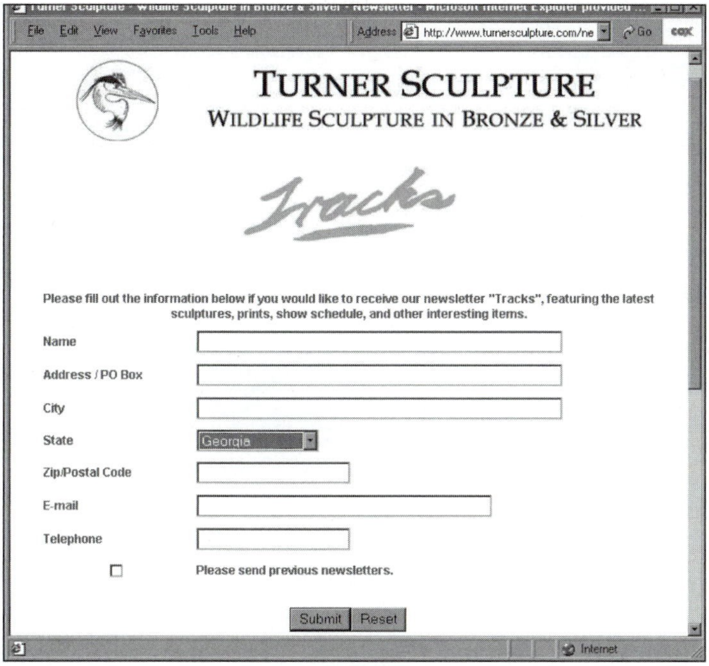

Figure 9.3

Online request for newsletter *Tracks.* Screen capture from http://www. turnersculpture.com/ newsletter.htm. All artwork, photographs, and web site design copyright Turner Sculpture 2002.

Turner's sends announcements of new sculptures, other art, or various special offers to the targeted addresses it has collected. Figure 9.4 shows an example of an e-mail announcement from Turner Sculpture. Notice that the content is attractive, interesting, and well designed, with a dash of Dr. Turner's dry wit for good measure. Note also that recipients are given instructions on unsubscribing from the mail list, along with the promise that the request will be honored immediately.

Summary

E-mail marketing should be tailored for specific audience(s) and goals. Although lists of e-mail addresses can be purchased or rented from magazines and other sources, more effective lists are developed by a business through its customer correspondence, opt-in newsletters and updates, and guest book registrations.

Avoid using spam techniques to recipients who may have no interest in your product or service. Although it may result in short-term sales, ultimately it will alienate people and reflect poorly on your company.

▽ **Subject:** **Bull & Bear - New Sculpture by William H. Turner**
    From: Turner Sculpture <turner@esva.net>
    Date: 10/30/2002 7:03 AM

TURNER SCULPTURE
WILDLIFE SCULPTURE IN BRONZE & SILVER

NEW EDITIONS

Turner Sculpture
P.O. Box 128
Onley, VA 23418

turner@esva.net
www.turnersculpture.com

Bull & Bear
by William H. Turner

Bull & Bear
William H. Turner
Reference # 560
Limited Edition of 150
14"l x 6"w x 8"h
$825.00

"I had been asked many times to create a sculpture depicting the Wall Street Bull & Bear theme. However, many artists have done this, so I was reluctant to do it.

Finally I conceived the idea to show the bull winning when viewed from one side and the bear winning when viewed from the other.

It is mounted on a walnut base with a turntable, so a touch of the finger will change it from bear market to bull market.

(Turning it in either direction does not affect the market)." *WHT*

View sculptures by William and David Turner on our website www.turnersculpture.com
Herons & Egrets | Waterfowl | Birds | Birds Of Prey | Owls | Game Birds
Fish | Dolphins & Manatees | Marine Life | Frogs | Turtles & Tortoises
African Wildlife | Big Cats | Elephants | American Wildlife | Bears
Childhood Memories | Farm Animals | Dogs | Horses
Squirrels & Mice | Rabbits | Foxes | Otters
Deer & Antelope | Rams

Secure Order Form
Home

🖭 Internet

Figure 9.4   E-Mail Message. "Bull & Bear: New Sculpture by William H. Turner."
Copyright Turner Sculpture 2002.

Review Questions

1. List three goals of e-mail marketing.
2. Why should e-mail marketing be directed toward specific groups of customers or potential customers?
3. Define the *recency* of a list.
4. Name four sources of e-mail addresses that are preferable to buying or renting one from a print magazine subscription list.
5. Why is an opt-in newsletter or product update service a good source of e-mail addresses?
6. Name three types of content that a business might include in e-mail marketing.
7. Define *double opt-in permission.*
8. What is "The Permission Rule"?
9. List three types of information you might wish to store in a database about your opt-in e-mail recipients.
10. What does an autoresponder do?

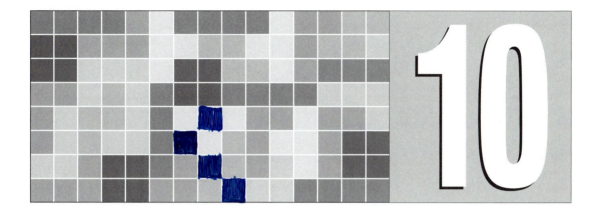

E-Mail Mechanics

The steps in communicating by e-mail are the same as those in written communications: addressing the message, composing it, and sending it. Likewise, e-mail recipients can do the same things with e-mail messages as they can with paper letters, memos, reports, and other documents: read them, discard them, answer them, forward them to someone else, and file them. They can also print them or quote them in other messages.

This chapter covers the basics of using e-mail. It also addresses mechanical issues specific to e-mail: links, attachments, and electronic formats.

THE BASICS

Experienced e-mail users may want to skip to "Beyond the Basics."

E-Mail Programs

The most popular e-mail programs in the United States include various versions of Qualcomm's *Eudora*, Netscape's *Communicator*, Microsoft's *Outlook*, or *Outlook Express*, and AOL mail. Many large companies, schools, government offices, and other organizations use proprietary programs for their Intranet (within the company) and Internet communications.

In addition to these programs, many Web-based e-mail programs are available, such as those offered by Yahoo!, Hotmail, and Spacemail. Users

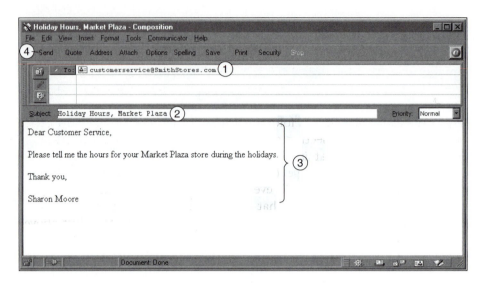

Figure 10.1   Outgoing message from Sharon to George.

can access their password-protected Web-based e-mail from any computer with an Internet connection and browser. Since Web-based e-mail uses the host's interface, a separate e-mail application program is not required. In addition to flexible anywhere, anytime access, Web-based e-mail reduces the risk of contracting e-mail viruses, since you can check and read messages without moving them onto your own computer's hard drive. Four disadvantages of Web-based e-mail are: (1) it can be slow and tedious; (2) some functions such as sending attachments are limited or not available; (3) it frequently carries advertising added by the sponsoring Web site; and (4) it conveys the implication of thriftiness, since most Web-based e-mail is free. In short, Web-based e-mail is not suitable for businesses.

The Mechanics of Creating E-Mail

The mechanics of creating an e-mail message are to open the New Message (or Create Message or Write Message or Compose Message) window of your e-mail program, fill in the e-mail address(es) of your recipients, fill in the topic of the message, and then enter the message text.

Figure 10.1 shows a message that Sharon Moore is planning to send.[1] She has addressed it to customerservice@SmithStores.com by typing that

---

[1]We show samples created in Netscape *Communicator.* Although the program you use might look a little different, the basic components will be the same. We do not mean to imply any advantage to or endorsement for Netscape *Communicator.* It is simply the program we are currently using.

e-mail address in the field next to the word "To." (1) She identifies the topic of the message as "Store Hours, Market Place" by typing that text in the field next to the word "SUBJECT." (2) She types her message of inquiry in the body of the e-mail. (3) Next she will click on the send button (4).

Figure 10.2 shows the message that George Manfors, who works in Customer Service at Smith Stores, received from Sharon. The top left section of George's e-mail screen lists folders that George has created for storing his messages. The top right section of George's screen lists messages George has placed in the folder that is currently open. The bottom portion of the screen shows Sharon's message. (The screen can be rearranged. Your screen might not look exactly like this, even if you are using the same e-mail program that we used here.) Now that George has received Sharon's message, he has several choices. Most choices are shown on the buttons just above the list of files and messages, including Reply, Reply All, Forward, File, Print, and Delete. George decides that he will forward Sharon's message to Eddie and ask him to confirm the information. George plans to reply to Sharon when he gets the final information.

Figure 10.3 shows George's message to Eddie. When George clicks on Forward several things happen: (1) the screen for creating a message opens; (2) the subject line is automatically included, along with the abbreviation "Fwd" to indicate that the message with that subject is being forwarded,

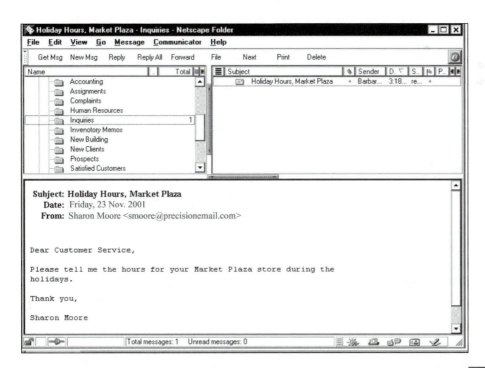

Sharon's message as it appears in George's in-box.

Figure 10.2

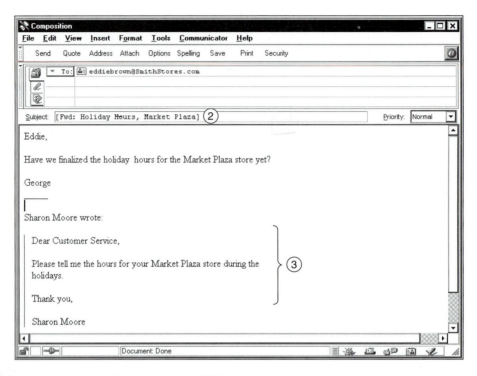

Figure 10.3   George's outgoing message to Eddie.

and (3) Sharon's message is automatically included in the body of the message sent to Eddie.

George types Eddie's e-mail address in the 'To' field. Then he places his cursor in the body of the message and types his question to Eddie. George could write a new message to Eddie, without forwarding Sharon's message. But in this case he decides that he wants Eddie to see why he is asking the question.

After Eddie confirms the hours for George, George goes back to Sharon's original message and clicks the 'Reply' button (Fig. 10.4). This time, Sharon's e-mail address is automatically entered in the 'To' field. The subject line is automatically included, along with the abbreviation "Re" to indicate that this is a reply to Sharon's message of that subject. Eddie needs only to type his message to Sharon in the body and send.

To quote Sharon's original message in the body of his message, George would click on the Quote button and Sharon's message would appear in the message body. This is often useful for short messages, as well as for busy business representatives who are helping a client solve a problem that may require a string of messages. The string of quoted messages remind the recipient of earlier questions and comments.

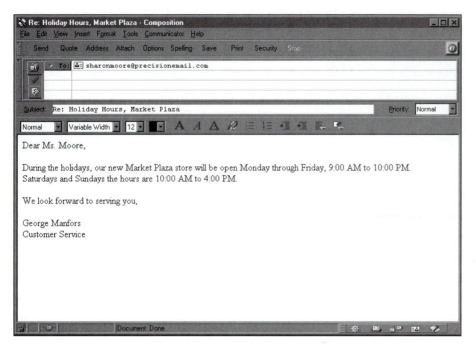

George's outgoing reply to Sharon.

Figure 10.4

Most e-mail programs allow users to quote the original message *always*, automatically. Generally this option is not recommended. It's a lot easier to click a Quote button when you want a message to show, or to copy/paste a sentence or two that you want to quote, than to high-light and delete long messages that you don't want to take up space in the e-mail.

One of the choices that did not apply to George's messages above is Reply All. The recipient of a message sent to two or more addressees may reply only to the original sender (Reply) or may reply to the original sender plus everyone who received the message (Reply All).

Here's an example that uses a few more options. Figure 10.5 shows a message in which Randy Kellam has sent a special offer to three cus-tomers; the e-mail addresses are shown in the fields next to the 'To' but-tons. Randy also sent a copy to the Sales and Marketing Department of Candy Hearts, perhaps so they would know about the special offer in case one of the customers contacted them. The e-mail address of the Sales and Marketing Department is shown in the field next to the Cc box. Finally, Randy sent a copy to his boss, but that one was a blind copy. The boss's e-mail address is shown next to the Bcc box. The other recipients of the

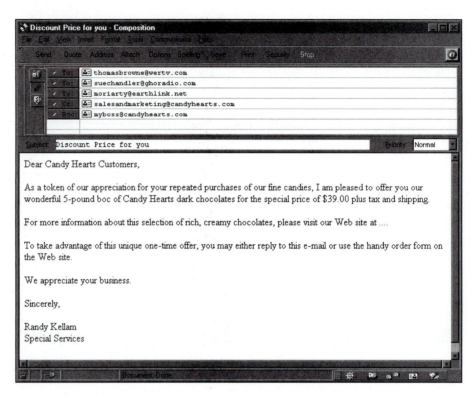

Dear Candy Hearts Customers,

As a token of our appreciation for your repeated purchases of our fine candies, I am pleased to offer you our wonderful 5-pound boc of Candy Hearts dark chocolates for the special price of $39.00 plus tax and shipping.

For more information about this selection of rich, creamy chocolates, please visit our Web site at ....

To take advantage of this unique one-time offer, you may either reply to this e-mail or use the handy order form on the Web site.

We appreciate your business.

Sincerely,

Randy Kellam
Special Services

Figure 10.5 Randy Kellam's e-mail message addressed to several recipients.

message—the direct recipients and those who received a Cc copy—cannot see that the message went to Randy's boss.

What's It For? As a self-check, describe what each of the following e-mail options does: Send, Reply, Reply All, Forward, To, Cc, Bcc, Subject.

BEYOND THE BASICS

Formatting E-Mail

Today's e-mail messages have much greater capability than they did just a few years ago. At the outset, all e-mail was plain text—only letters and numbers that always appeared in the same typeface and font. The advantage—if it could be interpreted as such—was that plain text messages do not take up much space: they travel through cyberspace quickly and load quickly into the recipients' e-mail program. Many messages still use plain text format, but increasingly users employ formatting options such as different fonts and incorporate links, images, and attachments. These options use html formatting, the same html that we discussed in regard to Web pages in Chapter 2.

What advantages do e-mails formatted in html offer to a marketer? Html e-mail can generate as many as 60 percent more responses or interactions than can plain text e-mail (see http://www.travelocity.com). As with printed advertising or brochures and flyers, people pay more attention to things that look interesting and are easy to absorb.

Compare the two e-mail messages shown in Figure 10.6. The formatted text makes important points stand out. The graphics help recipients see immediately what the sender is describing. Furthermore, the active links allow a user to click directly into the sender's Web site to get more information or place an order online.

```
We are pleased to announce the availability of our new
cleaning product, CleansAll. CleansAll will work miracles
on your sinks, tubs, showers, toilets, and tile. Never
again will you resort to strong abrasives or steel wool
to remove those tough stains or mineral deposits. And as
a special introductory offer, the coupon shown below may
be redeemed for one free container of CleansAll when you
buy one container of this new product at your local re-
tailer.
Try CleansAll today!  You'll be glad you did.
-----------------------------------------------------------
       Coupon   Coupon   Coupon   Coupon   Coupon   Coupon

          Redeem this special Coupon today.
               Buy One, Get One Free.
                   CleansAll.

Coupon registration number 1232456789
-----------------------------------------------------------
And don't forget to visit our Web site at
http://www.cleaneverythinginsight.com for more great
products!
```

Two examples of the same message

Figure 10.6

We are pleased to announce the availability of our new cleaning product,

CleansAll.

CleansAll will work miracles on your sinks, tubs, showers, toilets, and tile. Never again will you resort to strong abrasives or steel wool to remove those tough stains or mineral deposits. And as a **special introductory offer,** the coupon shown below may be redeemed for one *free* container of **CleansAll** when you buy one container of this new product at your local retailer.

Try **CleansAll** *today!* You'll be glad you did!

COUPON COUPON COUPON COUPON COUPON COUPON COUPON COUPON

Redeem this special **COUPON** today.

Buy One, Get One Free,

CleansAll.

Coupon registration number 1232456789

And don't forget to visit our Web site at **http://www.cleaneverythinginsight.com** for more great products! Simply click **HERE**.

Figure 10.6   Two examples of the same message (*continued*)

Examine the e-mail message below. List five ways to enhance the message by using html formatting.

> Relieve the stress of today's fast-paced living! Take a moment for just one cup of our delicious, soothing herb tea and the cares and tensions of the day will float away. Sip our Oh-So-Soothing Herb Tea, made with delicate chamomile flowers, and let your mind slip off to a peaceful meadow or sun-warmed hillside. Look for Oh-So-Soothing Herb Teas at specialty teashops, or order direct from our Web site.

Sending Links, Attachments, and Web Pages

E-mail offers several options for sending information beyond a message's text. The most popular are (1) links in the message that connect to Web pages with more information, and (2) photos and other files attached for the recipient to download and open.

MESSAGES WITH LINKS

Sending links to more information on the Web is very easy and quick—for you and for the recipient. To send a link, simply type the entire URL (as in http://www.koelzer.com/marketingtips.htm) into the body of the e-mail. A few older versions of e-mail programs will not read these URLs as active, clickable links, but most will.

If your team or company has posted detailed product information or the specifics of a special offer, for example, your e-mail message can be brief. The recipient will be able to click on the link to access the additional information.

Another useful way to serve a customer or prospect is to send helpful, relevant links to other sites. Such actions show that you know something about this person's industry and that you want to be helpful. Assume that you have clients who are interested in converting an old bank building into a restaurant. Some things you could send include:

- Links to sites containing general information on the pros and cons of using certain types of furniture in certain types of fast-food restaurants

- Links to sites with articles describing state-of-the-art ideas on how to configure restaurant cooking areas for maximum efficiency

- Links to information on the latest cleaning and maintenance techniques for back bar areas, cooking modules, refrigerators, floors, walls, etc.

- Links to the sites of manufacturers of the products that you carry as a distributor

TIP!	**E-MAIL BY VOICE**

Can't keyboard (type) well and don't want to learn? Voice-based alternatives are becoming increasingly bug-free, although some still require fairly new and fast computer equipment (see http://www.dragonsys.com for an example). The manufacturers of Dragon's Naturally-Speaking programs provide ways to *speech enable* many computer tasks.

Eudora products from Qualcomm have integrated voice e-mail into the regular e-mail program, so Eudora users have the choice of using character or voice to create messages (http://www.eudora.com).

ATTACHMENTS

You can save time and deliver critical information quickly by sending photos, charts or graphs, documents, spreadsheets, or other files as attachments to e-mail messages. Exercise caution, however, since some e-mail services will not accept or process attachments. Others allow the user to download the attachment, but inexperienced users may not know where to find the material they have downloaded or how to view it. Be sure that your recipients' e-mail program can handle your attachments easily in order to avoid frustration and bad feelings.

Avoid attaching large files that will significantly increase the time your contact spends downloading the message. How can you be sure you are not sending an attachment that is too large? One way is to send it to yourself first and see how long it takes to retrieve it. But remember that the recipient's computer, modem, or connection might not be as fast as yours.

To send an attachment, open a message composition window or click on Reply or Forward from an existing message. Click on the Attach button or the button showing a graphic of a paper clip. This will open a directory window from which you may select the file you wish to attach. Of course this means you must know what name you assigned the file and where you stored it. Click on the file once to select it and then click on the Open or Attach This File button. Notice that clicking on the Open button does not actually open the file; it simply attaches it to the e-mail. You may attach several files to one e-mail, but if you attach too many or files that are too large, the recipient's e-mail service (or yours) might refuse to process the message.

The key to sending attachments is *compatibility between the type of file that is sent and the programs available on the recipient's computer.* Valuable time and opportunity can be lost by spending time creating a handsome report in a format that the recipient cannot open. Efforts can also be wasted enhancing a terrific photograph and saving it in a format that the recipient cannot see.

Almost all users can see images that are .jpg or .gif files because these files are compatible with Internet browsers. If you send another type of image file, be sure the recipient has a program that will allow them to display your image.

Similarly, if you wish to send a Microsoft Excel file, determine that the recipient has the Microsoft Excel program. Even if they do not have Excel, most spreadsheet programs allow users to export the information to a file format that the recipient can open.

Sometimes a user can open a document, but will display it with poor line breaks, poor page breaks, misaligned images, and other visual problems because the receiving computer does not have fonts to match the ones used in the original document. One solution is the use of PDF files. *PDF* stands for portable document format, and the program that reads them is Adobe's Acrobat. Anyone, regardless of their computer platform—Mac, PC, UNIX, etc.—can download and install the Acrobat reader program for free from http://www.acrobat.com or http://www.adobe. com/products/acrobat/main.html. The free program is the *reader*. You must purchase the full program (or another Adobe product that includes it) if you want to *create* PDF files. The full Acrobat program converts many types of documents, complete with images and tables, to PDF files. In most cases, the fonts are embedded inside the PDF file so that, when the file opens, the document looks the way its maker intended it to look.

SENDING A WEB PAGE BY E-MAIL

This function is probably most useful for small businesses or individual professionals. If you are using a Netscape Navigator browser 3.0 or newer, try the File/SendPage or File/MailPage function. Sometimes the choice will be File/SendFrame, depending on the type of site you are visiting.

In Microsoft's Internet Explorer, the function is Send Page. What's so great about this function? You can send an entire Web page, graphics included, right from your browser. If you find a particular Web page of interest to one of your customers or prospective customers, just click on File and then on Send Page. Your e-mail program will open so that you can enter the person's e-mail address and a note, and then send the page. Or use a similar function, this time in the following order: File>Send>then choose, Link by E-mail or Send Link to send only a link in the e-mail message to direct the recipient to the site you found.

Imagine that, while you are surfing the Web, you find a railroad history site that looks interesting and remember that your purchasing agent customer, Susan, is a railroad history buff. So you send her a message about it. When Susan opens her e-mail, there's the railroad history page, or a link to it, waiting for her. She won't even have to type in the site address . . . another way you can show that you are listening.

Try It   A small business that sells home fixtures for enhancing safety for the elderly or disabled has a large line of rails, handles, ramps, etc. Name three types of useful Web sites that you could include (as links) in an informative e-mail to the company's customers.

Categorizing and Filing E-Mail

Where should you file e-mail messages from visitors to your site or from people who have found you by virtue of your other marketing? Where should you store your replies? In folders and subfolders that your e-mail software lets you create.

To create a folder in most e-mail programs, open the program's File menu, select New Folder from the drop-down menu, and then give the folder a name. In AOL, click on My Files, then select Personal Filing Cabinet from the drop-down menu, then click on Add Folder at the bottom of the Filing Cabinet screen.

To create subfolders, go to the folder you want the subfolders to belong to, right click on it, and then select New Folder from the pop-up menu. When the blank box appears, type in the name of the subfolder. Hit the Enter key or click on OK, and the folder is created. In AOL, highlight the parent folder, then click Add Folder at the bottom of that screen. Type in the name and click on OK. Voila! There's your contact's name in a subfolder. (Don't get carried away with levels of folders. A good guideline is to create no more than three levels.) To file a message, simply just drag it from the inbox to the target category.

Businesses with proprietary e-mail programs or with large sales or customer service departments may have already structured the files for team-members to use. The organization depends to a certain degree on the type of business and on the job of the individual in the company. For example, a sales team responsible for e-mail inquiries about a number of different products might set up an e-mail filing system that organizes the message according to the products for sale. A marketing team that handles responses to promotions might set up folders by promotion name or date. A very small business or an individual might organize folders by clients or prospective clients or past clients. Yet another way to categorize e-mail is according to characteristics of the senders—low, medium, or high frequency purchasers, for example. The advantage to the latter classification is that the information is ready to apply to a new promotion—an e-mail

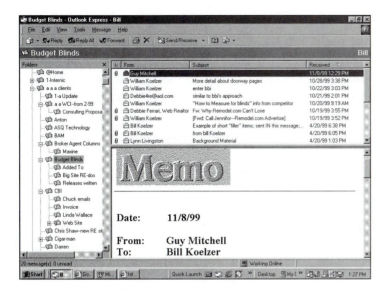

Figure 10.7

Bill's in-box.

announcement enticing low-frequency users to join a rewards program, for example.

Figure 10.7 shows an example of subfolders in an Outlook Express folder called Clients. From the list of messages you can see the importance of using a very specific subject on your e-mail messages—a subject that adequately describes the content of the message.

Make a list of folders and subfolders that would make sense for your business and your e-mail communications.

Try It

E-MAIL ETIQUETTE (*NETIQUETTE*)

1. E-mail isn't really so different from other forms of communication. The primary e-mail guideline is: Always remember that there's a person not just a computer, on the receiving end of your messages. Read and write e-mail accordingly.

2. Be sure to put your name, office, and phone/fax number at the end of each message. Many e-mail programs have an automated signature that does this for you. Why? It's good business communications style, and your name won't show on the From line unless your program is specifically set up to show it. Don't risk having your reader wonder who sent the message!

 Signatures can also be used to add links that might be useful to a recipient who might do business with your firm. For example, you can add links leading to the most current statistics on your industry.

3. Always enter a topic in the subject field. The readers of your e-mail see only your name/ e-mail address and the subject line when they retrieve their mail. Make the subject line work for you. It should encourage the recipient to open your mail. And it helps everyone see at a glance a particular e-mail for which they might be searching. "From Bob" is not a good subject. Better to be specific: "From Bob re: Modified Wiring on the Dialysis 500XKE350."

   Remember, too, that if you hit Reply to someone's e-mail, usually the information that you add to your reply will merit a different subject line than was on the e-mail you received. Thus, "MY Department's Role/Wiring/New Dialysis Machine" may be appropriate.

4. Use upper and lower case when typing in your message. The two reasons for this rule are that (1) USING ALL CAPS IN AN E-MAIL MESSAGE IS CONSIDERED SHOUTING; and (2) MESSAGES TYPED IN ALL CAPS ARE MORE DIFFICULT TO READ BECAUSE THE LETTERS ARE ALL THE SAME HEIGHT.

   Don't make your readers crabby by making your message harder to read! Do use upper-case letters for an occasional word or phrase for EMPHASIS.

5. Read and reread your outgoing messages before sending. If your e-mail program has a spell checker, be sure it is turned on and use it as well! If any of your statements can be taken two ways, one positive and one negative, inevitably the reader will understand it in the negative! Even if you don't believe that's true (although plenty of research shows that it is), don't take the chance.

6. Never, NEVER send e-mail in anger. You may find it difficult to retrieve your message or take back your angry statements after you've cooled off. (And what if you were wrong?) If you catch yourself dashing off an angry note, stop. Leave the room, turn off your computer, go get a snack or a drink, or—if you just can't stop writing—quickly change the address of the recipient to your own, so the message comes back to you. You'll have a chance to reconsider your statements later, when you're calmer.

7. Do use the common abbreviations and symbols that e-mail users like to include, but only if your reader has used them in messages to you first and you're sure your "shorthand" will be understood. Be very cautious because some recipients may consider the use of such symbols frivolous. Often, though, as in-house service people become more familiar with clients, a good deal of friendly banter ensues and perhaps more is exchanged in friendly e-mails than you'd care to know about. Here are a few examples of e-mail shorthand:

BTW	by the way
TTYL	talk to you later
SYL	see you later
:-)	smiley face (Read it sideways.)
;-)	winking ("Just kidding.")
:-X	Don't tell! (Tape over mouth.)

Naturally, college kids have invented thousands of these! Many are shown at http://www. pb.org/emoticon.html.

8. Include your e-mail and Web site addresses at the bottom of each e-mail message. Use your program's automatic signature to add your contact information.

9. Use extreme care when selecting who will receive a copy (cc) or blind copy (bcc) of an e-mail. Why? Because the message will display the e-mail addresses of all those you designated to receive a cc. It will not display the e-mail addresses of all those whom you designated to receive a blind copy. Listing someone as a cc (will display) when they should have been listed as a bcc (will not display) can sometimes prove embarrassing.

Enjoy using e-mail. It's a powerful, speedy, easy-to-use communication tool.

Summary

Use e-mail and e-mail tools to their greatest advantage. Links to additional information on the business's Web site or other pertinent sites on the Internet can be very helpful in getting recipients to interact with your information. Attached images or documents can also be useful, but be sure to send files that the recipient can open and that are not too large for their e-mail service to process.

Review Questions

1. Name three non-Web-based e-mail programs.
2. What is a disadvantage of Web-based e-mail?
3. What are the purposes of the fields next to the To, Cc, and Bcc labels in an outgoing e-mail message?
4. What is the meaning of Reply All?
5. Why might it be better to quote only a few lines of a long incoming message rather than quoting the entire message?
6. What is the difference between a plain text message and one formatted in html?
7. How do you include a link to a Web page in an e-mail message?
8. List the steps involved in sending an attachment with an e-mail message.
9. Why is it important to organize and file e-mail messages?
10. Explain how to move a message from one folder to another.

Composing E-Mail

Think of the Internet as a global conversation. In order to be successful on the Internet, companies must be part of that conversation. At some point in the not-too-distant future, we'll tune in to the Web and listen to a cacophony of human voices, or just several voices, or just one. We'll experience live Web meetings and feel as though we're sitting in the same room and at the same table with colleagues, worldwide sales staff, or clients. Scary? Maybe. Thrilling? Definitely. Before that happens, a lot of e-mail will be entirely e-voice. Meanwhile, however, you need to generate and respond to written e-mail.

Not all salespeople or customer service representatives or marketing assistants or independent professionals are great writers. Some are; some aren't. Some people who are great at talking to people on the phone seem reluctant to write an e-mail message longer than a few lines. Do you?

Many printed and online forms today simply ask for a checkmark in a box. But e-mail on a one-to-one basis is different. To answer a customer's e-mail inquiry adequately, at least a few short paragraphs are needed. Although composing e-mail may seem difficult to some people, it is becoming increasingly necessary to do it well. If your business can't communicate well with its clients and prospective clients, another business will. A single e-mail message may be all a recipient has for evaluating the knowledge, attitude, and professionalism of the sender. So writing skills count!

Some smaller firms assign team members with good writing skills to respond to incoming e-mails, and assign others to telephones. Other firms outsource the entire customer relationship management function or automate it internally using sophisticated software. Some managers scribble out the gist of a message and then ask a more grammar-wise team member to construct the final version.

If your writing skills are not at the level they should be, draft your messages and let someone who is better with words help you polish them. Follow model business letters, changing the facts to suit your intended message. Take a writing class. Meanwhile, review the writing tips in the next section.

This chapter will help you prepare effective e-mail messages related to marketing. "The Basics" sets out a list of tips for writing clear, unambiguous messages. "Beyond the Basics" provides you with a simple process that will assure that your messages are appropriate for your audience, cover sufficient information, and are as effective as possible. Sample e-mail messages are included to illustrate the key points and provide examples of types of e-mail messages.

THE BASICS

Communicating by E-Mail

Effective e-mail communications don't just happen. They require some thought about the audience, the purpose of the message, and what the message should include to accomplish that purpose. The following short list of steps and tips will help you write clear, unambiguous e-mail messages that will not be misunderstood—and that will help you get the results you want.

1. Plan. Know your purpose. Are you making a complaint or answering one? Are you trying to stimulate trials of a product? Are you providing facts and figures in response to an inquiry?

2. Plan. Know your audience. The amount of background information or detail you provide should be appropriate for the recipient. Provide sufficient information to enable the recipient to do what you want him or her to do. But don't provide information the recipient already has; that can be interpreted as being condescending. Knowing your audience will help you use an appropriate tone or level of formality. Do the buyers of your products or services tend to be rather formal? Do you know them on a first-name basis? The rule of thumb here is: when in doubt, follow the same business correspondence style that you would use for a printed letter.

3. Use short sentences. Reword sentences that are too long into two sentences. Use a simple, active subject-verb-object sentence structure when

possible—more like Hemingway than Shakespeare. Short sentences are easier for most readers to absorb and remember.

4. Use plain language—clear words that your reader can relate to. Look for terms that could be misunderstood and replace them or provide an explanation.

5. Eliminate phrases that could be interpreted as sarcastic, egocentric, critical, and so forth. A sentence that sounds fine when spoken may lose its intended effect when read by a recipient.

6. Use short paragraphs and skip a line between paragraphs to make the message easier to read and to emphasize main points.

7. State clearly what you want the recipient to *do!* Answer a question? Visit a Web site? Give you an opinion? (Don't assume that sending someone a list of facts will lead them to take action!)

8. Avoid long, involved descriptions and explanations. Send detailed information as an attachment or post it to a Web site and send the link.

9. Use "you," "your," or the person's name.

10. Read what you write! Always check all e-mail addresses and Web site addresses. Incorrect Web addresses are unreachable and will irritate your contacts. Until you gain experience, read each e-mail message aloud to yourself before you send it. This technique will help you identify statements or phrases that are vague or that could be misinterpreted.

BEYOND THE BASICS

Answer Promptly: Quick Follow-Up Says "Good Service" to Customers

When you receive e-mail and responses, follow up immediately to make a sale, satisfy a customer need, or move your recipient to whatever action you desire. And *continue* following up. Most sales are not made in the first contact, but rather through follow-up. The importance of following up is made clear in these statistics from the Association of Professional Salesmen and the National Sales Executive Association:

2% of sales are made on the first contact
3% of sales are made on the second contact
5% of sales are made on the third contact
10% of sales are made on the fourth contact
80% of sales are made on the fifth to twelfth contact

Obviously, firms that market online using one-time mass e-mailings will probably have only limited success. Help prospects reach a decision by presenting a viable, useful possibility that they might not have considered before. Follow up quickly on inquiries—even if you think you answered a question previously! Use every reasonable opportunity to provide information or service.

Plan Ahead

For decades, IBM printed the word THINK on its employee communications, on notepads, memos, sales reports—everything that its people read. This watchword applies nowhere better than to your communications, especially e-mail. Why especially e-mail? Because we are becoming so accustomed to the speed and conversational style of e-mail that some of the planning we use for letters, reports, proposals, and other communications isn't always applied.

The basic planning of e-mail is simple. Answer these questions:

1. To whom am I writing and what do they already know?

2. Why am I writing?

3. What do I want the reader to do?

4. What information do I need to give the reader that will improve the likelihood of their taking the desired course of action?

TO WHOM AM I WRITING?

Sounds simple, doesn't it? But sometimes there's a little more to it than knowing a person's name. Knowing the intended reader of a message may mean understanding their business culture, position or rank, product or service needs, likes and dislikes, priorities, financial resources, time pressures, responsibilities, authority, preferences, and more.

Assume that you work for a pharmaceutical company that has just received government approval for a new drug used to treat migraine headaches. You receive messages asking for more information about the drug. One is from a neurologist who specializes in treating migraines; one is from your company's advertising agency, which wants to promote the benefits of this drug to consumers; one is from a migraine sufferer who has "tried everything else under the sun." Will your response be the same to all three? Probably not, because each person has different needs and knowledge. To the neurologist, you might send detailed research reports on the drug's chemical properties, side effects, and effectiveness. To the advertising agency you might send a description of the primary benefits of the drug: what makes it better than other treatments, who stands to benefit the most from its use, and any disclaimers or warnings required by law.

And you might direct the migraine sufferer to general information that is available on the company Web site, or to a physician.

If you or your work team has been assigned the task of writing a message or messages for an e-mail marketing campaign, you will probably be writing to the audience you identified in Chapter 2, or some specific segment of that audience. Perhaps you are targeting only the people who visited your Web site and opted in for product updates; or purchasers of your basic product who are now eligible for a discount on the advanced, custom, or upgraded model; or customers who have made online purchases from your company's Web site at least twice in the past six months, . . . the possibilities are myriad.

1. What type of readers do you write to most frequently? Name three things you know about them that affect their decisions.
2. Assume that you work for Lou Burton Company, a designer and manufacturer of outdoor clothing. Burton sells its clothing through sporting goods stores that specialize in fishing and hunting gear. Your boss has asked you to write a message to your clients, the buyers who decide what clothing to carry in their stores. Name three things that would be important to those buyers.

Try It

WHY AM I WRITING?

Your purpose in writing a message may be determined in part by your profession, the type of company you work for, or the type of job you do. Product-marketing assistants for example, may write surveys to evaluate customer satisfaction, or send product updates to distributors nationwide, or prepare announcements about new campaigns to local offices or sales representatives. Technical support persons for a software program may write to help guide users experiencing difficulty with their company's product. Sellers of antiques and collectibles may write messages describing the characteristics and condition of items displayed on their Web site or in local classified ads. Workers in a tax accounting service may write messages asking for additional information or data, or telling inquirers about the background and expertise of the accountants in the firm.

WHAT DO I WANT THE READER TO DO?

Isn't this the same question as "Why am I writing?" Sometimes, yes. But, especially for marketing, it serves as a reminder that you want people to do something besides simply reading a message to gather information. Perhaps you want to answer some questions or provide updated information—both valid purposes. But you may *also* want the reader to forward the message to someone else, reply to it, confirm a meeting, send you a fax, print out the message, complete a survey, click on a link for more information or to register for something or to reserve or order something.

The long-standing "rule" of direct response marketing is to ask recipients to take some action. This rule applies to e-mail just as much as to direct mail or other media. Indeed, the additional options of linking to the Web to carry out other functions make e-mail the direct response marketer's dream. Be sure that your message asks the reader to take a particular action. Don't let your recipients wonder, "Now, why did they send me this message?"

Try It   Assume that your boss has asked you to review a message she wrote to inform customers about a new e-book. Her message describes the e-book and says that it is now available for $19.95. List three actions the message could ask the recipients of the e-mail to take.

WHAT INFORMATION SHOULD I PROVIDE?

The general answer to this question is: enough information for the reader to make a decision. Too much information may confuse or bore the reader; it can sometimes be interpreted as "talking down" to a reader. Too little information may lead the reader to believe that you are not well informed or that your message is simply not convincing. How do you decide? One way is to provide what you believe to be the minimum information to cover the important points and then include links to plenty of additional information on your Web site. You may wish to provide basic information and ask the reader to contact you personally for more details. Or you may wish to write a brief cover message with a report or other longer document attached.

Read Actively and Respond by Listening

Begin the process of creating effective e-mail by applying a technique known as *listening back*. In e-mail (as in all communication), how well you listen to others is actually more important than what you say to them.

When you get an e-mail message from a potential customer, read the message actively; that is, absorb it and focus on its details. Then listen back: respond to *each and every point* the sender made, leaving nothing out. Listening back assures that (a) your correspondent will know you understood the entire communication, and (b) you won't miss an opportunity to provide service.

Why respond to every point? Why not focus on the main point and disregard the others? Because if you make the judgment that a message writer is more concerned about *one* point than another, you may have judged incorrectly. You may have jumped on one issue or question, missing the point that might be the most important to the sender. Remember the cardinal rule: Never assume! Let's take an example: an e-mail inquiry from a prospect:

Dear (Companyname):

You are, no doubt, familiar with our firm, HotTime Hamburgers, with its 1,500 stores in the Pacific Northwest and Northcentral States. We are seeking additional economical sources for our choice of quality stainless steel kitchen fixtures, including griddles, deep fryers, ovens, reefers, and miscellaneous items for at least 240 units. Work would ideally begin in six weeks.

We are also considering remodeling many of our older units (110) in the motif of their local area. For this effort, we are interested in stylized food service booths, chairs, tables, counters, easy-clean salad bar gondolas, and related items. Since you are an area distributor, we know that you supply many of these items, but we are not sure that your Web site lists all that you can provide. Please tell us which of these items you can supply, what the delivery time would be, a bit about your past work in this product area, and your credit and billing practices. If we like what we see, we will send you an itemized list of what we need. Do not call. Please send the information attached to an e-mail. Thanks for your assistance.

John Prospect

Wowzers! What do you do now? Know what Mr. Prospect wants by "listening" for clues and ways to serve him, just as you would if you met him face to face. From the words used in the example, you can deduce that he probably has the following concerns:

- Ability to handle large volume purchases

- Your track record in his region

- Ability to serve big-order chains

- High quality products

- Ability to work closely with a chain's interior designers

- Ability to provide most of his needs from *one* source—you

- A wide choice of brands, configurations, and materials

- Style and wide choice

- Custom design capability

- Speed of delivery

- Price, but more importantly, value

- Easy-clean surfaces

- A list of similar past customers

- Your credit rating

- Billing terms and conditions

If you wonder how we could "listen" all of these items from the message Mr. John Prospect sent, you may need to practice your active reading. Try to find the information in the message that inspired us to add each point in the list.

Upon receipt of the e-mail message in the example above, the first step in your listening process is to make a list of all the concerns. You will refer to this concerns list—much as you would to an outline—when drafting your reply. Since the list is rather long, you should consider writing a short e-mail cover message and attaching a longer document with the details.

Do not be afraid to e-mail a prospect to ask for more specifics, adding "... so I can better pinpoint the kind of support that I know you want from us." Who can make you wrong for saying that?

Include URLs for sites or Web pages with more information about the topic under discussion. Say, for example, "Besides what I've included here, we've found that the type of chairs that you currently use in your HotTime units in our area can be found in wide variety at our supplier's site at: (Example: http://www.duraformcpi.com/seating.html). But, are these the precise type that you are thinking of for the remodeling?" (Tactics like these show the prospect that you are doing research—doing your homework.)

Try It   Brent is a sales assistant at the Millenium Music Store, which sells new and used instruments. Following is a message received by the store asking about a saxophone that was advertised for sale. Read the inquiry and Brent's response. Which of Brent's points address the customer's concerns? Which points could have been omitted? What did Brent miss?

> Dear Millenium Music:
> Did you sell the old saxophone you advertised Sunday? Is it still on sale for $435? What condition is it in? In the picture it looks as if it might be a C. G. Conn. Is it? Can you tell me more about it? Do you have the original case? I want it for a gift that has to arrive in Canada by Friday. Can you ship it so it gets there on time?
>
> Thanks,
> Allen Meyers
>
> Dear Allen:
> Yes, that terrific old alto saxophone is still available. It is, indeed, made by C. G. Conn. Ltd. The keys have mother of pearl on them, and there's beautiful art-deco-style engraving on it too. Condition is great. Even the silver color is mint: no worn-through places at all. This instrument is large and not good for kids to learn with. Besides, they don't take care of things and would ruin it. It has an old case that is scratched up pretty badly but fits it okay.
>
> That's it.
> Brent

Assume that you have received an e-mail asking if you sell kitchen faucets with built-in water filters. Your company sells three models of such faucets. List three pieces of information that you would include in your reply.

Try It

THE "DO'S" OF EFFECTIVE E-MAIL

1. If you do not have an e-mail account, get one *now.* Select an address that people can remember easily and type without making typos. BrownPipeManufacturinginfo@BrownPipe Manufacturing.com *is not* a good e-mail address; info@Brown.com *is.*

2. Set up different e-mail accounts for different people or divisions or departments rather than having all e-mail come to one address, requiring someone's time to sort and forward. Many smaller firms use "generic" e-mail addresses like the ones shown below:

   info@companyname.com   to answer general consumer or trade questions about the firm

   press@companyname.com   to respond to queries from the media

   sales@companyname.com   for use by the centralized sales department in a small firm

   tech@companyname.com or support@companyname.com   used by technical staff to providing customer service

   or customerservice@companyname.com, reservations@companyname. com, or orders@ companyname.com   for what their names imply.

3. Avoid using free e-mail accounts such as those from Hotmail, Yahoo!, or Bluelight. Such accounts do not help secure your identity and build recognition. Also, recipients may wonder why a successful firm or its personnel uses a free e-mail program. Furthermore, many of these programs limit the size of attachments, which customers (and you) will find annoying. Worse yet, most free e-mail providers display annoying ads on the screen and may attach them to messages you send. Why risk having a competitor's ad appear at the bottom of *your* e-mail message?

4. Check your e-mail regularly. Check it at least six times a day, since timing could be critical. Rapid responses to requests for information or assistance could make the difference in someone's decision about choosing a firm. Timely responses to questions could relieve anxiety and help a transaction go smoothly.

5. Respond to e-mail inquiries immediately, even if only to say, "I'll check into that and get back to you." If you promise to send something by a certain time, be sure that you do so.

6. Write clearly. Avoid sarcasm.

7. Send useful, helpful information in response to inquiries. Listen to what the sender's message said and repeat his or her list of needs or questions in your own words. This shows that you are paying attention and addressing the particular needs or situation.

8. Make two assumptions when drafting e-mail messages to people who have signed your firm's guest book on its Web site or requested more information at a trade show on a reader response card (*bingo card*):

1. that the recipient went there to get information about your products and services; and
2. that you have something of value to write about.

Tell them about new or useful Web pages that the company has added to its site. Tell them the firm has a newsletter they can receive by e-mail. Give them your trade show schedule, or the city-by-city itinerary of the sales or manufacturer's representatives for their territory. Give prospects the addresses of sites where they can get more information on your industry and on theirs. Select links that you think are related to what *they* want to know.

Likewise, take good care of vendors via e-mail. Keep them updated on inventory to avoid last-minute orders that place a burden on them. Send them URLs to sites they might find useful; this is similar to clipping a story from a newspaper to send to a friend.

In short, give everyone who deals in any way with your firm something that they will perceive as useful.

9. Use the signature function of your e-mail program effectively: to list Web sites (usually these can be active links) that will direct the recipient to certain of your pages or to other pages that you would like them to see.

10. Save the e-mail you receive and send. Save everything, including e-mails to or from any party involved with your transactions. Some correspondence may be subject to business or SEC statutes pertaining to required records retention. Also, a complete "paper" trail is critical to dispute resolution should a problem arise. Even the seemingly insignificant items you consider not worth saving at the moment may later prove to be the key that makes a huge difference to you or your customer or your attorney. (See Chapter 10 for more on managing e-mail.)

11. Promote your e-mail address. A rule of thumb: If your phone number is on it, put your e-mail address on it as well. And be sure that your e-mail address is short and easy to remember. Mention it in your outgoing voice mail recording. The easiest addresses for recipients to remember are ones including your name (assuming it is easy to spell) and "at-firmname-dot-com. Spoken, it would be "Thomas at firm name dot com." Enunciate.

If your last name is a tongue twister, use your first name and an initial in return e-mail addresses and voice messages. Instead of Sam Braunschweiger, become SamB@firmname.com. Also, avoid using underscores in e-mail addresses: Sam_B@firmname.com. Once the address is underlined, as in Sam_B@firmname.com, the underscore cannot be discerned easily, resulting in confusion.

The most powerful Internet marketing tool for a firm is neither its Web site nor directory advertising; it's e-mail. Your Web site may be graphically impressive and loaded with information, but what counts ultimately is the direct communication between you and your customers or prospective customers.

Sample Messages

The messages shown below are examples of the most common kinds of e-mail messages that businesses receive and answer. Modify them to fit your own needs and style.

The most important things about responding to customer, client, or prospect are: respond as soon as possible; write so that your recipients feel that you listened to what they said; convey to them that you or your product can do the job, that you care, and that you know how to help.

Advise buyers to visit your Web site, which is packed with hints and tips or frequently asked questions (FAQs), for additional information. Even if your page contains only links to *outside* Web sites that offer related information, your contact will feel that *you* provided all this information. This makes you a real "know-how" company when it comes to serving your contacts by e-mail.

Read through the following sample e-mail messages, making notes about why each bit of information was included or how you might modify it to suit your own purposes.

SAMPLE 1

From a real estate agent to a homebuyer who has e-mailed saying his family is planning to move to the agent's city. In the e-mail to the agent, the buyer gave fairly good criteria for the kind of home he wants. Here's the agent's response:

Dear (name):

Your e-mail was very clear about your desire for a single story, 3-bedroom, 3-bath home from 1,800 to 2,000 square feet with a big backyard, no freeway noise, and an extra-large lot, in the $200,000–$250,000 price range.

Attached is a file with information on seven homes that meet your criteria. Please have a look at the photos and property descriptions and then e-mail me the MLS numbers of the ones you like best. That will help me become clearer on exactly what residential styles and features you like.

Here are a few links to Web sites that have a good deal of information about this area: http://www.bigcitysiteonBedford.com http://www.bigregionsiteonWestchesterPutnam.com

Cordially,

Betty Topagent, GRI, CRS
bet4re@hometown.com
http://www.bet4rehometown.com
555-555-5555 or 555-555-5555.

P.S. And here's a page from my Web site with even more local links:
http://www.bet4rehometown.com/westchesterputnam.html

Comments:

1. The agent repeated the specific desires of the homebuyer so he would see that the agent fully understood his request.

2. The agent attached specific information that addresses the homebuyer's interests.

3. The agent told the homebuyer what she wanted him to do.

4. The agent gave additional resources (links to more information) to address concerns she expects of homebuyers new to the area.

SAMPLE 2

To a customer who visited the products section of your Wood Wise site and asked for more information.

Dear Mrs. Joynes:

You asked for more details on all-weather siding products that can be applied to a screened-in porch that will remain unenclosed during the winter. From what you said, [quote here], the following products will serve your needs—depending on what "look" you like best.

WinterWood #1123
AspenLook #1144
WillowWalk #1156
SpruceHill #1168

These products all share the following features:

Feature One
Feature Two
Feature Three
Price Range of X-Y

Please follow the link http://www.whatever444.com for a detailed comparison of the four products that I've placed there for you. If you would like to see "real" samples, contact Ron Smudley, who is the dealer nearest to you in Billings, Montana. You'll find him at Smudley Building Supplies, 224 College Blvd., Billings, Montana, (zip) Phone: 000-000-0000. Website: http://www.SmudleyBillings.com. E-mail: Smudley@Billings323.com.

Since you are interested in all-weather wood-look siding, you might also want to see our new line of (whatever is related) at http://www.Siding Company456.com. There you'll find full installation tips and hints, links to valuable home exterior protection information, and coupons that will save you considerable money on other home-related products.

Thanks for contacting me. Let me know if I can be of further assistance.

Cordially,

Glen Hammer
Wood Wise Home Improvement Specialist

Comments:

1. Glen referred specifically to the customer's needs.

2. He directed Mrs. Joynes to click on a link for further information.

3. He knows from experience that buyers want to see the "real thing" before deciding, so he provided contact information for the local dealer.

4. He provided additional helpful information that buyers of these products usually require.

SAMPLE 3

Web site complaint. This is the kind of letter that firms get by the hundreds every day. Even the misspellings are typical:

> Dear (Websitename)
> I was just in your website and tried to clik on the free jellybeans and when I did, it wouldn't go there. Is this a ripoff or do I need to do something else to get the jelly beans you sad I could get?
>
> Candyeater.

———————

> Answer:

> Dear Candyeater:
> We are sorry that you could not reach the page on our Web site that offers free jellybeans.
> Please click on this link, which will take you directly to the alternate jellybean page: www.jellybeancompany34.com/samples.
> Everything should work for you this time. And thanks for alerting us. Doing so makes the site work better for everyone.
>
> Milton Sweet
> Director of Customer Services
>
> P.S. Be sure to visit our new Web section on the history of jellybeans at www.jellybeancompany34/beanhistory.htm. There's even a coupon there that you can download for some nifty gift items. You can share it with your friends—just forward this link to them. Or, click HERE.

Comments:

1. Milton was quick to apologize for the inconvenience. Even if the problem was the user rather than the Web site, the apology conveys good business manners and (sometimes) helps calm an irritated visitor. (If you are a technology or software site, however, it may be important to distinguish between your error and customer misunderstanding.)

2. Except for the specific URL cited above, this same answer could apply to various problems that a customer has with a Web site. Companies often write stock answers for the typical e-mails they receive.

3. The e-mail reply provided a quick solution to the problem and told the reader what to do.

4. Milton added a P.S. to encourage Candyeater to visit the site again and use the special offer. He encouraged Candyeater to forward the offer to others, a *viral marketing* approach intended to increase traffic and encourage trials.

5. The paragraphs are short. This makes the e-mail *look* easy to read (and, in fact, it is).

6. The message is not from "The JellyBean Company," but from a real person. This makes the response more "real" and "personal" to the recipient, even though he may suspect that you have 200 people all answering e-mails the same way.

Hint: Here's a candy treat for *you*, Dear Reader. You can get free Jelly Belly brand jelly beans by visiting the firm's web site at http://www.jellybelly.com and clicking on Free Samples in the dropdown menu.

SAMPLE 4
Service complaint.

> Dear Companyname:
> About two weeks ago I ordered a (product) and it has not arrived yet. Was my order lost? Can you check and see if everything is okay? Has it been shipped yet? Please advise. I need this outfit!
>
> Scully
>
> 23456 Round Avenue
> Portland, Michigan 48875

————————————

> *Answer:*
>
> Dear Scully:
> Your order of (insert date) is in our computer and hasn't been lost. We checked the status and here's what we found.
> (Give appropriate explanation. See samples below.)
> The requested product was on backorder when you placed your order. Sadly, the product is *still* on backorder due to such heavy demand for it. We expect to have a new supply on _____, at which time we will immediately ship your order.
> OR

Your order was delayed because (give the reason here) and we now expect that it will be shipped to you on _____. (Or, it was shipped on _____.)

If you would like to modify or cancel your order, or order a different product, please follow this link to our Web site (give URL) and click on Status of my Order to make modifications. Or, if you prefer, simply reply to me now with your instructions.

To apologize for our delay, we have reserved a coupon in your name at (give URL). The coupon is worth $10 off any purchase from the Pre-Season Specials section of the Web site.

Sincerely,

Penelope Wardrobe
Customer Fashion Consultant

Comments:

1. Penelope addressed the problem head on—Scully's order was not lost.

2. She gave Scully information and assurances that the item would reach him.

3. She gave him power to change or cancel his order with relative ease.

4. She gave him an incentive to re-visit the Web site and a $10 discount coupon to promote goodwill.

SAMPLE 5
Service complaint.

Dear (Company):
What's the deal with my order? I ordered that hammer over a week ago and it was supposed to ship in a couple days. . . .

Disappointed,

Clem

Answer:

Dear Clem:
Your order has been located; here are the details.

The product was shipped to you on (date) via _____ and should arrive in several days.

OR

Your order requested a color/size that we do not make. You asked for a left-handed hammer in black, which we have never carried. We carry only natural wood, white, and red.

We have canceled your order and issued a credit to your credit card for the purchase price of $100.00. (You will receive a confirmation of the credit by regular mail.)

You are most welcome to return to our HammerMasters site at (give link) and order a hammer in the color that you prefer.

While you are at the site, take a look at our stunning new titanium-handle ambidextrous hammers. We manufacture them ourselves and, for regular customers like you who have registered at our web site, we are giving an introductory never-before-offered 50% discount.

Would your friends like a similar offer? To send them the offer direct from our Web site and to secure the offer yourself, click HERE.

Cordially,

Piers Plowman
Builder's Consultant
William Langland Corporation

E-Mail Masters

The addition of e-mail communication to a list of daily tasks may seem somewhat daunting at first. With practice, the process goes more quickly. One technique for speeding up the process is to create e-mail masters for various circumstances.

Use the sample messages in this chapter as models or create your own and save them as masters. Once your master e-mail messages are composed and typed, proofread, and spell-checked, save each one to your documents file with a document name that you will remember. Then you'll be able to use these e-mail masters to answer most e-mails and you won't have to type every reply from scratch. Just find and open the appropriate master e-mail message, copy all of it or pertinent portions of it, and paste it into your e-mail message body.

Add information or edit the text in the master so that you are "listening back," and then send it off. Some e-mail programs, such as Eudora or EudoraPro, allow users to save each master as Stationery.

Summary

Simple writing that communicates clearly remains an essential business tool. Like other written communications, e-mail should be composed based on an understanding of the readers' knowledge, needs, and priorities. Writers should be clear about their purpose for writing and about what they want the reader to do.

E-mail should be kept fairly short. Extensive or detailed information can be attached in a separate document or provided on a Web page.

Competent writing counts! A single message may be your only chance to make a positive impression or communicate an important fact or idea.

Review Questions

1. Why is there a greater chance of misunderstanding in e-mail communications than in face-to-face communications?
2. How can you avoid ambiguity or misunderstanding in e-mail messages?
3. Name three things to think about when planning an e-mail message.
4. Why is it preferable to use short sentences?
5. Why should you keep paragraphs short and leave spaces between them?
6. How could reading an e-mail aloud help you improve it?

Answers to Chapter Review Questions

CHAPTER 1

1. What are the four general categories of business Web sites? Company or corporate identity; product or service information; transaction oriented; relationship building

2. Who are the most common audiences for a corporate identity Web site? The employees and investors

3. Are product or service information Web sites built for high-pressure sales? No. They're built to disseminate information and to build awareness and positioning.

4. What feature is typical of a transaction-oriented Web site? It is built to sell products or services online to other businesses and to consumers.

5. What distinguishes a relationship-building site from other sites? A relationship-building site aims to work with its audiences beyond one single sale. It often emphasizes communication to keep clients informed and to learn from clients.

6. In what way is an old-fashioned hardware store similar to a good transaction-oriented site? Both aim to provide personal service and build long-term relationships.

7. List four interactive elements that a Web site can offer visitors. Answers may vary, but possibilities include: chat room, guest book, downloads, surveys/polls, registration for newsletter or other offers

8. Describe how typical C2C auction sites (such as eBay) work. Sellers post items to sell and buyers post bids on them. The highest bidder wins the item, assuming the bid meets a preset minimum amount. The auction site takes a small commission from the seller's credit card account for each item sold.

9. What percentage of online auction bidders have actually purchased something in an online auction? 83 percent

10. List four benefits that portals offer visitors.? Answers may vary, but possibilities include: search engine, Web-based e-mail, forums, shopping

11. In what ways may the data that portals provide not be objective? Portals control what users see and they are supported by advertisers. Therefore, the information they provide may favor their advertisers.

12. Define a *vortal* and describe how it differs from a portal. A vortal focuses on a particular topic. Portals are more general in focus.

13. What purpose might a business have for constructing a vortal? To build visitor traffic and visibility for the business, product, or service; also to demonstrate its expertise in a given field.

CHAPTER 2

The statements listed below are possible answers to the questions at the end of Chapter 2. The idea is important; the exact wording is not.

1. Why should your business distinguish itself from competitors? So customers and clients will have reason to select your products or services over those of your competitors

Answers for questions 2 through 6 will vary, but possibilities might include points such as those given below.

2. What are some ways in which your business is different from your competitors'? We're 20 percent faster. We offer more services (or more products). We deliver. We have more offices throughout this region. We're the largest. We're the oldest.

3. In what ways are your products different from those of your competitors? We offer more colors (or sizes, options, features, etc.)

4. How are your competitors trying to position themselves in the marketplace? They claim to be the people-friendly service provider. They claim to provide the most accurate research.

5. How do your competitors portray their products or services as different or better? They say their juice drink has the most juice. They say their paint covers anything in only one coat. They claim their lightbulbs give 50 percent more hours of illumination.

6. How does your positioning relate to your target audiences? Our target audience is movie video renters, and we are positioned as having the newest titles available first! Our video store is located in a high-tech employment area, so our target audience is fairly young and very technology savvy. We are positioned as having the most videos available on DVD. Our target audience is reptile owners, and we're positioned as the reptile-loving veterinarians.

7. How would you go about defining your target audiences? Build up a description based on information from market research, including demographics, psychographics, purchase behavior, buyer surveys, personal interactions, etc.

8. What is the "human element" that you must always remember when dealing with customers and prospects? Customers and prospects are people. The more you know about how they make decisions—their preferences and priorities—the more likely you will be to communicate messages that work.

9. List three common goals of most Web sites. To educate their customers/clients; to increase orders from existing customers; to get new customers

10. List three common Web site mistakes. Lack of clearly defined goal(s) for the Web site; lack of a clear message or direction for visitors; insufficient budget for launching or promoting the site

11. When planning a site, should people brainstorm together or by themselves? Brainstorming together increases the chances that various possibilities will be explored.

12. Why is it important to budget adequately for Web site promotion? Because a great Web site that nobody finds is not useful

13. What is *branding*? A clear, well-recognized position that your company, product, or service occupies in the minds of your audience; the features and benefits that the audience associates with the company, product, or service

14. What positioning has Maytag always sought (and achieved) for its products? Reliability.

15. What is a "lookie-me" Web site? A site that tells visitors about how wonderful the company or product is without providing useful or distinctive information or functions; an "ego" site.

16. What does a unique marketing position statement accomplish? It declares clearly how the product (or service or company) distinguishes itself.

17. Why are secondary target audiences important? They refer customers or clients.

18. Name your firm's secondary target audiences in order of importance. The answer depends entirely on your type of company, but see pages 41-43 for examples.

19. How will your Web site attract secondary target audiences? By including content and links to content that are of interest or importance to them; by promoting the site in places on the Web that are frequented by members of that audience.

20. Why do you suppose Jello chose Bill Cosby as its ad spokesman? Perhaps because linking Bill Cosby, a well-known comedian and head-of-family symbol, to Jello identifies or lends credibility to Jello as a fun family food.

CHAPTER 3

1. What features are common to many business Web sites? Description of the business and its history, its products and/or services, the employees, and information on how to contact the company

2. Name a few companies or products whose branding is so strong that they probably do not need a tagline to communicate it? Answers will vary, but might include IBM®, Kleenex®, McDonald®'s, Timex®, or Polaroid®.

3. Is it more important to talk about a firm's annual sales or about the visitors' interests? A firm's annual sales might be important for a few companies or certain select visitors, but in general Web sites should address visitors' interests.

4. How does the Web site for Lincoln automobiles communicate the product's positioning? It uses the word *luxury* as headline; it uses graphics that communicate the message of luxury.

5. What is the primary function of the headline of a Web site? To communicate the market positioning

6. What types of information should you expect to find on a corporate Web site? Information about the company history, news, management, franchises, subsidiaries, divisions, job opportunities, financial health, product/service lines, people.

7. How does the Lipitor Web site help Pfizer sell the product with no on-line selling? In four ways: (1) increasing brand awareness; (2) building the public's confidence in Pfizer and Lipitor; (3) increasing the degree to which people are accustomed to the idea of taking a drug for cholesterol; (4) repeatedly telling Web visitors to have their cholesterol levels checked and to ask their doctor about Lipitor.

8. What does a hot red background communicate about a product? Energy, excitement, thrills

9. What characteristics does including a company's 60-year history communicate to visitors? Stability, experience, reliability

10. What does including information about a firm's employees add to a Web site? The message that the company values its people, its human aspects; the message that the company understands that most people still want to deal with people

11. Why does a Budget Blinds franchisee's Web page appear to have more content than it really does? The franchisee Web sites display the corporate product information seamlessly.

12. Name three types of services or service-based companies that use Internet marketing extensively. Possibilities include banks and other financial institutions; travel-related businesses; shipping firms.

13. How can testimonials improve a Web site's effectiveness? By communicating the positive perceptions of clients and customers who appreciate the product or service's features, benefits, and positioning.

14. How do small antique and collectible dealers achieve some of the advantages of large businesses on the Web? By participating in Web malls.

15. What does a site's *stickiness* refer to? How long it keeps visitors engaged and how often they return

16. What factors help make a site more sticky? Specialty information; related tips; content that changes regularly; interactive functions such as surveys, puzzles, and polls

17. What types of content would you consider adding to a site that sells collectible California pottery? Answers will vary, but possibilities include history of pottery, types of clay, glazes, history of the potters, history of the artists, today's values, photos.

18. Why are some Web masters opposed to having links to outside sites? Because the links will take visitors away from the site, possibly never to return.

CHAPTER 4

1. Name three types of interactive Internet functions related to marketing and/or selling. Answers will vary, but may include such functions as interactive catalogs, order forms, shopping carts, downloads, teleconferencing, live chat, Webcasts.

2. What are the three primary components of an interactive Web catalog? Product browsing or search function (front end), database (back end), order mechanism (form, shopping cart, etc.)

3. Why would industrial firms making many, many products benefit from having an interactive Web catalog? An interactive Web catalog that allows users to search a large number of products will save the company sales representative and/or customer service rep time, will save possible catalog printing costs, and will give users easy access to all the products and their variations.

4. What does the "front end" of a shopping cart generally refer to? The browsing and searching functions that the Web visitor uses to find items.

5. What does the "back end" of a shopping cart generally refer to? The database that contains all the product images, descriptions, prices, etc.

6. What steps are involved in purchasing an item using an online shopping cart? Find the item with the front end, place it in the shopping cart, and check out by providing shipping and payment information.

7. How can publishing an online e-book and offering it as a free download help achieve a firm's marketing goals? Some possibilities include: may capture user e-mail addresses for future marketing; may provide incentive to buy the firm's products or use its services; may help differentiate the firm's product or pricing from competitors'; may keep the firm's name in front of the user for an extended period of time.

8. What is the function of PayPal.com? To give Web users the capability of purchasing an item online without giving various sellers a credit card number.

9. How can a small shop benefit from selling in an online catalog, considering the cost of an entire shopping cart system and all its programming? By participating in a "mall."

10. How can offering an item on an auction site such as eBay be considered a promotional activity? The item description in the auction can include information on the firm, the quality or variety of its products, locations, phone numbers, e-mail address(es), and—importantly—links to its Web site(s).

11. What dollar volume did eMarketer project for online auctions in year 2002? $12.1 billion

12. Why would you want to add human click to a Web site? To give users the ability to communicate in real time with a live person at your company.

13. List some costs that can be saved by using Webcasting rather than in-person meetings. travel, accommodations, meals, conference facilities, time spent away from the workplace

14. What is an *opt-in newsletter*? One that is sent only to users who request it.

CHAPTER 5

1. What is the most important criterion for Web site organization? Ease of navigation

2. What five general criteria are key to a Web site's accomplishment of its goals? It should reflect the market positioning, stand out from competitors' sites, be consistent from page to page, have clear navigation, and be interesting and colorful.

3. List three rules of effective Web site organization. The main page should have clear means for visitors to begin exploring the site. Directions for navigation should be clear and specific. The number of "layers" should be limited so users can find what they seek with only a few clicks.

4. Name three features that can help make a site's entry page look inviting. Good use of white space; a headline to tell visitors the purpose and positioning of the site; subheads or button links.

5. What sort of look 'n' feel would you expect a site selling expensive tropical fish and related equipment to have? Answers will vary, but might indicate blues and greens for water and aquarium plants with splashes of bright, rich color, probably on the fish; might include photos of large high-end aquariums, possibly in public places.

6. Why is an attractive site less important than one that addresses a firm's goals? A pretty site that doesn't address the firm's goals cannot accomplish the company's marketing goals.

7. Why is it useful for a site to be different from those of competitors? To help visitors develop a sense of the identity, features, and benefits of the company, product, or service; to help achieve recognition and awareness of your company, product, or service

8. Why should all pages in a Web site have some element that is consistent? So visitors are always aware that they are on that particular site; to increase visitors' recognition of the site.

9. Is it better to guide visitors carefully from page 1 through page 45 of a site or to let them go wherever they wish? Why? Visitors should be able to work their way through a site in whatever way suits them. They should not have to take the longest path to the information or function they're seeking.

10. Why does a Web page need to be *directive*? So visitors do not have to wonder about how to get to the information or function they seek or that you want them to find

11. Why is it better to use smaller images than larger ones? Images with a smaller file size load faster and avoid trying visitors' patience.

12. Why does a Web page need white space? To avoid looking cluttered or crowded; to help visitors see the content and navigation more easily.

13. What is the purpose of a site's headline? To communicate immediately the positioning of a company, product, or service, as well as the purpose of the site.

14. Why is it good to avoid gaudy *splash pages* and rich media effects on home pages? Some users with older browsers or slower Internet access may not be able to view the page or may become irritated waiting for it to display.

15. What are the dangers of a cluttered Web page? Visitors may not find what they are looking for and may leave.

16. Why should lines of text not fill the entire width of the monitor? Line lengths of 5 inches or less are easier to read.

17. Why is it important to ask visitors to *bookmark* a site? To increase the likelihood that they will return.

18. What is one advantage of using *framed* Web sites? Most framed sites put a navigation bar in one of the frames so visitors can always find their way to another section of the site.

19. What do the colors yellow, red, and orange usually communicate? warmth, energy

20. Give an example of mapping links to a graphic. (There are many possible answers.) A map of the United States with the area of each state linked to information about that state; a picture of a room with the furniture, carpet, windows, and other features linked to decorating ideas or suppliers of those items

CHAPTER 6

1. What type of site is used most frequently to find Internet Information? A portal

2. What two sources do people use most frequently to find Web data? Search engines and links

3. List similarities and differences between a vortal and a portal. A vortal is similar to a portal in that it is a launching point to find data. It is unlike a portal in that it contains data on only one subject.

4. A directory is similar to what printed publication found in most homes? Yellow Pages

5. Can a portal include one or more search engines? Why is this good? Yes. This is good because engines help people find information—and that's a portal's job.

6. What kind of tool for finding information employs humans to categorize sites? A directory

7. How does a search engine's *spider* or *robot* work? It scours the Web to find data that matches a searcher's request.

8. Does the Web currently have millions or trillions of Web pages? - trillions

9. Why is it important for a company that markets locally to include its city in its metatags? So that people searching for that company's product(s) in a given city will see the site.

10. Name two directories that your company should be listed in. Yahoo!, Open Directory Project, Looksmart, Galaxy

11. Why must one be especially careful when entering a URL into Yahoo!? Because a typographical error can take a very long time to correct

12. Is Excite.com a search engine, a directory, a portal, or all three? All three, but it acts primarily as a portal.

13. How does having many links pointing to your site give your company more recognition on search engines? Some search engines rank sites based on how many links point to them.

14. What does a meta-search engine do? Searches other search engines for results.

15. Why is it important to correct typos when adding your URL to sites? A mistake will cause your site not to be included.

CHAPTER 7

1. Why do site owners need to advertise their advertising? Even a terrific site is worthless without visitors, so site owners need to assure that their target audience learns of the site and accesses it.

2. What percentage of online small businesses gain sales from their local area? 48 percent

3. Describe the difference between a *listing* and an *enhanced listing*. A listing provides a company name and possibly an address, phone number, and e-mail address. An enhanced listing has additional features, such as an active link to a Web site, a tagline, boldface type, and descriptive text.

4. Name two objectives of banner ads. Build recognition and generate site visits (click-throughs)

5. What percentage of people who see banners actually click on them? Less than one percent

6. Give two examples of *specialty sites*. Answers will vary. Possibilities include garden.com, realtor.com, epicurion.com, and seafood.com.

7. Name one disadvantage of exchanging banners with other sites. Answers will vary. Possibilities include slowing the display of a Web page on the visitor's browser and the potential for enticing a visitor away to another site.

8. What kind of search engine is Overture.com? A bid-for-position search engine

9. What is the difference between CPC and CPM? CPC refers to "cost per click"; that is, you pay only when someone actually clicks on the link leading to your site. CPM refers to "cost per thousand" impressions; that is, you pay each time a user sees the page your ad is on, whether or not that user clicks on the link to go to your site.

10. Explain how context-based presentation of banners or tile ads works. The banner or tile ad appears only to visitors who have searched for certain related keywords, purchased certain related items, or visited certain related Web pages.

11. How do standard banner sizes make planning of online advertising easier? Standard banner sizes help advertisers compare prices for banner and tile ads. They may also reduce the number of banner or tile designs a company needs to create for various placements.

12. Is the price of advertising that reaches a carefully defined target audience higher or lower than advertising to a larger but more general audience? Higher

13. Why does an ad on a page that is five clicks away from a home page cost less? Fewer users will see the ad.

14. Why is it worthwhile to advertise on Web sites of internet service providers? ISPs often have local or regional traffic. Sometimes they build this traffic by providing their customers with a personal home page portal that displays each time the customer connects to the Internet.

15. Do people use search engines or links more often to find pages on the Web? Links are used more often than search engines, but only by a small margin.

16. Why is it usually not worth creating an affiliation to sell products of another firm on a business site? Answers will vary, but, like banner exchanges, affiliate icons slow the page loading and entice visitors away from the hosting site.

CHAPTER 8

1. What is "good performance publicly appreciated"? A definition of *public relations*

2. What does *newsworthy* mean in the context of public relations? Facts that are timely, interesting, or educational to the audience that receives them

3. Why would a golf equipment manufacturer want to show 360-degree views of golf courses on its Web site? To bring golfers, the target audience for golf equipment, to the site.

4. Which is better remembered, an ad or an editorial item? An editorial item

5. What is the most common type of business press release? Announcement of new products or services

6. Why is a case history describing a problem solved by the use of your products or services a powerful marketing tool? Such case histories

can help position a firm as an industry leader, an authority on solving customer problems, a company that understands its customers' needs.

7. Why does an audience give you more credibility when they read a favorable article about your firm or its products? Articles by another author are generally viewed as being more objective than one by the subject company.

8. Why is it easier to get publicity into local media than into national media? Often local media have fewer resources for obtaining content and welcome new material.

9. What is meant by a story's "angle" or "hook"? The fact or interpretation that will interest the audience—that will motivate the audience to read the article or go to the Web site to get more information

10. Are newsgroups time consuming, or do they save you time? They probably take up more of your time than they're worth.

11. Is advertising encouraged in usegroup postings? No. In fact, blatant commercials will receive a negative reaction.

12. How does a Web site's guest book work? What benefits can it offer a company? Visitors leave comments that are displayed with previous entries. Good comments can add to a company's (or product or service's) credibility.

13. Name two services that Web site owners can provide to your firm. Answers may vary. Possibilities include: increase your visibility with links or banners; keep you advised of advertising opportunities; refer related inquiries to you.

14. What should appear on your business cards, fliers, brochures, e-mails, newsletters—basically on everything that your company publishes about itself? Web address, e-mail address, and your unique positioning statement or brand

15. Why should you offer specific reasons for your audiences to visit your site? To give them a strong reason to do so

16. How can adding humorous or lighthearted content improve your Web site? It can relieve the seriousness or the monotony of boring text.

17. What is the value of displaying your URL and a tagline on your firm's vehicles? Visibility to the local target audience(s)

18. What is meant by offering something valuable *to the audience at hand*? Tailor the message to the audience that will be sure to see or hear it

19. Why would you announce a special new edition of Web site content to your audiences? To give them a specific reason to visit or re-visit the site

20. Name two things that you can learn about your Web site visitors from the site's traffic statistics. Answers may vary. Possibilities include:

number of visitors, number of repeat visits, time spent on various pages in the site, path of travel through the site, point at which visitors entered and where they entered from, geographic location of visitors, browser they use

CHAPTER 9

1. List three goals of e-mail marketing. Answers may vary. Possibilities include: acquire new customers, retain existing customers, increase sales from existing customers, build brand awareness, reinforce positioning, gather data.

2. Why should e-mail marketing be directed toward specific groups of customers or potential customers? Targeting specific audiences is more effective than the shotgun approach because messages can be tailored according to audience and goals.

3. Define the *recency* of a list. The age of a list or how recently it has been updated. Older lists have more addresses that do not function or that users do not access.

4. Name four sources of e-mail addresses that are preferable to buying or renting one from a print magazine subscription list. Correspondence with customers, product registration cards, order forms (on- and offline), guest book entries, and e-mail inquiries

5. Why is an opt-in newsletter or product update service a good source of e-mail addresses? This strategy targets users who self-select themselves to receive the e-mails, obtains the *permission* of the recipients for the e-mailings, and limits sending of unwanted spam (junk e-mail).

6. Name three types of content that a business might include in e-mail marketing. Answers will vary. Possibilities include: product/service/ company announcements; press releases, newsletters; product or other tips, surveys, sales/specials; Web site updates.

7. Define *double opt-in permission.* Opt-in clients or prospects confirm by e-mail or Web page that they did, indeed, opt in.

8. What is "The Permission Rule"? Never send unsolicited e-mail messages. Always get the permission of a recipient before e-mailing anything.

9. List three types of information you might wish to store in a database about your opt-in e-mail recipients? Answers will vary. Possibilities include: whether the recipient purchased from you, requested more information about a specific product or service, requested a print catalog, did not respond at all.

10. What does an autoresponder do? An autoresponder sends prepared e-mail messages in response to (a) a user's request from a Web site; or (b) an e-mail to a particular address.

CHAPTER 10

1. Name three non-Web-based e-mail programs. Eudora®, Communicator®, Outlook®

2. What is a disadvantage of Web-based e-mail? Possible answers include: advertising; slowness; unbusinesslike impression

3. What are the purposes of the fields next to the To, Cc, and Bcc labels in an outgoing e-mail message? The To field is for the recipients e-mail address. The Cc field is for the e-mail address(es) of persons who will receive a copy of the message. The Bcc field is for the e-mail addresses of persons who will receive a copy of the message but whose address will not appear to the other recipients.

4. What is the meaning of Reply All? Reply All refers to sending a response to a message to everyone listed in the To and Cc fields on the original message.

5. Why might it be better to quote only a few lines of a long incoming message rather than quoting the entire message? Quoting a few relevant lines gives the reader the information needed to understand the context of your message without having to read or download a very long message.

6. What is the difference between a plain text message and one formatted in html? A message formatted in html can use various fonts, colors, images, links, etc. Plain messages contain only text. Plain messages load more quickly.

7. How do you include a link to a Web page in an e-mail message? Use the File/Send Link function of your browser or type the entire and exact URL of the link you wish to include in the body of your message.

8. List the steps involved in sending an attachment with an e-mail message.
   - Open a message composition window or click on Reply or Forward from an existing message.
   - Click on the Attach button or the button that has a graphic of a paper clip on it.
   - From the directory window that opens, select the file you wish to attach.
   - Click on the file once to select it.
   - Click on the Open or Attach this File button.

9. Why is it important to organize and file e-mail messages? E-mail messages accumulate quickly. A great deal of time can be wasted searching for a particular message if they're all left in the main inbox.

10. Explain how to move a message from one folder to another? Drag and drop.

CHAPTER 11

1. Why is there a greater chance of misunderstanding in e-mail communications than in face-to-face communications? Face-to-face communications provide tone-of-voice cues, facial expressions, and body language to help listeners understand the message. Written communications do not provide these cues.

2. How can you avoid ambiguity or misunderstanding in e-mail messages? Plan carefully, use straightforward language, write short sentences, read what you've written aloud, and avoid sarcasm.

3. Name three things to think about when planning an e-mail message. Your relationship to your audience, what your audience already knows, your purpose in writing.

4. Why is it preferable to use short sentences? Short sentences are easier for most readers to absorb and remember.

5. Why should you keep paragraphs short and leave spaces between them? To make the message easier to read and to emphasize main points

6. How could reading an e-mail aloud help you improve it? You may hear statements or phrases that are vague or that could be misinterpreted.

Appendix A
Create an Internet
Marketing Action Plan

STARTING A PLAN

Your Internet marketing plan can be developed in concert with your existing (or new) business marketing plan. The two plans will probably share many of the same goals Nonetheless, it is critical to develop a distinctly separate plan for online marketing—one that seeks to position and brand your business online in ways that connect with your target audiences.

In earlier chapters, you gathered your thoughts about the unique marketing position you wish to occupy in the minds of your target audience. You've written a profile for your primary and secondary target audiences and done some thinking about what your online goals really ought to be, given your company's status and capabilities.

You have also considered what kind of site might be best for your business and thought about where and how to advertise your site. You already know more about Web site design than most managers, because you have a clear understanding of content, appearance, organization, navigability, colors, and getting found.

The tools in this appendix will help you organize your newly earned knowledge and get it down on paper, an activity that looks suspiciously like making an actual plan.

Why bother? Companies that plan have fewer crises and dramatically reduce the need for meetings. They avoid the "siege mentality" that plagues many firms operating in today's highly competitive and fast-paced markets. Everyone on the team enjoys a sense of direction, knows the goals and steps, and can evaluate their effectiveness. Planning—in writing—and communicating that plan to all team members throughout the business is a sign of good management. Develop the plan with input from everyone possible in your company. Not only does this help assure that everyone feels invested in the plan and increase the likelihood that it will be communicated and carried out; it also increases the likelihood that the plan will be based on consideration of all possible approaches and outcomes. More than ever before—because the Internet is still foreign territory to many experienced professionals—knowledge and information reside throughout a company, not only with management.

The tools provided here are probably best suited to a small business. The principles and questions, however, apply even to large organizations with large divisions or subsidiaries or partners. Decide at the outset which company or division or product or service you are marketing, and whether you need to develop several interrelated plans.

PHASE 1: TASKS, TIMETABLE, BUDGET

Start by making a commitment to a set of tasks, an approximate timeline for accomplishing them, and an estimate of costs. Conceptualization of the tasks will take place in the checklists on the next two pages, where they are divided into four groups: Preliminaries; First Steps, Web Site; First Steps, E-mail; and Building Your Internet Presence.

Use the checklists to develop an overview of what you will need to do and as a to-do list. Check off completed tasks as you go. Set target dates for completion of each group of tasks and write the date in the My Deadline space provided at the top of each section. Also, estimate and write in the costs of the various pieces so that you begin to develop an idea of your Internet marketing budget.

Important: These checklists are a general guide. If they do not fit your company, alter them. Make your own checklists. For example, the first item, "Obtain e-mail account and Internet access," might need to read "Install network with e-mail and Internet access via T-1 line throughout all buildings."

PHASE 2: ESTABLISH YOUR WEB PRESENCE

After you have completed this phase of your action plan, you will have a solid foundation on the Web. You'll have a Web site and search engines will find it. This is the point at which many executives stop. If you stop here, you've wasted your time and money. Your objectives are:

1. Construct (or hire construction of) or improve your Web site and make sure it is registered with search engines.

Internet Marketing: Planning Checklist

Preliminaries _____

My Deadline

❏ Obtain e-mail account and Internet access. $_____

❏ Search for industry's leading associations, trade groups, exchanges, B2B marketplaces, RFQ, RFP, and other sites. Identify those primary and secondary target audiences that will be most likely to visit. Make a list of their names and URLs. (For now, simply make a list and put it in a secure place. Later, a detailed review will determine where to get free links, banner exchanges, and paid ads.)

First Steps: Web Site _____

My Deadline

❏ Create positioning statement

❏ Complete target audience profiles

❏ Make Web site wish list (look 'n' feel, content, links, etc.)

❏ Select/assemble graphics, photos, testimonials, résumé or "about" information, other content

❏ Select a Web site creator and a Web site host

❏ Register URL ($70 max. for two years)

❏ Web site created and working $_____
$\qquad$ (Budget)

❏ Register site with search engines

❏ Review the list of sites that you made (above). Be sure it includes the various kinds of potential advertising sites and opportunities mentioned in Chapter 7, including:

- _____ Regional and community sites (city, county, state, U.S. region)
- _____ Industry associations
- _____ Directories
- _____ Yellow pages directories
- _____ Bid-type search engines
- _____ Online mini-stores (Yahoo! etc.)
- _____ Noncompeting firms in industry that might exchange links with you
- _____ Regional industrial suppliers/vendors to target audiences who might do the same
- _____ Large content/media sites such as About.com, eFront.com, etc., and media placement firms such as DoubleClick.com and others
- _____ Foreign country sites (if you market internationally)

Note: Many sites post their advertising rates. For others, send an e-mail requesting ad rates. You will want to refer to rates later as you make decisions about revisions to your online marketing program. Also, look for industry sites that offer free links, banner exchanges, etc., including your trade organization or association.

❑ Printing, with e-mail and Web site address
   _____ Business cards
   _____ Stationery
   _____ Tablets
   _____ Sign riders
   _____ Other signs
   _____ Other
❑ Record voice-mail message
❑ Plan any additional media visibility (with advertising or marketing agency if appropriate)

First Steps: E-Mail _____

                                                          My Deadline

❑ Create "signatures"
❑ Create specific folders for filing customer/prospect messages
❑ Write e-mail message masters and templates for letters

Building Your Internet Presence _____

                                                          My Deadline

❑ Enhanced links in directories and association sites $_____
                                          (Budget)

❑ Banner or tile ads
   _____ Free or Exchanged   _____ Paid $_____
                                                      (Budget)

Additional presence on Web sites

_____ Search engines   _____Online stores (Yahoo!, etc.)
_____ Content sites (About.com, etc.)   _____Major directories (Looksmart, etc.)
_____ Yellow pages (GTE, etc.)   _____Statewide sites
_____ Countywide sites   _____City sites
_____ Foreign sites   _____Other
_____ Your home office's site, if you are a division, subsidiary, etc.
_____ Each site belonging to a division, subsidiary if you are the home office
_____ Noncompeting vendors who serve your target audiences with goods/services
_____ Bid-type search engines (overture.com, Sprinks.com, 7search.com, Kanoodle.com)
_____ Other marketing of your Web presence
_____ Other marketing of your Web presence
_____ Other marketing of your Web presence
                          $_____
                          (Budget)

❑ Other marketing of your Internet presence
1. _____
2. _____
3. _____
4. _____
5. _____
6. _____

$ _____
(Budget)

2. Establish a link or banner ad in at least one specialty site serving your field.

3. Add your Web site and e-mail addresses to your print materials and re-record your outgoing voice-mail messages to add "Visit our web site at xxx_.com" and "Send e-mail to me at xxxx@name.com."

To get started, you need to establish a reasonable "working" presence on the Internet. You should not wait months until your elaborate, end-all, whiz-bang $300,000 new Web site is complete. Nor should you mount a Web site before it is complete or in revision and say "under construction"; that only frustrates visitors. If you currently have no site, establish a Web presence as soon as you can. But transfer the URL you're using for your working site to your final site. This will enable you to add your two Web addresses to all your off-Web materials, starting now.

TIP!	**USE CAUTION WITH HUMAN-EDITED DIRECTORIES**

At this point, avoid adding outdated or temporary Web sites to human-edited directories (Yahoo.com, DMZ.org, Looksmart.com, About.com, etc.) because they will rank your site *lower* based on what little content they see now, rather than higher based on the magnificently valuable content-packed site that you *intend* to build.

Steps to Establishing Your Web Site

1. Review your positioning (See Chapter 2).

2. Make a list of the content items and functions you want to include on your site (See Chapters 3 and 4).

3. Make a list of sites you want your site to link to (See Chapter 3).

4. Assemble all photos you want to include in your site, along with related product descriptions, model numbers, etc.

5. Gather testimonials and information about your firm and products/services.

6. Write a list of words that describe how you want your site to look and feel (see Chapter 5).

7. Identify the company (or your future Web master) that will build and host your site. (Some companies perform both functions.) To help decide on a company, visit your competitors' sites and note what appeals to you and what does not. Also, speak with executives in noncompetitor firms about their level of satisfaction with the firm they use.

8. Select an available Web site address (URL) and register it, or have your Web master do this for you. Put considerable thought into choosing your domain name so that, ideally, it is easy to recall, easy to write or say, and yet still identifies your firm or type of business.

9. Make it your Web master's job to register your Web site with all major search engines on a regular (approximately every three weeks) basis.

10. Get listed and hold a dominant position on major bid-type search engines. The most well-known pay-per-click search engines are:

> http://www.overture.com (formerly GoTo.com)
> http://www.Sprinks.com
> http://www.Bay9.com (previously called RocketLinks)
> http://www.FindWhat.com
> http://www.7Search.com
> http://www.Kanoodle.com
> http://www.Ah-ha.com

Firms that market internationally should consider adding their site to foreign sites and search engines. (Note that translation services will likely be needed for non-English-speaking countries.) Some of the United Kingdom sites listed here are sub-sites of the major search engines and directories.

> http://www.UKSprite.com
> http://www.Godado.co.uk
> http://www.eSpotting.com
> http://www.Splut.com

Your First Online Presence in Your Industry

Order a banner, page, or link to your site on one or more of the major Web sites serving your industry. Which site first? The biggest and best one you can find—probably the site of the leading trade organization or association for your industry. Use a search engine to help you identify such sites.

PHASE 3: EXPAND YOUR INTERNET PRESENCE

Add Your E-Mail and Web Addresses to Your Key Print Materials

Have your Web site address and your e-mail address added to all your printed promotional materials, including your business cards, stationery, brochures, retail displays, cartons, packages, labels, notepads, calendars, and flyers. Don't forget the signs in front of corporate offices or divisions. Remember: Everything that has your phone number on it should also have your Web site address and your e-mail address.

1. To reach your primary target audience, add your Web site address—ideally a banner or enhanced link—to every industry-related directory and Web site address that is visited regularly by and appeals to that audience. Be there "waiting" for them and offer them a real reason in your links and banners to visit your site.

2. To reach your secondary target audiences, follow the instructions in #1 for sites frequented by them.

3. Create a signature (or many signature versions you can use alternately, depending on the intended recipient) to use in your outgoing e-mail. Place these signatures in your e-mail Options program as defaults and alternatives. Save them also in a word processing document in case your e-mail platform crashes. Spend considerable time creating your signature, which should contain much more than your name, title, and contact information.

4. Learn how to capture links to sites that may be of interest to prospective or current clients, or send those clients entire Web pages, easily accomplished using current versions of browsers. Practice this task until it becomes an easy, natural function.

5. Review the hit statistics or visitor information for your Web site. Are major search engines finding you? If not, check to see if your site is

still registered with them. If it is, perhaps your keywords, metatags, page titles, or other site information need revision.

How long are visitors staying on your site? Are any particular pages more popular than others? Are visitors not finding a particular page? What path do most take, page to page, when touring your site? Does the number of unique visitors rise immediately after you send out e-marketing newsletters or viral e-mails? Does the count go up when you launch a new print ad campaign? By how much? Does a certain type of ad or newsletter result in more visitors than do other types? Use this information to refine your ads, your newsletters, your site content, and navigation.

6. Visit your site as though you are a first-time visitor. (Clear your browser's cache and start fresh.) Ask others in the company, as well as relatives or neighbors, to do the same and take notes for you.) Is your positioning statement clear? Does the headline *grab*? Does the site need more content pages? Photos? Links? Does it load quickly and grab your attention? To find out how fast your page downloads for visitors at various modem speeds, go to WebsiteGarage.com (http://www.website garage.com) and conduct a free critical performance diagnostics check of your Web page.

7. List three site-marketing strategies that you want to use, and carry them out.

8. Repeat steps 5, 6, and 7 about every three months. You'll be adding marketing tools and tasks to your Web arsenal on a regular basis.

9. Answer all e-mails promptly and completely!

Appendix B
Resources on the Web

Resources on the Internet multiply daily. They also change, relocate, are replaced, or are deleted. Avoid purchasing books that purport to be Internet directories because change happens so quickly. Nonetheless, following is a list of Web sites that are current as of November 2001. We have used some of these sites for many months, and so we are fairly sure of their stability. Others are relative newcomers. Understand that the list is neither exhaustive nor permanent. Use it as a guide to get you started.

The resources are categorized into five sections, some of which contain subgroups. The major sections are:

1. General sites with local information

2. City, county, and state web sites

3. Tools to improve your positioning

4. Tools for building and maintaining your Web site

5. Popular links to add to your site

GENERAL SITES WITH LOCAL INFORMATION

Many valuable sites with general or national information also provide that material for local areas. Weather information, maps, local accommodations for home hunters, demographics, movies, and other information can be found on the Web. Be sure to drill down far enough within a site to find the page that pertains to your area, and then create your link directly to that interior page.

Weather	http://www.weather.com
Track Storms	http://www.storm98.com
U.S. City Information	http://www.usacitylink.com

Worldwide Cities	http://www.timeout.com
Travelocity	http://www.travelocity.com
MapQuest	http://www.mapquest.com
Yahoo Maps	http://maps.yahoo.com/py/maps.py
TV Schedule	http://www.tvguide.com
Movie Schedule	http://www.moviefone.com
Grocery Coupons	http://www.valupage.com
Employment	http://www.monsterboard.com
Gov. Recreation Lands	http://www.recreation.gov
Aerial Views of Anywhere	http://www.terraserver.microsoft.com
Vacations and Your Pets	http://www.vetinfo.com
One Stop Stock Information	http://www.stocksheet.com
Seniors	http://www.senior.com
World Wide Recipes	http://www.wwrecipes.com
Official Baseball Leagues	http://www.majorleaguebaseball.com
Visit 20,000 Online Stores	http://www.shopguide.com
World Travel Web Sites	http://www.leonardsworlds.com/camera.html
City Pollution by Zip Code	http://www.scorecard.org
Universities Online	http://www.mit.edu:8001/people/cdemello/univ.html
Farmers Almanac	http://www.almanac.com
U.S. Museums	http://www.museumca.org/usa/state.html
Child Care Sources	http://www.careguide.net

CITY, COUNTY, AND STATE WEB SITES

Include sites with city, county, and state information for buyers who are considering relocating to your area. Large cities may have dozens of city sites. One is probably a site maintained by the city itself. Others are built for commercial or other purposes. Some state or regional sites have a page or set of pages for their cities that may also be helpful.

Some states use a Web address format that has been set aside for them. The address is usually expressed with the standard beginning "http://www.state," followed by the state abbreviation and ".us." For example, Georgia's URL is http://www.state.ga.us; Washington's is http://www.state.wa.us; and Massachusetts's is http://www.state.ma.us. Simply change the abbreviation for the state to see if your state has a Web site using this standard Web address format. A variation on the state URL is followed by some cities, as in http://www.ci.boston.ma.us or http://www.ci.saint-petersburg.fl.us.

The following list of city and state Web sites is far from exhaustive, but it will give you an idea about where to start looking. These addresses are current as of January 2002.

Alaska	http://www.state.ak.us
Anchorage, AK	http://www.ci.anchorage.ak.us
Juneau, AK	http://www.juneau.lib.ak.us
Arkansas	http://www.state.ar.us
Phoenix, AZ	http://www.ci.phoenix.az.us
Los Angeles, CA	http://www.ci.la.ca.us
	http://www.losangeles.com
San Diego, CA	http://www.sandiego.com
	http://www.sandiego.org
Santa Barbara, CA	http://www.ci.santa-barbara.ca.us
Riverside, CA	http://www.ci.riverside.ca.us
Denver, CO	http://www.denver.com
Hartford, CT	http://ci.hartford.ct.us
	http://home.digitalcity.com/hartford
Florida	http://www.state.fl.us
Tampa, FL	http://888tellnet.com
Atlanta, GA	http://www.gausa.com
Idaho	http://www.accessidaho.org
Davenport, IA	http://www.ci.davenport.ia.us

TOOLS TO IMPROVE YOUR POSITIONING

One clever tactic to improve your market positioning is to display your URL and/or e-mail address on your car's trunk or fender (really!). http://www.primelinx.com

Another tactic is to make free or nearly free bridge pages. A bridge page makes more of *your* pages available for search engines to find. Once found, the bridge page simply redirects visitors to your main Web site. Some examples include:

> http://www.switchboard.com
> http://site.yahoo.com
> http://agtr.com/act-main.htm
> http://hometown.aol.com/hmtwn123/index.htm
> http://angelfire.lycos.com
> http://www.freeyellow.com
> http://www.webspawner.com
> http://www.theglobe.com
> http://www.webdiner.com/templates/index.htm
> http://www.hms.harvard.edu/it/www/templates/index.html

TOOLS TO BUILD AND MAINTAIN YOUR WEB SITE

Save yourself considerable time and money by using these free sources of Web site analysis or valuable marketing information based on *your* input.

- Learn which keywords are most efficient in searches:
  http://inventory.overture.com/d/searchinventory/suggestion/
  http://www.searchspy.com

- Make your keywords count: http://www.keywordcount.com.

- See Keywords being used this minute:
  http://www.metaspy.com
  http://voyeur.mckinley.com/cgi-bin/voyeur.cgi

- Make your images load more quickly:
  http://www.gifworks.com
  http://websitegarage.netscape.com

- Check the spelling on a Web page:
  http://www.jimtools.com

- See how search engines rank your company:
  http://www.top-10.com/freevisrprt.html
  http://www.jimtools.com
  http://www.topdogg.com

- Web site traffic analyzers are available at:
  http://www.hitbox.com
  http://www.webtrends.com

- Is your HTML code accurate?
  http://www.anybrowser.com
  http://www.websitegarage.com

- Detect dead links:
  http://websitegarage.netscape.com/O=wsg/tuneup_plus/index.html
  http://www.SevenTwentyfour.com
  http://www.jimtools.com/link.html

- Determine how many links point to your company:
  http://www.linkpopularity.com/
  http://www.linkstoyou.com

- Learn how people find your site:
  http://www.radiation.com/products/linktrakker

- Find out how fast your site displays:
  http://www.netmechanic.com/index.htm

- Buy or sell domain names:
  http://www.buydomains.com
  http://www.greatdomains.com
  http://www.thedomainexchange.com
  http://www.domainnames.com

- Learn from these free newsletters:
  http://www.dummiesdaily.com
  http://bottomlinesecrets.com
  http://www.netmechanic.com
  http://www.webpromote.com
  http://searchenginewatch.internet.com
  http://www.emarketer.com
  http://www.zdnet.com
  http://www.internettrafficreport.com
  http://www.webposition.com/newsletter.htm
  http://www.forrester.com
  http://e-newsletters.internet.com
  http://www.nielsen-netratings.com
  http://www.britannica.com

- Make free banners: http://www.mediabuilder.com

- Obtain free graphics for your Site: http://www.hey-you.com

- Let people recommend your site: http://www.recommend-it.com

- Add a free guestbook: http://www.guestbook.nu

- Add clock and weather to your site: http://www.onyoursite.com

- Keep current with the latest search engine updates:
  http://searchengineforums.com/bin/Ultimate.cgi
  http://www.searchenginewatch.com
  http://www.laisha.com/search

- Make meta tags and learn how to use them:
  http://WDVL.com/Authoring/HTML/Head/Meta
  http://searchenginewatch.internet.com/webmasters/meta.html
  http://hotwired.lycos.com/webmonkey/html/96/51/index2a.html
  http://www.scrubtheweb.com/abs/builder.html
  http://www.ineedhits.com/metatag

- Add links to map sites:
  Yahoo Maps, Driving Directions, at http://maps.yahoo.com/py/
      maps.py
  Maps of all Kinds, at http://www.mapquest.com
  Zip Codes; Distances Between at http://link-usa.com/zipcode
  How Far From (City) to (City) at http://www.indo.com/distance
  Thomas Brothers Maps at http://www.thomasguide.com
  National Parks at http://www.gorp.com/gorp/resource/
      us_national_park/main.htm

POPULAR LINKS TO ADD TO YOUR SITE

Constantly changing content is a major factor that attracts repeat visitors to your site. Along with local area information, add links to popular topics that virtually anyone can enjoy. Here are a few idea builders to help you to get started.

Best of the Web

Top Ten Lists: 725 Categories   http://www.toptenlinks.com
Directory of World's Online Web Cams   http://www.earthcam.net
Best Web Sites on Internet   http://www.webbyawards.com
Top 100 Sites for Kids   http://www.100hot.com/kids/

Top 100 Sites for Sports   http://www.100hot.com/sports/
Top 100 Sites To Make Drinks   http://www.100hot.com/alcohol/
Top 100 Sites for Travel   http://www.100hot.com/travel/
Top 100 Sites for Autos   http://www.100hot.com/autos/

Home and Garden

All About Home Care   http://www.allabouthome.com
Handy Home Uses of Common Foods   http://www.wackyuses.com
Home Maintenance and Repair from MSU   http://www.msue.msu.
    edu/msue/imp/mod02/master02.html
Tim Carter's Home Maintenance   http://www.askbuild.com
What's Recyclable; What Is Not   http://www.obviously.com/recycle/
    guides/shortest.html
Fix Anything Anywhere   http://www.misterfixit.com
HouseNet Home and Garden   http://www.housenet.com
House Beautiful   http://www.housebeautiful.com
Basic Gardening   http://www.gardening.com
All About Pianos   http://www.pianoworld.com
Do It Yourself   http://doityourself.com

Food

Culinaria Online Recipes Galore   http://www.culinaria.com
Find Recipes for Anything   http://www.lycos.com/search/recipedia.
    html
Cake Recipes   http://www.cakerecipe.com
Cookie Recipes   http://www.cookierecipe.com
Calzone Recipes   http://www.calendarzone.com/recipes/
Coffee Lovers   http://www.coffeescience.org
Garlic Facts and Fun   http://www.thegarlicstore.com
New to Wine? Enjoy Learning   http://www.enjoywine.com
Fast Food Facts Calories, Hints   http://www.olen.com/food/
7,600 Recipes for Cooking   http://www.epicurious.com
Flying Noodle Pasta Recipes   http://www.flyingnoodle.com
Oriental Food Recipes, Hints   http://www.orientalfood.com
Recipe Exchange   http://www.recipeXchange.com
Wine Spectator's for Oenophiles   http://www.winespectator.com
Vegetarians   http://www.vrg.org

Pets

Have Fish Tank? Get Top Info Here   http://www.actwin.com/fish/faq/tanksize.html

Dog & Cat Vet Advice   http://www.vetinfo.com

Glossary

@ Symbol most often seen in e-mail addresses, as in "johnandjane@eartnet. com"; in general, the Internet symbol @ means "located at."

alternative text Sometimes called *mouseovers* or *alt tags*. Words that display while an image is loading and when the user places the mouse/pointer over an image. Unless the Web site owner/creator changes the alternative text, the name of the graphic file, such as house.gif, will show. However, any text may be used, such as, "Sam Brown, Realtor for first-time home buyers in Bowling Green, Kentucky." Some search engines read this alternative text along with visible text to help determine a site's relevance to specific keywords.

animated.gif A type of graphic that appears to move. An animated .gif combines several images, each slightly different from the previous one, that appear one after another automatically, giving the appearance of motion—similar to motion pictures.

attachment A file attached to an e-mail message. The file may be a photo, text, a Web page, or any other type of file. Do not send files unless you are certain the recipient can find them, view them, and open them. If your e-mail recipients can browse the Internet, then .jpg and .gif graphics files, html files, and simple text files will work fine.

Adobe Acrobat is an excellent tool for exchanging documents over the Internet if you and your recipient do not have the same software. Acrobat will create a .pdf file (portable document file) which can be viewed using the Acrobat Reader, a program downloadable for free. Such .pdf files can be read even across platforms (that is, whether you are using a PC or a Macintosh computer system).

auction site A site that makes available for sale items that visitors bid on. At a predetermined time, the auction closes and the high bidder wins the auction and pays the seller. Many variations are now available, but the significant player is eBay, at http://www.ebay.com.

audio books Books that are downloadable from the Internet or available on disk, that can be listened to by users through their computer's audio program. Similar to books on tape, audio books differ from e-books in that audio books are heard by users, whereas e-books are read by users.

autoresponder A function on a computer that sends an automated response to a command from a Web site or to an e-mail recipient with a particular addressee or subject line.

B2B Business to business. B2B sites sell business products and/or services to other businesses.

B2C Business to consumer. B2C sites are constructed by businesses to sell their products and/or services to consumers.

banner ad   A small, rectangular, usually horizontal ad that appears on Internet pages. Banner ads usually link the visitor to the Web site or page of the banner owner (advertiser).

banner exchange   Reciprocal banner display, characterized by the statement: "I'll put your banner on my site if you'll put my banner on yours." Banners often, but not always, include an active link to the target site, becoming link exchanges.

bcc   Abbreviation for *blind carbon copy* or *blind copy*; indicates a copy of an e-mail message sent to recipients whose addresses do not show on the message. Think of a blind copy as a "secret" copy. For example, if Mr. Agent sends a message to Mr. Buyer with a copy (cc) to Ms. Broker and a blind copy (bcc) to Mrs. Attorney, only Mr. Agent and Mrs. Attorney know he sent her a copy; Mr. Buyer and Ms. Broker do not see Mrs. Attorney's name or e-mail address on the message.

bridge page   A Web page that leads visitors to another site, hence, a bridge. Several sites offer free pages; tripod.com and geocities.com are among the better known sources. Often, but not always, these pages carry their own metatags and their URLs can be registered with search engines. Because some search engines penalize such pages in their rankings, the Web savvy put at least some new or different information on each bridge page, rather than simply a list of links to pages in the target site.

bulletin board   A Web page that displays messages submitted by users. Most bulletin boards are specific to a particular topic.

cgi form   A form on a Web page filled in by Internet users and then sent to the owner of the Web site or some other designated recipient. Examples of cgi forms are guest books or surveys on the Internet. CGI is an acronym for Common Gateway Interface.

chat room   A Web site function that allows a group of people to type statements in such a way that all members of the group can see everything written by every other member.

community site   (1) A Web site featuring content that is primarily for or about a given city. In a broader sense, this term includes county, regional, and state sites. This book uses the phrase *community site* in this sense. (2) A Web site created and maintained by a community of users, or a group of formally linked Web sites on a common topic.

corporate identity site   A Web site whose purpose is to communicate with a company's employees and/or investors. Corporate identity sites promote their market positioning and philosophy and present information on their history, size, leadership, dedications, and so forth.

C2C   Consumer to consumer. C2C sites are constructed by individuals to sell products and/or services to consumers. C2C sales also occur commonly on auction sites, such as eBay.com.

customer relationship management (CRM)   A type of marketing based on the goal of building long-term relationships with customers or clients. Web sites built to support CRM goals provide features to communicate with visitors; engage them in "conversation"; demonstrate that they understand visitors' priorities, preferences, and needs; provide visitor-friendly ways to purchase items; provide fast or real-time communications between customer service or marketing representatives and visitors, and so forth.

dealership   Display of a graphic and link to an e-commerce site in return for a commission on items sold to visitors using that particular link. Sites with large inventories sold in a catalog format are the most frequent offerers of dealerships.

directory A list similar to your familiar Yellow Pages, with links and Web site information organized according to categories. General directories, like Yahoo!, are broadbased and include thousands of topics. Some directories focus on a given topic, and may be considered vertical portals, or *vortals*.

domain name The main part of an Internet address, including its extension. In the address http://www.disney.com/news/pocahontas.htm, for example, "disney.com" is the domain name. Until late 1999, domain names were limited to 26 characters; now they may include as many as 76 characters.

Domain name extensions (suffixes) indicate the *top-level domain* (TLD) to which the name belongs. For example: .com indicates a commercial business; .net indicates a company that specializes in networks; .gov is used by government sites, local, state, or national; .org indicates an organization, usually nonprofit; .edu is used by educational institutions, school districts, and schools; .mil stands for "military." Some extensions indicate the country where the site is based, .mx for Mexico or .ca for Canada, for example. Early in the year 2000, .md was added for use by physicians, hospitals, and other medical-related entities. In 2001, more extensions were added, such as .biz, .pers, and .ent.

downloadable Capable of being copied from a computer connected to the Internet to a user's computer.

e-books Electronic books, downloadable from the Internet or available on disk, that can be read by various reading devices such as Adobe Acrobat eBook Reader. E-books differ from audio

books in that audio books are heard by users, whereas e-books are read by users.

emoticon Term coined for *emotion icon*; a small icon composed of punctuation and other characters, such as colons and parentheses. For example, :-) is the symbol for a smiley face (look at it sideways). If the colon is changed to a semicolon, ;-), the emoticon is winking, indicating jest or humor.

folder An object in a graphical interface, such as Windows, that can contain multiple documents or other types of files. Folders are useful for organizing or holding e-mail messages, graphics, scanned photographs, and documents created with a word processing or other application.

forward To send an incoming e-mail message to another recipient or recipients.

.gif A file extension indicating a type of compressed file used for photos and other graphics on the Internet. .gif (pronounced "gif," as in *gift*) files are more frequently used for graphics than for photos. GIF is an acronym for Graphics Interchange Format.

hidden text Text written in the coding of an Internet page that does not display on the site. Common examples are the METAtags with title, keywords, site description, and other information that some search engines read and store in their databases.

home page The front or main page of a Web site. A home page often acts as a starting point leading to other documents stored at the site. A page that precedes the main, navigation-oriented, traditional home page is often called a *splash page*.

home search site Web sites that enable consumers to search for and view text and photos of homes for sale that match their criteria. Examples: Home-seekers.com, Realtor.com.

host (1) To store a customer's Web site on a server, thus making the site available to everyone with Web access. (2) A computer system that stores data, such as a Web site, and that is accessed by a user or users from a remote location.

.htm A file extension indicating a page prepared in hypertext markup language (html); one of the most common types of Web pages.

html Acronym for HyperText Markup Language, an authoring language used to create documents for viewing with an Internet browser.

interactive catalog A database of items with a "front end" that allows visitors to search for an item and provides some means of online ordering.

interactive functions Functions on a Web site that allow visitors to interact with the site, that is, visitors take some action (clicking on something, for example), and the Web site performs some action in response, usually clicking to go to another page (although technically causing the Web site to do something is not included in this definition since it is so common). Examples include visitors' adding items to shopping carts, using an online order form, participating in a chat room, or starting a video stream.

.jpg A file extension indicating a type of file used for photos and other graphics on the Internet. .jpg (pronounced "jay-peg") files are usually used for photos, but sometimes they are also used for graphics. .jpg files are compressed so that photos appear on the user's monitor more quickly. Photos compressed as .jpg files can be reduced to about 5 percent of their normal size, but some detail is lost in the compression. .jpg stands for Joint Photographic

Experts Group, for which the compression technique is named.

keywords Words people enter into search engines to find information on the Web. Most search engines match words being searched for with Web pages that have them. A typical consumer keywords search might be "Manhattan, NY real estate" (no quotes). Keywords are also listed in the METAtags (hidden text) of Web site pages for reading by search engines.

link A connection between a location on a page and another location on the same or a different page on the Internet. When a user clicks on a link with the mouse, the location connected to the link is displayed. Text links are often underlined and shown in blue. Graphics can also be linked. When the mouse is pointed at a link, the mouse pointer usually changes to a pointing hand.

link exchange Reciprocal linking between or among sites, usually without exchange of fee or other consideration.

listen back To reply to an e-mail message only after verifying that you have understood and noted ("listened to") every point that the sender made, and have responded completely, point by point.

live chat or **live customer service** A Web site function that allows a user to communicate with a customer service representative or other person by typing messages back and forth. Compare with *chat room*.

mall A Web site consisting of many individually owned sections or *store fronts* selling products and services.

MAPI Acronym for messaging application programming interface, a built-in Microsoft Windows system that enables various e-mail applications

(MAPI-enabled ones) to send and receive messages.

metatag Sometimes written METAtag. Coding with information about an Internet page or site. These tags tell what the page is about (META Title and META Description) and provide keywords (META Keywords) that represent the page or site content and more. Many search engines use metatag information to determine ranking of a site in displayed search results.

portal A Web site that serves as a gateway to the world of the Internet by providing a directory or directories of links, featured links, and a search engine or engines to help visitors find what they seek (or what the owner of the portal wishes them to find). Portals offer a very broad range of choices to help visitors locate almost anything imaginable on the Web.

position, positioning A specific place held in the minds of the public or a given audience (or market segment) concerning a product or service. Chez LaFayette, for example, may have positioning as the best upscale French restaurant in a given town, whereas MacGregor's may be positioned as a family style, low-cost, easy-access fast food vendor. Positioning is similar, in many ways, to reputation.

product or service information site A Web site that provides information on the features and benefits of products or services, but that falls short of helping visitors purchase those products or services.

Reply, Reply All To answer an incoming e-mail message. Reply sends the response only to the address of the originating message; Reply All sends the response to the original writer and to everyone who received a copy (cc) of the original message.

robot A program that runs automatically. Some Web pages contain hidden text telling robots what to do; for example, "return every 7 days" or "do not catalog this page." See also *spider*.

screen saver A program that displays animated graphics on a computer's monitor when the computer is turned on but has not been used for a period of time. Screen savers are small programs that can be easily downloaded.

search engine An Internet site, function, or program that maintains databases of Internet pages, with their keywords and URLs, and retrieves the information according to keywords entered by users, displaying a list of Internet sites and/or pages. Examples include Excite, Infoseek, Google, and Webcrawler.

server A computer or device on a network that manages that network's resources. Your Internet service provider and all the people who belong to it share the use of its servers. Basically, a server "serves" the e-mail and Web browsing needs of those who use it.

shopping cart A selecting and ordering mechanism used on some sites that sell products and services. A shopping cart usually allows visitors to select items to put in the shopping cart or basket and later check out using a credit card or other payment mechanism.

signature Generally, a statement and a selection of links and/or images that are automatically attached at the end of outgoing e-mail messages.

signature link Text, graphics, and/ or links added automatically at the end of outgoing e-mail messages.

spam Electronic junk mail or junk newsgroup postings. Unsolicited, advertising-oriented e-mail comprises most *e-junk*.

specialty site Any site that deals almost entirely with one topic; for example, http://www.gardening.com is a gardening specialty site.

spider A program that automatically retrieves Web page information for use by search engines; a type of robot.

sponsor A site, individual, or company that receives highly visible credit for supporting a section of a Web site. For example, Goodyear Tires might sponsor a section in AOL called Tires & Auto Accessories.

streaming media Technology that transmits (streams) audio and/or video from a server to a user's computer. Streaming video is played on the user's computer as it is received from the server.

teleconferencing Voice conferencing using an Internet connection and a microphone and speakers connected to users' computers rather than to telephones.

tile ad A small, usually square ad that appears on Internet pages and usually links the visitor to the Web site of the advertiser.

transaction-oriented site A Web site that provides some level of online purchasing capability so visitors can buy products or services, make reservations, or transact other business. Transaction-oriented sites emphasize the selling of their products or services, but fall short of providing visitor-friendly information and communications tools.

UMPS Acronym for unique marketing positioning statement; a concise statement intended to express the characteristics that combine to make up your position. Examples are: "Hershey—The Number One Chocolate Bar in the World" and "The Top-Selling Ocean-View-Home Real Estate Agent in Maine."

URL Acronym for Universal Resource Locator, the World Wide address of Web pages, Web images, documents, and other Web resources. For example, the URL for the main entry page of Burpee Seeds' site is http://www.burpee.com. Each page and image or graphic on the Internet has its own URL. The URL for Burpee's logo image on its home page is: http://www.burpee.com/image/global/wwwlogo.gif. Learn more about URLs at: http://www.w3.org/Addressing/Addressing.html.

URL registration Reservation of a main Internet site address (domain name). Internic, more recently called Network Solutions, is an entity officially authorized to regulate assignment of domain names.

user-controlled catalogs A catalog that allows users to custom design or select particular models, colors, or pieces. See http://www.makeoverstudios.com for an example.

video conferencing Similar to teleconferencing via the Internet, but allows transmission of video as well. Video conferencing can be used between two people or can connect several people in different locations at one time.

vortal A *Vertical portal*; a Web site that serves as an Internet gateway to pages and sites related to a particular topic or interest.

Webcasting Internet broadcasting; tranmission of live or prerecorded audio and/or video to users connected to the Internet.

Web fax, Internet fax A Web site function that allows visitors to send a document from their computer to another person's fax machine.

Web page A page in a site on the World Wide Web. Every Web page is identified by a unique address, or URL (Universal Resource Locator). A page is often considered to be 11 inches long, but actually pages can be very long, indeed, and can take up many paper pages when printed.

Web site An organized, related, interconnected group of Web pages. Sites typically include a *home page*, which is the first page seen by someone entering the site, and subsequent pages reachable from the home page and internal links.

Index